Criminal Conduct and
Substance Abuse Treatment

Criminal Conduct and Substance Abuse Treatment

Strategies for Self-Improvement and Change

pathways to responsible living

2nd Edition

THE PARTICIPANT'S WORKBOOK

Kenneth W. Wanberg
Center for Addictions Research and Evaluation, Denver, Colorado

Harvey B. Milkman
Metropolitan State College of Denver

SAGE Publications
Thousand Oaks ▪ London ▪ New Delhi

Preparation and development of this edition of *Criminal Conduct and Substance Abuse Treatment: Strategies for Self-Improvement and Change, Pathways to Responsible Living - The Provider's Guide and The Participant's Workbook* were funded by: The Center for Addictions Research and Evaluation; The Center for Interdisciplinary Studies; and Sage Publications, Inc.; and the time, efforts and resources of the authors.

Support for the preparation and development for the 1996 version of Criminal Conduct and Substance Abuse Treatment: Strategies for Self-Improvement and Change came from: The Colorado Alcohol and Drug Abuse Division, Department of Human Services (Contracts 957230 and 960671); The Division of Criminal Justice, Colorado Department of Public Safety from the Edward Byrne Memorial State and Local Law Enforcement Assistance Program Formula Grant to Colorado from the U.S. Department of Justice (Contacts 94-DB-15A-58-1 and 95-DB-15A-58-2); and the time and efforts of the authors.

The copyright holders and authors grant to the State of Colorado, Alcohol and Drug Abuse Division, the rights to reproduce *Criminal Conduct and Substance Treatment: Strategies for Self-Improvement and Change, Pathways to Responsible Living - The Provider's Guide and The Participant's Workbook (2nd ed.)*, - for use in treatment, probation, judicial and correctional programs within the State of Colorado.

For information:

Sage Publications, Inc.
2455 Teller Road
Thousand Oaks, California 91320
E-mail: order@sagepub.com

Sage Publications Ltd.
1 Oliver's Yard
55 City Road
London EC1Y 1SP
United Kingdom

Sage Publications India Pvt. Ltd.
B-42 Panchsheel Enclave
Post Box 4109
New Delhi 110017
India

Printed in the United States of America

Library of Congress Cataloging-in-Publication Data

Wanberg, Kenneth W., Milkman, Harvey B., Criminal Conduct and Substance Abuse Treatment: Strategies for Self-Improvement and Change, Pathways to Responsible Living, 2nd ed.

ISBN 978-1-4129-0591-6

Direct correspondence should be sent to:

The Center for Interdisciplinary Services   or   Center for Addictions Research and Evaluation - CARE
P.O. Box 16745   P.O. Box 1975
Golden, CO   80402-6012   Arvada, CO   80001-1975

11 12 9 8 7

Kenneth W. Wanberg, Th.D., Ph.D., is a private practice psychologist and the Director of the Center for Addictions Research and Evaluation (CARE), Arvada, CO. Harvey B. Milkman, Ph.D., is Professor of Psychology at Metropolitan State College of Denver and Director of the Center for Interdisciplinary Services, Denver, CO.

Acquisitions Editor: Arthur Pomponio
Editorial Assistant: Veronica Novak
Graphic Design and Layout: Karyn Sader

TABLE OF CONTENTS

PROGRAM CLOSURE: CONTINUING YOUR JOURNEY OF RESPONSIBLE LIVING

LIST OF WORKSHEETS

LIST OF FIGURES

LIST OF PROFILES

LIST OF TABLES

LIST OF PROGRAM GUIDES

INTRODUCTION

Strategies for Self-Improvement and Change

Pathways to
Responsible Living

*"The greatest discovery of my
generation is that a human being
can change his life by changing his
attitude."*

-WILLIAM JAMES

Welcome to *Strategies for Self-improvement and Change (SSC): Pathways to Responsible Living.* This program will take you on a journey of change. It is a journey of making changes in your life in order to get positive outcomes for yourself and for your community. This may be the biggest journey of your life. Thousands of people on probation, parole, in community correction settings or in prison have benefited from the ideas and skills they learned in this program.

You may have been sent to this program as part of your overall plan of correcting and changing:

◆ Your past involvement in criminal conduct (CC); and

◆ Your involvement in alcohol or other drugs that has led to harmful outcomes.

But most important, you enrolled in this program because you were concerned about your past criminal conduct (CC) and your past alcohol or other drug (AOD) use problems. You were seen as someone who wanted to change the direction of your life.

Yet, part of you may not want to be here. Tell us about that part of you. We want to understand those thoughts and feelings. But we know that part of you **does** want to be here and wants to change the course of your life so that you can have better outcomes in your life. We also want you to tell us about that part of you. That is the part of you that we want to support and help grow.

This *Workbook* is your guide in *SSC (Strategies for Self-Improvement and Change).* It is an important part of your life while you are attending *SSC.* You are asked to bring the *Workbook* to each treatment session. It is a symbol for the improvements and changes you are making in your life and a symbol of **responsible living.**

SSC is divided into three treatment phases, 12 different modules and 50 treatment sessions. There is a short introduction to each phase and each module of the program. Each module has specific treatment sessions. In each session, objectives are outlined, key ideas of each session are presented, and exercises and worksheets are provided to help apply the topics and material to your own situation.

We want you to take an active part in each session through sharing what you learn in the exercises and worksheets. We would like you to read the content of each session before group and complete the classroom worksheets in group.

Module 1 is the introduction to the *SSC* program. All clients will receive this module before continuing into the program. *Module 1* may be done on an individual basis, or in an orientation group.

We now begin our journey - a journey of change, a journey that leads us to personal fulfillment and **responsible living.**

Change takes place in steps or phases. These steps are like a spiral. We may slip back to an earlier stage of change, but never back to where we started. The spiral or cycle of change is different for different areas of change. We might be in one stage of the spiral for changing criminal thinking, and another stage for changing our AOD use pattern. Our main targets of change are criminal conduct and substance abuse. Other targets are improving our relationship with others, managing emotions and being more responsible to the community.

Change is not easy. Sometimes it comes in small steps or stages. For example, babies learn to walk in stages. They struggle to take a few steps, then realize they can crawl faster - and it's not as much work. They get up again and try to walk and take a few more steps. Imagine if a baby decided that crawling forever would be better than walking. Sounds silly, but that's where people get stuck - not wanting to change, but knowing change might improve their life and lead to better outcomes.

The *SSC* program is provided in steps or phases that are developed around three stages in the spiral of change. We begin our journey by looking at these phases.

Phase I: Challenge to Change

We make changes when we are challenged. This is the first stage of change and the first phase of this program: *Challenge to Change.* We are challenged to change when our thinking and behaviors have led to bad outcomes, for example, losing an important relationship or **losing our freedom.**

In *Phase I,* we build knowledge and skills in several important areas.

▶ Build **trust** in your *SSC* provider, those who are in the program with you, and in *SSC* itself.

▶ **Learn how thoughts, feelings and actions are related.**

▶ **Learn about AOD** (alcohol and other drugs) **use and abuse** and your own history and pattern of AOD use.

▶ **Learn about antisocial and criminal behavior,** the cycles of criminal conduct, and your past criminal conduct.

▶ Be **more aware of yourself,** your AOD use and CC (criminal conduct) thinking, feelings and actions and to make a commitment to long-term change in these areas.

▶ Understand the **pathways to relapse and recidivism** (R&R) and to R&R prevention.

▶ We **develop a plan** for building on your strengths and changing specific areas of your life.

Phase I is the **Challenge** stage of change - it is also the start of your journey of commitment to change. There are 20 sessions in this phase. Some *SSC* programs will offer *Phase I* sessions once a week; others may do two or even three or four sessions a week.

Phase II: Commitment to Change

Phase II, Commitment to Change, focuses on strengthening your knowledge and skills in bringing about changes that lead to a more **responsible and fulfilling life.** These skills will help you to:

▶ Change and restructure your thinking to have better and more positive emotional and behavior outcomes;

▶ Learn and practice interpersonal and social skills that give you better outcomes in your relationship with others;

▶ Learn skills that help you to be more responsible to your community and society; and

▶ Stick to your plan of recidivism and relapse prevention.

Phase II also focuses on your personal strengths and the problems you identified in *Phase I,* **Challenge to Change.** You sort out and put name tags on your thoughts, attitudes, beliefs, feelings and your actions, and continue learning skills to bring about change. You look at yourself in more depth and you are confronted as to who you are and what you do. You begin to make a decision to change and take action to change. You test out and practice changes in your actions. You become much more aware of yourself, your AOD use and your CC (criminal conduct). You discover what you want and need to change about yourself. In this phase you take part in special skill building sessions to learn to change thoughts and behaviors and develop self-control to live in a more responsible way. You get stronger in your ability to live a **drug-free** and **crime-free** life. You begin taking ownership of your change. You think: "these changes belong to me."

There are 22 sessions in *Phase II.* Some *SSC* programs will offer these once a week; others two or more times a week.

Phase III: Taking Ownership for Your Change

Phase III moves you to greater ownership of your change. You

▶ develop critical reasoning skills;

▶ learn how to resolve conflicts with others and the community;

▶ learn about life-styles and activities that help maintain change;

▶ look at work and job issues;

▶ learn how to become a guide or mentor for others.

You discover the power of the ideas, skills, thoughts and the actions that you learn and make them work for you. You have ownership of your change. It belongs to you. And that ownership gets stronger when you become a guide, mentor and example for others. You will find new pleasure from comfortable and responsible living. There are 8 sessions in *Phase III.*

PHASE I
challenge to change

**Building Knowledge
and Skills for
Responsible Living**

*We learn
strategies for
self-improvement,
change and
responsible living.*

Phase I **has seven modules**

Module 1: Orientation: How this Program Works

Module 2: Cognitive-Behavioral Approach to Change and Responsible Living

Module 3: Alcohol and Other Drug (AOD) Use Patterns and Outcomes

Module 4: Understanding and Changing Criminal Thinking and Behaviors

Module 5: Sharing and Listening: Communication Pathways to Self-Awareness and
Other-Awareness

Module 6: Understanding and Preventing Relapse and Recidivism

Module 7: Steps, Stages and Skills for Self-Improvement and Change

"Our life is what our thoughts make it."
-MARCUS AURELIUS

Phase I sets the stage for self-improvement and change. The first step is self-disclosure which leads to self-awareness. Self-awareness comes through feedback from others, learning how we change, and what we need to change. Then we learn skills to make change happen. **Self-disclosure leads to self-awareness and self-awareness leads to change.**

Trust helps you share your thoughts, feelings and your past. We want you to share your past drug use and past criminal behavior, your worries and fears, your problems and troubles. There are limits as to how confidential the information is you share. The law requires that your counselor or provider must report suspected child abuse and direct threat of harm to yourself or another person.

Phase I inspires us to change. Effort requires inspiration and motivation. However, being inspired is not enough. *Phase I* gives you maps that help guide your effort to change. You learn how thinking and acting fit into self-improvement, self-control and change.

We need to know what we are going to change and have knowledge about the areas we are going to change. This means **learning about alcohol and other drugs,** the outcomes of their use and the cycles of addiction. It is also important to know about **antisocial and criminal behavior,** the cycles of criminal conduct, and about your own patterns of criminal conduct. Antisocial refers to behavior that goes against the rules and good of society. Your criminal actions have been antisocial.

We learn and practice communication skills that help us understand ourselves and to improve our relationship with others. We look at how our thinking errors lead to substance abuse and criminal conduct. We focus on understanding and preventing relapse (returning to thinking and actions which lead to AOD abuse) and recidivism (returning to thinking and actions which lead to criminal conduct).

In *Phase I* you learn the rules and tools of change and identify the targets for change. You begin your *Master Profile (MP)* and *Master Assessment Plan (MAP)* in *Session 2.* In *Session 20,* you use your MP and MAP to complete a deeper assessment on yourself. You look at other problems in your life besides those related to AOD use and CC. Your MP is a portrait of your problems and strengths and your MAP is your guide for your SSC journey. Here are the goals for *Phase I.*

> ▶ Understand who *SSC* is for and how it works.
>
> ▶ Learn the basic ideas, rules and the map of cognitive-behavioral change.
>
> ▶ Learn about AOD use patterns and cycles and harmful outcomes.
>
> ▶ Learn about the patterns and cycles of criminal conduct (CC).
>
> ▶ Learning the pathways to self-disclosure and change and the skills to bring about changes.
>
> ▶ Learn the pathways to relapse and recidivism (R&R) and R&R prevention.
>
> ▶ Learn the stages that people go through when making changes.
>
> ▶ Learn to use the tools for change outlined above.
>
> ▶ Develop your MAP - your plan for change.

MODULE 1

It is important that we get off to a good start. We want you to understand who this program is for, what we would like for you to get out of the program, and to understand its approach. We want you to understand how change takes place and the rules, tools and targets of change. These tools and the changes you make help you develop patterns and pathways for responsible living and to live a meaningful and fulfilling life.

Orientation: How This Program Works - the Rules, Tools and Targets for Change

Module 1 **has two sessions.**

Session 1: Getting started: How *SSC* Works and Developing Trust and a Working Relationship

Session 2: Rules, Tools and Targets for Change

INTRODUCTION AND OBJECTIVES

This is the first of two orientation sessions for *Strategies for Self-Improvement and Change (SSC) - Pathways to Responsible Living.*

> ### OBJECTIVES
>
> ➡ Understand the purpose and objectives of SSC and the basic approach of the SSC program.
>
> ➡ Begin building trust and respect among group members and with provider staff.
>
> ➡ Have you do a brief evaluation of how you see your AOD use and your criminal history.

SESSION CONTENT AND FOCUS

WHO IS THIS PROGRAM FOR?

SSC is for persons who have a history of criminal conduct and AOD use problems. From 60 to 75 percent of those in the criminal justice system have AOD problems. As many as 80 percent of those locked up for robbery, burglary or assault did those crimes when using alcohol or other drugs.

Participants in *SSC* may be on probation or parole, or in a residential or community correctional setting. Although they differ as to the kind of AOD use problems and criminal conduct, all have in common a history of AOD use and abuse and a history of criminal conduct (CC).

HOW IS THIS PROGRAM SET-UP?

SSC is divided into three phases and 12 modules. Each module has separate sessions. In *Phase I* you are challenged to begin the steps of change: self-disclosure and developing self-awareness. You are also challenged to **commit to prevent future involvement in CC or AOD use.** The first two sessions are *SSC* orientation and are given in either an individual or group session.

Most programs offer *Phase I* in an open group set-up. After orientation, you are placed in a *Phase I* group that is going through the various sessions. You enter *SSC* at whatever session the group is on and continue until you have completed all *Phase I* sessions. In a closed group set-up, you go from *Session 1* through *Session 20* in the same group.

After *Phase I,* you and your counselor(s) decide whether to continue into *Phase II* and *Phase III.* After a brief orientation you continue in a *Phase II* group. Most *SSC* programs provide *Phase II* and *III* in an open group set-up. Some *SSC* programs combine *Phase II* and *Phase III.* Other programs have a separate open group for *Phase III.*

GOALS OF SSC

SSC has three main goals.

▶ To **prevent recidivism** into criminal thinking and criminal conduct - **to be prosocial**

▶ To **prevent relapse** into a pattern of alcohol or other drug (AOD) use that is harmful and disruptive to normal living and was part of your criminal behavior

▶ **To help you live a responsible and meaningful life.**

Preventing recidivism

Recidivism starts when you take part in criminal thinking or put yourself in situations where you risk taking part in criminal acts. Preventing recidivism is a society goal. It is not just your goal. It is the goal of never again taking part in criminal conduct or actions that break the law.

> **COMMUNITY COMMITMENT GOAL:** TO NEVER TAKE PART IN CRIMINAL CONDUCT

Exercise: Put your recidivism prevention goal in the space below. Then, compare your goal with the COMMUNITY GOAL stated above. Is it the same?

> **HERE IS MY RECIDIVISM PREVENTION GOAL:**
>
> _____
>
> _____

Preventing relapse

Relapse and recidivism are closely tied together. But, they are not the same. AOD use is not always related to the crime. What does relapse mean?

▶ *Relapse begins when you take part in thinking about, or putting yourself in, situations* that could cause you to return to a harmful pattern of AOD use.

▶ A **lapse** is *going back to AOD use that leads* to harming yourself or others after you have committed to a non-harmful pattern **or** to no use at all.

▶ A **full relapse** is *going back to having further problems* from AOD use or to a harmful pattern of AOD use - which may or may not involve criminal conduct.

There are two relapse prevention goals you can choose from.

- Never use alcohol or other legal drugs to the extent that they cause harm to you, to others or your community, and to abstain from the use of all illegal drugs.

- Live an alcohol and drug-free life - to abstain from the use of all mind-behavior altering drugs unless prescribed by a medical specialist. This should be the goal for those:

  - Whose AOD use has caused their life to be disturbed or upset;

  - Whose AOD use was part of their criminal conduct;

  - Who want to be at zero risk for having future AOD problems.

RELAPSE PREVENTION GOAL I: PREVENT AOD USE FROM CAUSING HARM, UPSETTING AND DISTURBING YOUR LIFE AND/OR THE LIVES OF OTHERS AND ABSTAIN FROM ILLEGAL DRUG USE

RELAPSE PREVENTION GOAL II: TO LIVE AN ALCOHOL AND DRUG FREE LIFE - TO ABSTAIN FROM THE USE OF ALCOHOL OR OTHER MIND-BEHAVIOR CHANGING DRUGS

There is also a community responsibility relapse prevention goal: to never be involved in AOD use that violates the law or is criminal conduct. Here are some examples.

- To never drive while your blood alcohol is beyond legal limits or while under the influence of drugs.

- To be AOD free while you are under judicial supervision.

- To never possess and use illegal drugs.

AOD COMMUNITY COMMITMENT GOAL: TO NEVER TO BE INVOLVED IN AOD USE WHEN IT IS A VIOLATION OF THE LAW OR THE TERMS OF YOUR JUDICIAL SENTENCE

Exercise: Write your relapse prevention and community commitment goals. Are they different from those described above?

HERE ARE MY RELAPSE PREVENTION AND COMMUNITY COMMITMENT GOALS:

_____

_____

_____

OBJECTIVES AND BENEFITS OF THIS PROGRAM

▶ Prevent recidivism and relapse.

▶ Have full awareness of your AOD use and criminal conduct history.

▶ Learn to change your thinking, beliefs and attitudes which control your actions.

▶ Understand how AOD use and abuse affect your mind, body, social behaviors, relationship with others, and your responsibilities toward the community.

▶ Understand the impact of criminal conduct on your personal life and on the community.

▶ See the value of a "zero risk" goal around AOD use - commit to living an AOD problem-free life.

▶ Have a more positive relationship with yourself, with others and with your community.

▶ Learn strategies and skills to live a more responsible and meaningful life.

Figure 1 describes the three main goals of *SSC*. These goals are met through three sets of skills.

▶ Cognitive or mental self-control skills.

▶ Social and relationship skills.

▶ Community responsibility skills.

These goals and skills rest on the *SSC* theme that self-control and self-management lead to positive outcomes and **responsible living** and change.

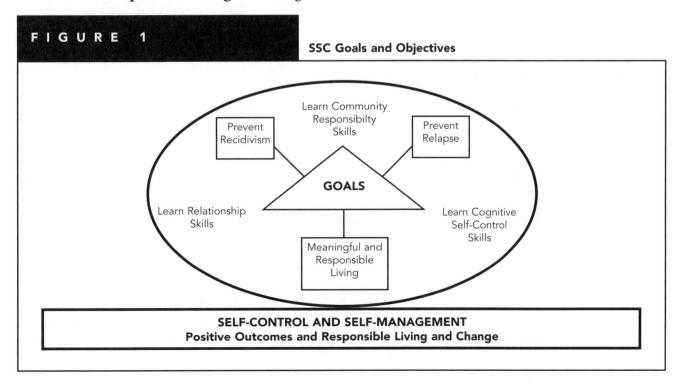

FIGURE 1   SSC Goals and Objectives

EXPECTATIONS OF EACH OTHER: PROGRAM AGREEMENTS AND GUIDELINES

> ▶ Be on time and attend each session.
>
> ▶ Take an active part in the group activities and exercises.
>
> ▶ Have a positive attitude and be respectful toward other group members and leaders.
>
> ▶ Keep names and all information you learn about other people in trust and confidence.
>
> ▶ Complete classroom worksheets and homework and make up any missed sessions.
>
> ▶ Agree to not use alcohol or any mind altering drugs while in the program.
>
> ▶ If you lapse into AOD use, agree to not come to group while using.
>
> ▶ Agree to discuss your use of alcohol or other drugs with your group leader.
>
> ▶ Take part in alcohol or other drug testing required by your sentence or this agency.
>
> ▶ Not take part in illegal activity or criminal conduct including driving with a revoked license.

YOUR GOALS AND OBJECTIVES

What would you like to get from this program? **Exercise:** Using *Worksheet 1* on page 17, write down what you want to get out of SSC. Share what you wrote with the group.

WHAT IS THE APPROACH OF SSC?

We have learned that most people who are involved in criminal conduct and substance abuse **have not learned** important lessons and skills that:

▶ Give them self-control over their thinking and actions;

▶ Help them be effective in relating to others and dealing with relationship conflicts; and

▶ Help them to develop and maintain responsible behaviors in the community.

This program will lead you down the path of learning lessons and building on the lessons you have learned to have more self-control, to be stronger in relating to others and to be more responsible to your community. Your providers - group leaders and counselors - are educators, coaches, and teachers who guide you and help you learn skills so that you can guide yourself in responsible living and change.

We have been taught that experience is a good teacher. **Is this true?** We learn from experience and it is important as we practice the skills that give us self-control and help us live in a responsible and caring way. **But, experience alone is usually not a good teacher. For, with experience, we often**

get the test before the lesson. A good teacher first gives you the lesson, then you have a better chance of passing the test. Too often, we are faced with many life-tests but did not have the lessons to pass them.

As counselors, teachers and coaches, we want to help you strengthen the lessons you have learned and to learn new lessons that prevent criminal conduct and harmful AOD use. We use several **strategies** (approaches) to meet these goals and objectives.

FIRST, we want you to tell us about yourself. What has happened that brought you to this point where you ended up in the criminal justice system? We want you to talk about your history of AOD use and criminal conduct through worksheets and in group.

SECOND, *SSC* is built on a **cognitive-behavioral approach** to preventing future involvement in criminal behavior or a pattern of harmful AOD use. Here is what this approach means.

▶ We make changes in our actions by changing how we think and what we believe about ourselves and the world.

▶ Change and improvement begins in our mind. Your thoughts, attitudes and beliefs - not what happens around you or to you - cause you to act in a certain way. It was your thinking that led you to criminal behavior. We learn how to change our mental world to give us control over our life and prevent repeating the thought habits and behaviors that led to criminal actions and AOD problems.

You learn three types of skills:

▶ Skills to change your thinking, attitudes and beliefs to give you self-control over your actions - **mental restructuring or thought changing;**

▶ Skills that change your social and relationship behaviors to give you more self-control over and respect for your relationships with others - **social and relationship skills training;**

▶ Skills that increase your responsible actions in the community - **community responsibility skills.**

Figure 2 is the cognitive-behavioral (CB) map showing how thoughts lead to feelings and actions. When faced with a situation or an event - a memory or something that happens outside of us - we usually respond **with automatic thoughts or thought habits.** Underlying these thoughts are our attitudes, values (what is important to us) and beliefs. These thoughts then lead to feelings and actions (behaviors). These actions may be adaptive - work for positive or good outcomes, or maladaptive - they lead to negative or bad outcomes.

▶ Whether a good or bad outcome, the thoughts that lead to the behavior are strengthened. This is shown by the arrowed lines going from positive or negative outcomes back to automatic thoughts.

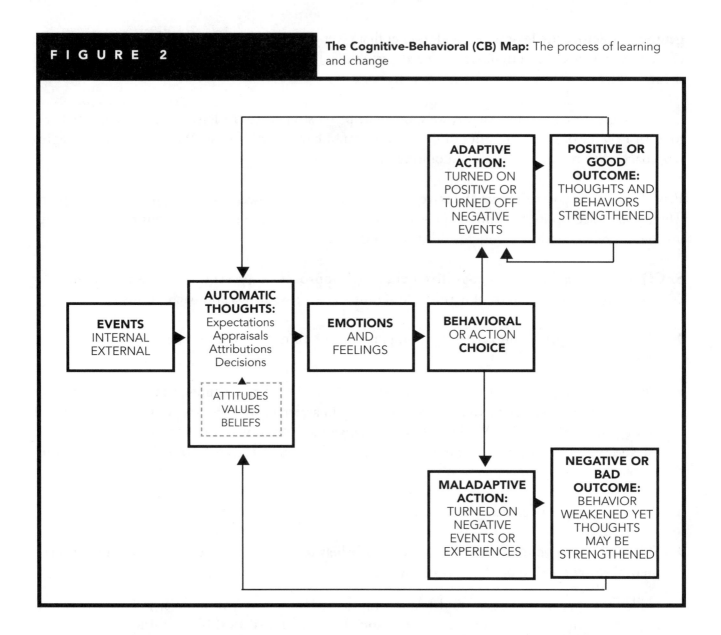

▶ If the outcome is good or positive, the adaptive or positive behaviors get strengthened - shown by the arrow going from positive or good outcomes to adaptive actions or behaviors.

When making changes, we start with our automatic thoughts or thought habits. To make changes stick, we change our underlying attitudes, values, and beliefs. *Figure 2* shows how this happens. We will use it for an exercise in almost every session. We call this the *Cognitive-Behavior (CB) Map Exercise.* We take a deeper look at this in *Sessions 3* and *4.*

Exercise: A group member will be asked to identify an event, and then the counselor will walk the group member through the *CB Map Exercise.*

THIRD, *SSC* gives facts and information about the patterns, cycles and problems of AOD use. You also learn about the outcomes and cycles of criminal conduct, how change takes place, about relapse and recidivism and relapse and recidivism prevention.

Our FOURTH approach is to give specific ways to prevent relapse and recidivism (R&R). All efforts to change and improve ourselves have R&R prevention as their final goal.

WHAT DOES THE CB MAP TELL US ABOUT OUR AOD USE?

▶ First, we expect (thoughts) positive outcomes from substance use - feeling better, having more pleasure, feeling more powerful, feeling socially relaxed, shutting down stress and bad events - and we get them. **AOD use is strengthened** - it is learned.

▶ We come to rely heavily on AOD use to get these outcomes - we **get dependent** or **addicted.**

▶ Although AOD use may lead to bad outcomes, we continue to use because we **expect positive outcomes** - to feel good or not feel bad - which strengthens our dependence. But, we continue to use and to get bad outcomes. We have mental cravings and urges that keep us using.

▶ As a result of using substances, we get into trouble with the law, with our emotions, with other people. We are **challenged.** We decide this is not good and we need to stop, to change.

▶ To get out of this cycle, we have to change our thinking. **Choice:** change thinking or continue to be dependent. Change is in our mind.

SSC helps us learn CB approaches to make changes and learn and practice skills to prevent harmful patterns of AOD use. It helps us deal with beliefs and expectations that lead to AOD use. It gives us self-control. **Self-control leads to positive outcomes.**

WHAT DOES THE CB MAP TELL US ABOUT OUR CRIMINAL CONDUCT (CC)?

▶ Like AOD use, criminal conduct is learned because we **think** it leads to positive outcomes - helps us cope with our problems, takes away stress, makes us feel better, gives us pleasure, make us feel more powerful, gives us a place to fit in. When these outcomes are fulfilled, our criminal thinking is strengthened - learned. **But, the learning is based on very short-term benefits and long-term problems.**

▶ We come to rely on criminal conduct to get these outcomes. We **get dependent or addicted** to CC even though it leads to bad outcomes. We continue to expect good outcomes from CC.

▶ We have mental cravings and urges, powerful thoughts that keep us into criminal thinking and criminal ways. As a result of our criminal thoughts we get into trouble with the law, with other people. We decide to stop and change. We are **challenged.**

▶ To get out of this cycle, we have to change our thinking. **Choice:** change our thinking or continue to be dependent on CC. Change begins in our mind.

SSC helps us learn cognitive-behavioral (CB) approaches to make these changes and learn and practice skills to handle high risk exposures that lead to criminal thinking and criminal conduct. It helps us to deal with the beliefs and expectations that lead to CC. It boils down to self-control. **Self-control leads to positive outcomes.**

HOW DOES SSC CONNECT SUBSTANCE ABUSE WITH CRIMINAL CONDUCT?

By entering *SSC,* you are saying you want to live a life free of problems related to AOD use. You have a choice as to your relapse prevention goals: to live an AOD-free life; or a life free of problems related to AOD use. By entering *SSC,* you are saying you want to live a crime-free life. Your **relapse prevention goal is person centered.** It is your choice. Your **recidivism prevention goal is not** *just* **your choice.** It is also **society's choice.**

Addiction to alcohol and other drugs (AOD) and criminal conduct (CC) have much in common. Both give us rewards right away - a rush or high from the act itself. Both can make us feel good. Both are followed by feelings or thoughts that are not pleasant such as anxiety, guilt, social disapproval or punishment. Both AOD-free and crime-free living are threatened by high-risk situations or high-risk thinking. Both lead to problems and pain in our lives, the lives of others and our community.

BUILDING TRUST AND (RAPPORT) HARMONY

Exercise: You are asked to introduce yourself and share the following:

▶ Some facts about yourself including your age, where you work, and the significant people in your life;

▶ What brings you to the program;

▶ What do you want to get out of the program;

▶ Your concerns or worries about being in the program.

Building Trust and Rapport

Exercise: Using *Worksheet 2,* page 18, write down some concerns you have about trust and your participation in the *SSC* program. Share these with the group.

BEING ALCOHOL AND DRUG FREE

We are expecting you to be AOD free while in *SSC.* Given that your AOD use has been part of your criminal conduct history, we ask you to consider living an AOD-free life - as your relapse prevention goal. This may be a big challenge. Think about it.

HOW DO YOU SEE YOURSELF AROUND AOD USE AND YOUR HISTORY OF CRIMINAL CONDUCT?

Exercise: We now want you to complete a short test - *Client Self-Assessment Scale (CSAS), Worksheet 3,* page 18. There are no right or wrong answers - we want to know how you see yourself. You are asked to score the test. We will look at these results again in *Session 14.*

EVALUATING YOUR NEEDS, PROGRESS AND CHANGE

At the start of SSC and during the program, you are asked to complete self-evaluation questionnaires. These questionnaires will help you and your counselor understand your specific situation and needs as you start the program. You and your counselor will also evaluate your progress and change during the SSC program. At the end of the program, you will be asked to complete the *SSC Program Closure Inventory (PCI)*. Some clients may be contacted following their completion of *SSC* to see how they are doing. Your counselor will explain this evaluation process during orientation.

SUMMARY OF SESSION ACTIVITIES AND HOMEWORK

1. Complete *Worksheets 1 through 3.*

2. For *Homework,* begin working on *Worksheet 4,* page 19, *List of Problems to Work on during SSC.* You will add to this list during your *SSC* sessions. Read the material in *Session 2* for the next session.

SESSION CLOSURE

Share with the group your thoughts about trust, and how you know who you can trust. Talk about your thoughts and feelings about your relapse and recidivism prevention goals. Share what you want to get out of SSC.

WORKSHEET 1	List and number your goals for SSC or what you want to get out the program

_____

_____

_____

_____

_____

_____

_____

Write down some concerns you have about trust and your taking part in the SSC program

_____

_____

_____

_____

_____

Client Self-Assessment Scale (CSAS): Rate yourself on each question. For every check in the "1" column, give yourself a 1, for every check in the "2" column, give yourself a 2, for every check in the "3" column, give yourself a 3, and for every check in the "4" column, give yourself a 4. Total your score.

Rate yourself on each of the following questions	0 None	1 Low	2 Moderate	3 High	4 Very High
1. Degree of problems you have had with the use of alcohol?					
2. Degree of problems you have had with drugs other than alcohol?					
3. Degree of problems you have had with criminal conduct in the past?					
4. Degree of help you need to keep from having further problems with alcohol or other drug use?					
5. Degree of help you need to keep you from being involved in criminal behavior?					
6. To what degree do you want to make changes in your life?					
7. To what degree do you think **that you have** made changes in your life?					
YOUR SCORE FOR EACH COLUMN					
YOUR TOTAL SCORE					

List of problems to work on in SSC

A. Problems you have carried over from childhood and youth

_____

_____

_____

_____

_____

B. Problems with alcohol or other drug use

_____

_____

_____

_____

_____

C. Problems with criminal thinking and behavior

_____

_____

_____

_____

_____

D. Problem thinking and feeling patterns and errors

_____

_____

_____

_____

_____

E. Current life situation problems

    1. Employment and job problems:

    _____

    _____

    2. Social and relationship problems:

    _____

    _____

    3. Marital problems:

    _____

    _____

    4. Family problems:

    _____

    _____

    5. Emotional and psychological problems:

    _____

    _____

    6. Physical health and medical problems:

    _____

    _____

    7. Being involved in treatment and counseling:

    _____

    _____

F. List your strong points and strengths

1. _____   4. _____   7. _____

2. _____   5. _____   8. _____

3. _____   6. _____   9. _____

INTRODUCTION AND OBJECTIVES

Orientation Session 1 told how *SSC* works and how it brings about change. This session provides rules, tools and targets for change.

OBJECTIVES

➡ Understand and apply six rules of change.

➡ Learn and practice the *CB Map Exercise.*

➡ Go over what you will include in your *Autobiography.*

➡ Introduce the *Master Skills List (MSL) for Responsible Living and Change.*

➡ Introduce the *Master Profile (MP).*

➡ Introduce the *Master Assessment Plan (MAP).*

➡ Go over the *Thinking and Action Patterns (TAP)* charting.

➡ Learn to do a *Thinking* and *Re-Thinking Report.*

➡ Learn to use the *SSC Scale* to measure changes in knowledge and skills.

SESSION CONTENT AND FOCUS

SIX RULES THAT GUIDE CHANGE

Change Rule One: Your thoughts, attitudes and beliefs - not what happens outside of you - control your emotions, actions and behaviors

We make changes in our lives when we change mental events: our thoughts, attitudes and beliefs. We briefly look at these events now. We do a deeper study of them in *Session 3.*

▶ **Automatic thoughts:** a **thinking pattern or thought habit** already formed inside our heads. These are **thought habits.**

▶ **Attitude:** a thought for or against a situation, person, idea or object outside of ourselves. It directs how we think, feel and act.

▶ **Belief:** a value or idea used to judge or evaluate outside events, situations, people or ourselves. A belief bonds you to outside events. **It is more powerful than an attitude.** It directs attitudes towards things or people. We have a set of core beliefs. Think about the beliefs you have that led to your criminal conduct.

Change Rule Two: We resist or fight changing our thinking, attitudes and beliefs

When you were arrested for your last offense, what were your thoughts? "Life's not fair?" "I've never had a fair chance!" "The cops are out to get me!" When we clasp to a belief, even though it leads to bad outcomes, we call this the **Belief Clutch.** It is a "do or die" view of ourselves. Remember the Flying Walendas. The father taught all of the troupe to always hold on to the balancing pole. "It's your life or death!" When walking between two buildings on a high wire, a gust of wind caught him. He fell to his death. The balancing pole had to be pried loose from his hands. Had he let go of the pole and caught the wire, he might have lived. Sometimes we clutch to a belief even to the point of our own destruction.

Exercise: Write in the spaces below one belief clutch that you hold on to that led to AOD use problems and one belief clutch that led to criminal thinking and behavior.

```
┌─────────────────────────────────────────────────────────────────────┐
│  BELIEF CLUTCH THAT LED TO AOD USE PROBLEMS                          │
│                                                                     │
│  _____   │
│                                                                     │
│  _____   │
└─────────────────────────────────────────────────────────────────────┘
```

```
┌─────────────────────────────────────────────────────────────────────┐
│  BELIEF CLUTCH THAT LED TO CRIMINAL THINKING AND BEHAVIOR            │
│                                                                     │
│  _____   │
│                                                                     │
│  _____   │
└─────────────────────────────────────────────────────────────────────┘
```

Change Rule Three: We have mixed thoughts and go back and forth about change

This is **ambivalence.** We get over our wavering or **ambivalence** when we learn that some of our thoughts, attitudes and beliefs lead to bad outcomes - they give us more pain than pleasure. It is then that we give them up or change them.

Change Rule Four: We choose the thoughts we have about ourselves and the outside world that lead to our actions

Look at the process of change shown in the *Cognitive-Behavioral (CB) Map, Figure 2,* page 14. A thought goes before every feeling and every behavior - and we choose those thoughts. You chose to let your thought habits or automatic thoughts about the events that took place before you committed a crime control your mind and your behavior. You also have a choice to change those thoughts. You control your thoughts. You control your actions.

Exercise: What are some choices you made that led to bad outcomes?

```
┌──────────────────────────────────────────────────────────────────┐
│  CHOICES I MADE THAT LED TO BAD OUTCOMES                           │
│  _____   │
│                                                                    │
│  _____   │
│                                                                    │
│  _____   │
│                                                                    │
└──────────────────────────────────────────────────────────────────┘
```

Exercise: What are some choices you made that led to good outcomes?

```
┌──────────────────────────────────────────────────────────────────┐
│  CHOICES I MADE THAT LED TO GOOD OUTCOMES                          │
│  _____   │
│                                                                    │
│  _____   │
│                                                                    │
│  _____   │
│                                                                    │
└──────────────────────────────────────────────────────────────────┘
```

Change Rule Five: We go though steps or stages when we make changes

These steps work as a spiral. When we change, we never go back where we started.

- **The challenge.** Something "hits us between the eyes." We get put in jail; lose our freedom.

- **The commitment.** We decide to change and put effort into it.

- **The ownership.** We learn ways to keep change going. Change belongs to you.

Change Rule Six: Think and act in terms of your best interest and the long-term look

We take part in using drugs or crime many times on the spur of the moment. We don't think "what is in my best interest? What are my long-term interests?" We don't think "I want a family but I can't if I'm in jail." The "long-term look" helps us think about consequences.

TOOLS AND TARGETS FOR CHANGE

There are two pathways to self-awareness: **self-disclosure** - sharing our personal experiences; and **receiving feedback** - having others tell us how they see us. The following **nine tools** and targets for change are based on these two pathways. They are your *Program Guides for Change* used throughout *SSC*.

1. Cognitive-Behavioral (CB) Map Exercise

Almost every session in *Phase I* starts with the *CB Map Exercise,* using *Figure 2,* page 14. This exercise works on past, present and future events. **Exercise:** Using *Figure 2,* one person takes a recent event, then identifies the thoughts, emotions, actions and outcomes related to that event.

2. Autobiography

There are three parts to our mental life: **memories,** the **here-and-now,** and our **dreams.** Our *autobiography* is based on our **memories.** We control our memories by how we choose to live each day. Our *autobiography* describes our roots and our past experiences. A tree stands on its roots and trunk - its history. We cannot stand in the present in any meaningful way without memory - our history. Our *autobiography* looks at the unpleasant and the pleasant parts of our history. If you have an autobiography, read it and add parts that may be missing. You are asked to write your autobiography in a separate spiral notebook over the next six to eight weeks. Here are the areas we want you to include.

- The family you grew up in.
- Your childhood through teen years.
- Your education, jobs, marriage(s) and interests.

- Your AOD use and abuse history
- Your criminal conduct history.
- What brought you into this program.

3. Master Skills List (MSL)

Program Guide 1, in the back of your *Workbook,* page 291, gives you the *Master Skills List.* After each session, you are asked to write in the date you started working on the skill, rate your level of mastery in using the skill and update your level of mastery on skills you learned. There are three groups of skills: **mental restructuring skills, relationship skills and society responsibility skills.**

Some *Master Skills* target change in both areas of relationship and society. For example, *empathy* can increase positive relationships with others and responsible actions in society. The goal is to reach a **Very Good** level of mastery for all skills. **Exercise:** In *Session 1,* you worked on the *Cognitive Behavior (CB) Map,* skill number 1 in *Program Guide 1,* page 291. Put the date you attended *Session 1* and rate your mastery level on this skill on *Program Guide 1.*

4. Master Profile (MP)

Your homework this week was *Worksheet 4,* page 19, listing problems to work on in *SSC.* We use this information to work on the your *Master Profile (MP).* **You are asked to complete your MP during the first month in this program.** Here are the areas of assessment in the MP.

I.   Your patterns of AOD use and abuse.

II.   Your criminal and antisocial thinking/conduct.

III. Your thinking, feeling and attitude patterns.

IV.   Problems of childhood and youth.

V. Your life-situation problems and conditions such as job, relationships.

VI. Your motivation for treatment and change.

Exercise: Look over your *Master Profile* in *Program Guide 2,* page 292. You are asked to complete the MP in the first month of the program. In *Session 20,* you rate yourself again.

5. Master Assessment Plan (MAP) - Targets for Change

The MAP is your *Program Guide for Change.* We use the MP to build our *Master Assessment Plan* (MAP). The MAP gives specific thinking, belief and action targets for change. It is your **plan for change** and map for your pathway of **responsible living.** **Exercise:** Look over your MAP, *Program Guide 3,* page 295. Start by writing in one problem area for *Alcohol and Other Drugs,* and one for *Criminal Thinking and Conduct.* In some sessions, we work on the MP and the MAP. **You are asked to complete the MAP in the first month of this program.**

6. Weekly Thinking and Action Patterns (TAP) Charting

You are asked not to use alcohol or other drugs while in *SSC,* and not violate the terms of your judicial sentence or get involved in a criminal act. A lot of our clients think about AOD use or find themselves in an AOD use situation; some may "lapse" into use or a pattern of use. They might think about committing a crime or violating the terms of their judicial sentence. Most clients use skills to prevent AOD use or criminal conduct outcomes. The *TAP Charting* keeps check on these possibilities. It includes the **week you did your charting,** whether you **thought about using alcohol or other drugs,** times you were **in a situation where you could drink or used drugs,** whether you actually **used alcohol/ drugs,** whether you **thought about violating the law,** and in the last column, **skills you used to prevent AOD use or criminal conduct.**

Exercise: We take a few minutes to look over the *TAP Charting Form, Program Guide 4,* page 300, in the back of this *Workbook.* You will be asked to do *TAP Charting* between each *SSC* session.

7. Thinking Report

The *Thinking Report* is your response to the here-and-now and has five parts. It is based on the main parts of the *CB Map, Figure 2,* page 14.

▶ **Event:** Describe in a few words the situation. Be factual and describe what you see.

▶ **Thoughts:** What thoughts do you remember? Do not explain, blame or make excuses.

▶ **Attitudes and Beliefs:** What attitudes and beliefs lead to or underlie your thoughts and feelings?

▶ **Feelings:** What were your emotions related to your thoughts about the event? Nervous, angry, irritated?

▶ **Outcome:** What was your choice, outcome action and behavior. Were they positive or negative?

8. Your Re-Thinking Report

The *Re-Thinking Report* changes our responses to the events that we experience. It has the same parts as the *Thinking Report,* but changes them to produce positive or good outcomes.

9. Measuring Your Knowledge and Skill Development: The Strategies for Self-Improvement and Change Scale (SSC Scale)

In each session you work on strategies and skills for self-improvement and change. At the end of each session, you are asked to measure your level of knowledge and skill using the *SSC Scale*. The scale is from "zero" to 10. The markers are "low," "medium," or "high" levels of knowledge and skill use. Sometimes, you are asked to measure your level of understanding of certain ideas. You start using the *SSC Scale* by showing the degree to which you understand the *SSC* program and the degree to which you think you will take part in the program. Put an X at the level that best fits you.

Understanding SSC program	0	1	2	3	4	5	6	7	8	9	10
	LOW					MEDIUM					HIGH

Degree you will take part in SSC	0	1	2	3	4	5	6	7	8	9	10
	LOW					MEDIUM					HIGH

SUMMARY OF SESSION ACTIVITIES OR HOMEWORK ASSIGNMENTS

1. Do the *CB Map Exercise.*

2. Go over the parts of the *Autobiography.*

3. Go over and begin the *Program Guide 1,* page 291, the *Master Skills List (MSL).*

4. Go over *Program Guide 2,* page 292, your *Master Profile (MP)* and do your first rating.

5. Go over *Program Guide 3,* page 295, the *Master Assessment Plan (MAP).* You are asked to add one problem in the AOD area and one to the criminal conduct area.

6. Go over the *TAP Charting, Program Guide 4,* page 300 and do this week's *TAP Charting.*

SESSION CLOSURE

Share with the group an important idea you learned this session. Discuss barriers or ways you are resisting change in your AOD use habits and in your criminal thinking or attitudes. Be honest. It's for your benefit.

MODULE 2

OVERVIEW

In order to change and develop responsible behavior in our community, we need knowledge and awareness of how we change and what we change. This knowledge will direct us on the path of responsible living. This module provides the basic understanding as to how thinking and behavior are learned and changed. Here are the goals for *Module 2*.

Cognitive-Behavioral Approach to Change and Responsible Living

◆ Understand how thinking and emotions fit into self-improvement and change.

◆ Understand how our behavior and actions are learned and changed.

Module 2 **has two sessions.**

Session 3: How Our Thinking, Attitudes and Beliefs Control Our Actions

Session 4: How Behavior is Learned and Changed

Change starts in our mind

SESSION INTRODUCTION AND OBJECTIVES

The Orientation sessions told how *SSC* works and gave you **rules, tools and targets** for change. We now look at how we can get positive emotional and behavior outcomes by changing our thoughts.

OBJECTIVES

➡ Understand how thoughts, attitudes and beliefs control our emotions and behaviors.

➡ Learn and apply five rules of thinking that lead to actions and behaviors.

➡ Learn the map for how thoughts are strengthened.

➡ Learn the steps and pathways to change thinking.

GETTING STARTED

▶ *CB MAP Exercise.* Share your *Thinking and Action Plan (TAP) Charting, Program Guide 4,* page 300, you did this week. Each member is asked to share one *SSC* goal from *Worksheet 1,* page 17.

▶ Key words: automatic thoughts, attitudes, beliefs, belief clutch, thought habit, thinking errors, outcomes, expectations, appraisals, attributions, decisions.

SESSION CONTENT AND FOCUS

FIVE RULES OF THINKING THAT LEAD TO ACTIONS OR BEHAVIORS

In *SSC Orientation,* we looked at six rules that guide change. Now, we look at **five rules of thinking** that lead to actions or behaviors. The first three rules of thinking are also rules of change in *Session 2.*

Thinking Rule 1: Thoughts control emotions and behaviors

Your thoughts, attitudes and beliefs - not what happens outside of you - control your emotions, actions and behaviors - and lead you to AOD use problems and criminal conduct.

▶ **Automatic thoughts - a thinking pattern or thought habit.** A mental reaction to outside events or our memories. They operate like an automatic car transmission that shifts gears on its own. Here are some automatic thoughts that lead to AOD abuse or CC: "I haven't had that much." "They've got more than they need." "I can get away with it. I'll take a chance." **Exercise:** Think about the last time you broke the law. Write two thoughts you had.

TWO THOUGHTS YOU HAD THE LAST TIME YOU BROKE THE LAW

_____

_____

▶ **Attitudes** - thoughts for or against a situation, person or idea. They direct our thinking. They are positions we take. They are hooked into feelings. Attitudes are "good" or "bad." Attitudes become so strong they form **attitude habits.** The right attitude of an airplane is to be lined up with the horizon. A pilot with the "wrong" attitude may "crash." Here are some "bad" attitudes that can lead to AOD problems or CC and cause a "crash."

"Nobody cares about me. The hell with it."

"No one's going to tell me what to do."

"Everyone's trying to screw me over." "They deserve it."

"I'll drink as much as I want." "I won't get caught."

Wrong attitudes can lead to a crash.

Exercise: Write down an attitude that led your AOD use or criminal conduct (CC).

AN ATTITUDE THAT LED YOU TO AOD USE OR CC

_____

_____

Attitudes also lead to good and successful outcomes. "I'm enjoying life." "I'm going to have a great day." **Exercise:** Write down an attitude that helps you have positive outcomes or success.

AN ATTITUDE YOU HAVE THAT LEADS TO POSITIVE OUTCOMES

_____

_____

◗ **Core Beliefs** are ideas we use to judge or evaluate events, people or ourselves. They bond us to outside events or people. "All people are created equal." "I believe in God." "I can go it alone." They are thought of as "truths." They become so strong they become **belief habits.** Here are some beliefs that lead to AOD abuse or CC. "I won't get caught." "I never get drunk." "The cops are out to get me." **Exercise:** Write down a core belief that led you to AOD abuse and CC.

A CORE BELIEF THAT LED TO AOD ABUSE AND CRIMINAL CONDUCT

_____

_____

Our core beliefs also lead to good outcomes. "I am an honest person." "People should do their best." "I am a happy person." "I am a good citizen." "I am a hard worker." **Exercise:** Write down a core belief that led you to positive outcomes or success.

CORE BELIEF YOU HAVE THAT LED TO POSITIVE OUTCOMES

_____

_____

Thinking Rule 2: We fight or resist changing our thinking

This is stubborn thinking. When we fight changing our thinking, we are defending our view of ourselves. Even though you have had pain from past criminal conduct, do you still **think** at times, "I can get away with it"? Even though drug use caused you problems, do you still think, "It's not going to hurt to get high once in while"? This is also *Change Rule Two*, page 22 in *Session 2*. **Exercise:** Write down how you fight changing your thinking about AOD use. Be honest.

HOW HAVE YOU FOUGHT CHANGING YOUR THINKING ABOUT AOD USE?

_____

_____

Think again about the Flying Walendas and the *belief clutch*. Share your belief clutches that lead to AOD abuse or CC . When you clutch to a belief and think "I'm right," remember each person sees the world and themselves differently. **"Two men looked out from prison bars; one saw mud, the other saw stars." No one view of the world is necessarily right or wrong.** Yet we do form common beliefs that become rules or laws. We begin to have legal problems when our actions resulting from our beliefs and our thinking patterns go against these common rules or laws.

Thinking Rule 3: We choose our thoughts

A thought goes before every feeling and behavior - and we choose those thoughts. Are you still *thinking,* "I didn't choose the thoughts that led to my legal problems?" This is also *Change Rule Four.* Look over the work you did on this rule in *Session 2,* page 22.

Thinking Rule 4: Our thoughts can become distorted and illogical (new rule)

These are errors in logic or thinking that can lead to problem emotions and behaviors. Here are some examples. "My way is the only way." "I know more than the other person." "You can't trust anyone." "They deserve it." **Exercise:** *Worksheet 5,* page 35, is a list of thinking errors. Check if you use these errors. Then, check if the thinking error was part of your AOD problems or CC.

Thinking Rule 5: Good and bad outcomes strengthen thoughts (new rule)

Both good **and** bad outcomes can strengthen the thoughts that lead to those outcomes. **Example:** The thought "she doesn't care, nobody cares," may lead you to get high and say hurtful things. The person responds by saying hurtful things back. You think: "See, she doesn't care." The bad outcome only makes the thought that leads to that outcome stronger.

MAPPING THE PATHWAY TO CHANGE OUR THINKING

Recall: what happens outside of you can bring automatic thoughts based on your beliefs and attitudes. Those thoughts may bring on feelings and a behavior or action response. That action response may be maladaptive - cause you to act in an irresponsible way, lead to CC or AOD abuse. Or the response may be a positive coping behavior. But **we have a choice before we act: To think before we act.**

Figure 3, page 32, is a *CB Map* like *Figure 2* that you saw in *Session 1.* *Figure 3,* however, shows how thoughts get strengthened or reinforced - the arrowed lines going back from the positive or negative outcome boxes to the automatic thoughts. It shows four kinds of **automatic thoughts.**

- ▶ **Expectations** are what we expect if we do a certain thing. "If I take a drink, I'll relax." "If I commit this crime, I'll feel more powerful." "If I work hard, I'll get ahead."

- ▶ **Appraisals** give meaning to ourselves, to what happens to us and to what we do. They are judgments and based on beliefs. "This is unfair," "I've lost something very important" or "I'm not that drunk." Some appraisals cause us to be irresponsible, angry, sad, happy, joyful.

- ▶ **Attributions** are thoughts that explain, credit or blame why things happen to us. **External:** "I got arrested because the cops were out to get me." **Internal:** "I drink because I can't handle life."

- ▶ **Decisions thoughts:** Big decisions that get us into trouble are built on many small decisions. Stopping to see a "friend" who does crimes results in committing a crime. You might say, "I didn't decide to get high. It just happened." Every behavior is based on a thought-decision.

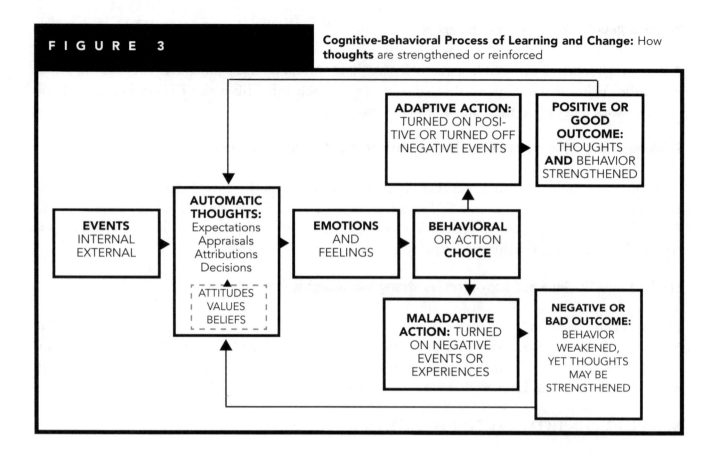

FIGURE 3

Cognitive-Behavioral Process of Learning and Change: How **thoughts** are strengthened or reinforced

Example: the boss wants to see you. Automatic thought - **expectation:** "He's going to tell me I'm slacking off." **Appraisal:** "He's always looking for something wrong." **Attribution:** "It's his fault, he's working me too hard." Your **attitude** is defensive and you make excuses. Underneath these thoughts and attitudes is a **core belief** "I can't do anything right." These thoughts, attitudes and beliefs lead to a maladaptive response that works against a good outcome. The boss is even more critical than he might have been. His actions only strengthen your thinking. "See, I was right, he's always on my back. I can't do anything right." Even bad outcomes strengthen the thoughts that lead to those outcomes.

You get a better outcome by *changing your thinking.* "At best, he may tell me I'm doing a good job. At worst, he may give me some constructive criticism." You say "I'm doing a good job." This leads to a positive belief about your own worth. Now you approach the meeting with strength and self-control. You may get negative feedback, but you take it as a way to improve. This leads to positive comments from the boss. Good outcomes strengthen the thoughts that lead to them. This is shown by the arrowed line from positive outcomes to our automatic thoughts in *Figure 3.*

Example: John had a fight with his wife. On his way home he thinks - **expectation:** "If I stop off and have a few I'll feel better." **Appraisals:** "She doesn't care. Nobody cares." **Belief:** "Life isn't fair." His **attitude:** "To hell with it, the hell with everybody, screw it." These thoughts lead to feeling discouraged - sorry for himself. More **appraisals:** "My friends at the bar care about me." He has a few more. Another **expectation:** "If I go home now I'll get chewed out." A "friend" at the bar says, "It'd be easy to break into the Quick-Shop down the street. Get enough beer for a month." The **beliefs** "life isn't fair and not being cared about" and the attitude "screw it," lead to his **appraisals:** "We can pull if off. Anyway, I don't care." **Expectation:** "I won't get caught." He gets caught and charged with burglary. This event strengthens his **thought** "nobody cares," his **attitude** of "screw it," and his **belief** "life isn't fair."

Figure 3 shows that positive (good) and negative (bad) outcomes strengthen thoughts that lead to those outcomes. If John changes his thought to "I'm going to listen to what she has to say," he will have a positive outcome. The thought gets strengthened. This is the arrowed line that leads from the POSITIVE OUTCOME back to the automatic thoughts. The bad outcome of getting arrested only strengthens the thoughts of "I'm not being treated fairly, it's not fair," - the very thoughts that led to his criminal actions.

THOUGHTS, EMOTIONS AND ACTIONS INTERACT OR AFFECT EACH OTHER

Emotions and moods can lead to thoughts; actions can influence how one thinks or feels; emotions can lead to behaviors. *Figure 4* below explains this. Yet, the key is: **Thoughts control our emotions and actions.**

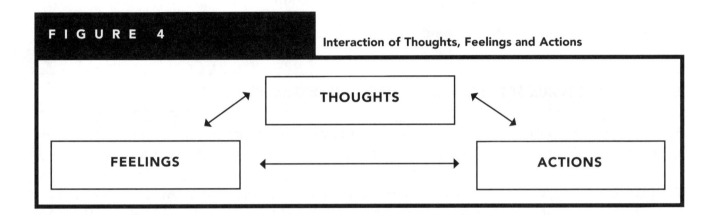

FIGURE 4   Interaction of Thoughts, Feelings and Actions

STEPS TO HOW THOUGHTS LEAD TO ACTIONS

Using *Figure 3,* follow these steps in seeing how thoughts lead to actions and behaviors.

Step 1: Choose an **event** that was followed by drinking. Say, an argument with your spouse.

Step 2: What were your **automatic thoughts?** "I'll have a couple to relax"? "She doesn't' care"?

Step 3: What was your **attitude?** "To hell with it." What was your **belief?** "Women are hard to get along with"? "You can't trust men"?

Step 4: What were your **feelings?** Anger? Sadness?

Step 5: What was your **action** or behavior? Did you get drunk? Storm out of the house? Argue or fight?

Step 6: What was the **outcome?** Did you not talk for days? Were there more problems? Did the behavior serve your best interest? Was it a good or bad outcome?

STEPS TO CHANGING YOUR THOUGHTS

Step 1: **Recognize thoughts** that lead to problem behaviors or bad outcomes.

Step 2: **Change those thoughts.** Imagine the positive behavior that can follow those thoughts. Go from automatic thinking to **non-automatic or self-controlled thinking. Think about thinking and think for a change.**

Step 3: **Identify your attitude** that produced those thoughts. Change that attitude.

Step 4: **Identify your beliefs** that underlie that attitude and the thoughts that show that attitude. Replace that belief with one that leads to more positive thinking and better outcomes.

Step 5: **Know the target behavior** you want that leads to better outcomes. Are your new thoughts, attitudes and beliefs going to result in that behavior?

Step 6: **What outcome do you want?** Will it give you self-control? Will it benefit others?

SUMMARY OF SESSION ACTIVITIES, HOMEWORK AND SESSION CLOSURE

1. **Exercise:** Do *Worksheet 5.* Do these errors in thinking cause problems at your work? In your relationships? Do they lead to AOD problems and CC? Which ones do you use most?

2. **Exercise:** Using *Worksheet 6,* write an event that took place before your last arrest. On the left side of the THOUGHTS space, put your negative thoughts. On the left side of the BELIEFS, ATTITUDES, FEELINGS space, put a belief, attitude and feeling that supported those thoughts. In the ACTION CHOICE space, there is written "chose to commit a crime." In the NEGA-TIVE ACTION space, there is written "broke the law." The NEGATIVE OUTCOMES space has "caught and arrested." Were you jailed? Did this outcome strengthen your thoughts that led to criminal behavior? **Now, go back to** the THOUGHTS space following the event. On the right side, change your thoughts that will lead to positive outcomes. Replace the attitudes and beliefs with those that are more positive and that will lead to a more positive choice that leads to a positive action. Does the outcome reinforce or strengthen the thoughts and beliefs that you changed? Work on this in class and share it with your group.

3. Update your *Master Skills List (MSL),* page 291 and your *MAP,* page 295. Do your *TAP Charting* for this week, page 300.

4. *SSC Scale:* Rate your level of understanding and knowledge of how thoughts lead to our behaviors and actions.

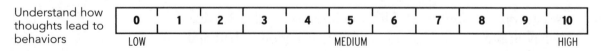

Understand how thoughts lead to behaviors	0	1	2	3	4	5	6	7	8	9	10
	LOW					MEDIUM					HIGH

5. Share with the group what behaviors will be hardest for you to change.

Checklist for your use in identifying your errors in thinking

ERRORS IN THINKING	NEVER THINK THIS	SOMETIMES THINK THIS	THINK THIS A LOT	PART OF MY CC/AOD USE
POWER THRUST: Better than others				
ZERO STATE: Feeling of no value				
VICTIM STANCE: Blaming others, poor me				
PRIDE: Feel superior to others				
DON'T CARE: Lack concern how others are affected				
PARANOID: People are out to get you				
DISTRUST: Can't depend on anyone				
DEMAND: You want it right now				
SOLO: Don't need help				
PROCRASTINATE: Put off things				
STUBBORN: Won't change your ideas or give in, no way				
RIGID: I'm right, you're wrong				
CATASTROPHIZE: Mountains out of molehills, worst will happen				
PICKED ON: Feel singled out				
JUST DESERTS: They deserve it or have it coming				
FAIR DESERTS: I deserve more than what I'm getting				
CHEATED: I was short changed, didn't get what I had coming				
SCREWED: Feeling mistreated				
MAGNIFY: Blow things out of proportion				
WEAK: Can't stand up to what is best for yourself				
LYING: Exaggerating truth, almost automatic for you				
HOSTILE: Unfriendly, lack of empathy				

Cognitive-behavioral outcome of your last arrest. Take the events that took place right before your arrest. On the left side of the rectangle, note your thoughts, attitudes, beliefs and feelings leading up to the arrest. Go back and change your thoughts, beliefs, attitudes and feelings. Now write in a positive action and the outcome.

EVENT

THOUGHTS

BELIEFS, ATTITUDES, FEELINGS

ACTION CHOICE?

Chose to commit a crime

NEGATIVE ACTION

Broke the law

POSITIVE ACTION

NEGATIVE OUTCOMES: WHAT THOUGHTS WERE REINFORCED?

Caught-arrested

POSITIVE OUTCOMES: WHAT THOUGHTS WERE REINFORCED?

SESSION INTRODUCTION AND OBJECTIVES

In *Session 3,* we learned the rules and the process of how **thought habits, attitude habits and belief habits** are formed and strengthened. Now we learn three rules that decide how **action or behavior habits - automatic actions** are formed.

> **OBJECTIVES**
>
> ➠ Learn and apply the rules of how we learn behavior.
>
> ➠ Understand how learning behavior fits into cognitive-behavioral change and self-control.

GETTING STARTED

▶ Group begins with the *CB Map Exercise.* Share your *TAP Charting.*

▶ Key words: thought habits, behavior habits, behavior strengthened or reinforced, CB change.

SESSION CONTENT AND FOCUS

REVIEW: HOW THOUGHTS AND BELIEFS GET STRENGTHENED

Thoughts and beliefs that lead to a positive or good outcome can get strengthened or reinforced.

Example: Betty has a conflict with someone at work. She stops and thinks, "I'm not going to argue, I'm going to listen and give him my view and work it out with him." This leads to a good outcome and the outcome strengthens the thoughts, "I'm going to listen and work it out with him." It also strengthens her belief that she has self-control and self-mastery.

Thoughts and beliefs that lead to negative or bad outcomes can get strengthened or reinforced.

Look at the example in *Session 3*, page 32. Conflict with his spouse led John to thinking "no one cares, nothing good happens to me." He thought, "what I need are a few drinks with friends who understand me." This led to having several drinks with a criminal-minded friend. He **decided** to do a crime with him and was arrested. This outcome led to the thoughts "things are unfair, nothing good does happen to me," which strengthened the original thoughts that "things are not fair, no one cares." The thoughts - expectations, attributions, appraisals, decisions - get strengthened.

The first pathway to learning is when thoughts are strengthened and we form thought habits.

RULES OF HOW BEHAVIORS OR ACTIONS ARE LEARNED

The second pathway to learning is when the behavior itself gets strengthened and learned, forming **behavior habits.** Once an action takes place, any of these can happen.

- The behavior may never repeat itself or never happen again.

- The behavior may repeat itself, but not on any steady basis or in any consistent pattern.

- The behavior may form a pattern or what we call a **behavior habit or action habit.** We can compare this to a **thought habit** or what we have called automatic thoughts.

Learning Rule 1: Turning on positive events or outcomes

If a behavior turns on positive events such as a pleasant feeling, a sense of well-being, that behavior gets strengthened. It repeats itself. It becomes an action habit. If drinking alcohol turns on positive outcomes, drinking is strengthened (reinforced). We do it again. This is how it works.

Exercise: In the first space below, write in a specific behavior you do often that turns on something positive for you. In the second space, describe the positive events - thoughts or feelings - that are turned on by that behavior. Then, check to what **degree of strength** that habit or behavior has in your life - *high degree of strength, moderate or low degree of strength (weak).*

Learning Rule 2: Turning off negative events

If a behavior turns off a negative event - something unpleasant, or painful - that behavior gets strengthened and is learned. It becomes a behavioral habit. This is a powerful way to strengthen behavior. We feel stressed, take a drink, the stress goes away. This strengthens the drinking behavior. This is how it works.

Exercise: In the first space below, write a specific behavior you do that shuts down something unpleasant. In the second space, put the negative events - thoughts or feelings - turned off by that behavior. Check what **degree of strength** that behavior has in your life - high degree, moderate or low degree (weak).

Learning Rule 3: Turning on negative events or outcomes

If a behavior turns on a negative event - something unpleasant such as pain or stress - that behavior is weakened, and will probably not occur at some point in the future. We drink too much, get sick, have a hangover. This rule says we should not drink again. This is how it works.

Exercise: In the first space below, write a specific behavior or action that turned on some negative or unpleasant event for you. Put the unpleasant event, feeling or thought that the behavior turned on in the second space. Check to what degree of strength that habit pattern or behavior has in your life - high degree of strength, moderate or low degree of strength (weak).

WHY DOESN'T RULE 3 - TURNING OFF NEGATIVE EVENTS - ALWAYS WORK?

For the behavior you gave in the last exercise, you might have checked "moderate" or even "high." If this rule worked, you should have checked "low." The behavior should have been weakened or no longer used. Why doesn't **Learning Rule 3** always work? Why continue behaviors that cause us problems? Why drink to excess again if you got sick from drinking? Here's why.

First, it's the power of Rules 1 and 2

Behaviors that turn on positive events or turn off negative events give us immediate rewards even though those behaviors can lead to bad outcomes. Immediate rewards may cause thinking errors. You go to a bar to "drown" your sorrows. You want relief right now, even though you know you will have a hangover tomorrow. Remember the country-western song: "A heartache tonight or a headache tomorrow." We are going to choose the headache tomorrow to get rid of the "heartache" tonight.

The power of **Rules 1 and 2** can prevent seeing serious outcomes of a behavior pattern. Why do over half of those persons convicted of a crime commit another crime after the pain of arrest, conviction and jail? Immediate or quick benefits of criminal conduct or AOD use are powerful rewards.

Second, it's the power of thoughts that lead to the outcomes

Learning Rule 3 doesn't always work because the bad results from a behavior also strengthen the automatic thoughts and beliefs that lead to the behaviors.

Exercise: Think of an example that shows how this works. Share this with the group.

Third, bad behaviors do not always lead to bad outcomes

We say, "I've had too much to drink, but I can get by with it. I've done it a lot and not gotten into trouble." We have committed crimes and not gotten caught or punished. This strengthens the thought "I can get away with it."

HOW THINKING AND BEHAVIOR ARE LEARNED AND STRENGTHENED

Let's put together the puzzle of how thinking and acting lead to *learning thought habits* (automatic thoughts) and to *learning behavior or action habits*. *Figure 5* below shows how this happens.

▶ The behavior may turn on a positive event. It may turn off a negative event (pain, stress). The behavior is strengthened - or it is learned. It becomes an action habit. **This is the arrowed line going from "positive or good outcome" back to "adaptive action: turned on positive or turned off negative events."**

▶ The outcome may be negative. In this case, the behavior should not get learned or strengthened. **There is no arrowed line going from "negative or bad outcome" to "maladaptive actions or turned on negative events."** But, regardless of the outcome - positive or negative, good or bad - the **thought, attitude and belief habits are reinforced** or strengthened.

Look again at the example in *Session 3*, page 32, of John getting involved in a crime. Can you see how both John's behaviors and his thinking were strengthened? Let's change John's thought **decision** from "I'll stop off for a couple," to "I'm going home to talk to her about our fight." He also uses new **appraisals:** "She's also upset, it's not worth fighting about," "I can handle this;" and **expectations:** "If we talk it out, I'll feel better and so will she." The **attitude,** "screw it" is changed to "it can work out." This builds John's belief "when I put effort into something, it works out." His **adaptive** - positive action of using communication skills and talking things out leads to a positive outcome. These action skills get **strengthened.** His thoughts, "I can make things work out," get strengthened.

Learning Rule 3 holds that John's criminal conduct should be weakened because it turned on bad things in his life. **Unless John changes his thinking, attitudes and beliefs that lead to criminal conduct, he is high risk for committing another crime and being involved in AOD use.** Repeat offenders have not changed their thinking, attitudes or beliefs.

PRACTICING COGNITIVE-BEHAVIORAL CHANGE

Exercise: Using *Worksheet 7*, page 42, take a situation that happened to you in the past that *resulted in a bad or negative outcome*. Write in the EVENT. On the left side of the THOUGHTS space, write down thoughts that resulted from the event. On the left side of the ATTITUDES, BELIEFS, FEELINGS space, write down an attitude and a belief that supported those thoughts and a feeling that was an outcome of your thoughts. On the left side of the BEHAVIOR CHOICE space, write an action you chose, and in the NEGATIVE BEHAVIOR space, the actual behavior. If the outcome was negative, the behavior was most likely negative. Write in the NEGATIVE OUTCOME. Did the outcome strengthen the thoughts, attitudes and beliefs?

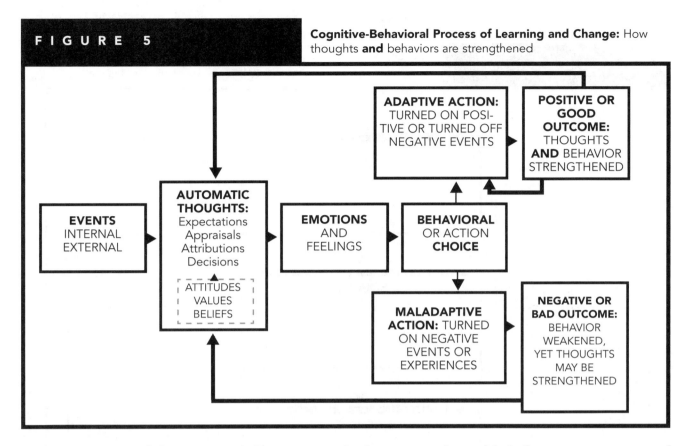

Exercise: Use *Worksheet 7* again. Change your thinking, attitudes and beliefs to get a positive and good outcome. Write a thought that counters the original thought, and the changed attitudes and beliefs that support those thoughts. What feelings come from these new thoughts and beliefs? What will the adaptive or positive behavior and outcome be? Does that outcome strengthen the new behavior and changed thoughts?

SUMMARY OF SESSION ACTIVITIES OR HOMEWORK ASSIGNMENTS AND SESSION CLOSURE

1. Complete *Worksheet 7*. Update your *Master Skills List (MSL)*, page 291, your *Master Assessment Plan,* page 295, and do your *TAP* Charting for this week, page 300. Read *Session 5* for next week.

2. Using the *SSC Scale,* rate your level of understanding of how thoughts and behaviors are strengthened and your skill level of changing thinking. Put an x at the level that best fits you.

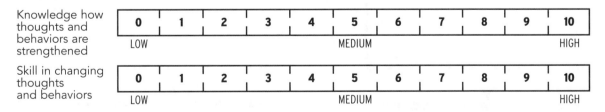

3. For closing group: Discuss what thoughts you will have to change when a friend offers you drugs.

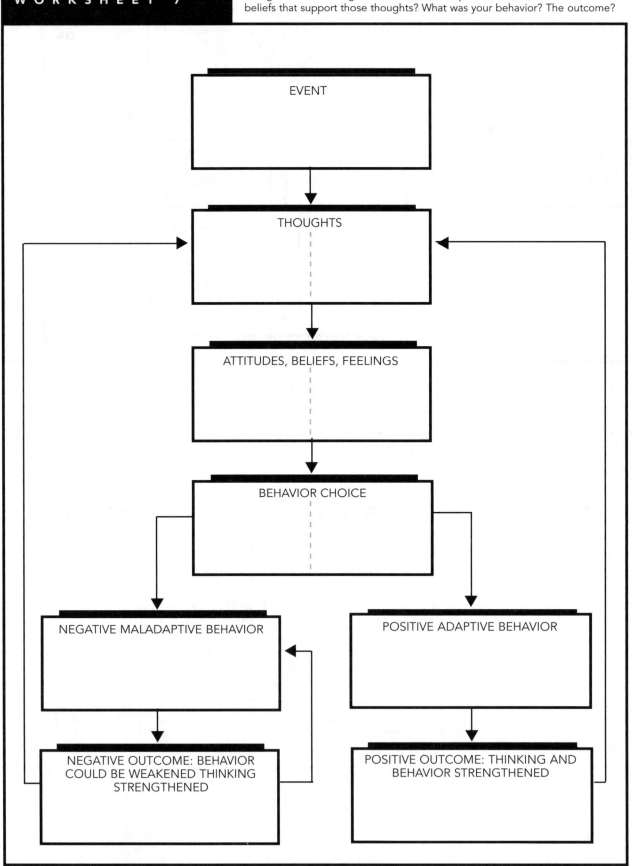

Practicing cognitive-behavioral change: Take an event that led to a bad outcome. Describe your automatic thoughts, feelings and beliefs, your behavior and the bad outcome. Start over. Replace those thoughts with positive thoughts. Those thoughts should lead to a positive outcome. What are some beliefs that support those thoughts? What was your behavior? The outcome?

WORKSHEET 7

EVENT

THOUGHTS

ATTITUDES, BELIEFS, FEELINGS

BEHAVIOR CHOICE

NEGATIVE MALADAPTIVE BEHAVIOR

POSITIVE ADAPTIVE BEHAVIOR

NEGATIVE OUTCOME: BEHAVIOR COULD BE WEAKENED THINKING STRENGTHENED

POSITIVE OUTCOME: THINKING AND BEHAVIOR STRENGTHENED

MODULE 3

OVERVIEW

An important goal of this program is to prevent relapse back into patterns of use that result in negative and disruptive outcomes.

Knowledge about alcohol and other drugs gives us a basis for preventing relapse. In this Module, we look at some basic facts and ideas about alcohol and other drugs. We then see how this knowledge applies to our own personal situation. On completion of *Module 3,* you will have a good idea of your AOD use and abuse patterns. You will be more aware of the problems and dangers of these patterns. Here are the specific goals of this module.

Alcohol and Other Drug (AOD) Use Patterns and Outcomes

◆ Gain basic understandings about AOD use and abuse.

◆ Understand the patterns of AOD use and abuse.

◆ Understand the pathways to disruptive AOD use outcomes and addiction.

◆ Have a clear picture of your own patterns of use and abuse.

Module 3 **has four sessions.**

Session 5: Alcohol and Other Drugs: How Do the Facts Fit You?

Session 6: Understanding Alcohol or Other Drug Use Patterns: How Do They Fit You?

Session 7: AOD Impaired Control Cycles: Pathways to AOD Problem Outcomes and Addiction

Session 8: AOD Use Problem Outcomes - Patterns of Misuse and Abuse: How Do They Fit You?

SESSION INTRODUCTION AND OBJECTIVES

> ### OBJECTIVES
>
> ➠ Learn some basic facts about alcohol and other drugs.
>
> ➠ Help you see how the facts and ideas fit you.

GETTING STARTED

▶ *CB Map Exercise.* Share your *Thinking and Action Plan (TAP) Charting,* page 300, that you did this week.

▶ Take a thinking rule in *Session 3* and apply that to an event that happened to you this past week.

▶ For thought and discussion: What is an alcohol problem? What is a drug problem? What causes alcohol and drug use problems?

▶ Key words: drug types, enhancers, suppressors, direct and indirect effects, tolerance, BAC, health risk, physical damage.

SESSION CONTENT AND FOCUS

BASIC FACTS AND KNOWLEDGE ABOUT DRUGS

1. **Definition:** A drug is a substance that changes or alters the way a person feels, thinks or acts.

2. **Drugs work** by changing the flow of electricity and the release of the body's natural nerve chemicals called neurochemicals.

3. **Table 1, page 46, shows five types or classes of drug**

   ▶ **Sedatives, depressants or downers** slow down our nervous system. These are **system suppressor** drugs and include alcohol, barbiturates, sleeping pills and other sedatives, and inhalants.

   ▶ **Narcotics or opiates** reduce pain and increase sense of pleasure and euphoria. These are also system suppressors. They slow down sensitivity to pain and internal and external stress.

   ▶ **Stimulants or uppers** speed up or excite the nervous system. These are **system enhancers:** cocaine, amphetamines, ecstasy, caffeine. They speed up both the mind and the body.

   ▶ **Hallucinogens** change or alter our perception and sense of reality. These are **mental enhancers**, but they enhance and change the mind.

▶ **Marijuana** can **both enhance and suppress the system.** The beginning effects are stimulation, pulse rate increases, some anxiety and tension which is followed by a pleasant feeling of well being and relaxation.

Nicotine is in a separate category, and has the effect of stimulating (initial) and relaxing the system. All five classes of drugs can be seen as either system enhancers, system suppressors, or both.

4. Drugs have a direct and indirect (withdrawal) effect

The **direct effects** happen when using the drug: they may be physical (sleepiness); psychological (feel good). The **indirect effects** happen when the drug wears off. This is the **withdrawal** or abstinence reaction.

5. Different drugs have different direct and indirect effects

The direct effect of a drug is usually opposite the indirect effect. **Alcohol: direct** - slows you down (go to sleep); **indirect** - speeds you up, shaky, nervous, can't sleep. **Cocaine: direct** - speeds you up; **indirect** - (withdrawal) slows you down. Both direct and indirect effects can cause problems. *Table 1* below gives the direct and indirect effects of the five types of drugs. The indirect effects are related to withdrawal. <u>Exercise:</u> Using *Table 1,* complete *Worksheet 8,* page 58. Write down the drugs you have used and the **direct** or intoxicating effects and the **indirect** effects from these drugs. Include alcohol.

6. Alcohol and other drugs make the body toxic

The body may become **dependent** on the drug, if it is in the system for a period of time. When the body withdraws from the drug, the system may go into shock. It is mental and physical. The shock to the nervous system can result in an epileptic seizure.

7. AOD tolerance causes physical and mental drug dependence

Tolerance is needing more and more of the drug to get the same results or the same amount gives less of what you expect. You may need four drinks now to get a "buzz," where once it took only two. It may take 10 times the amount of a narcotic

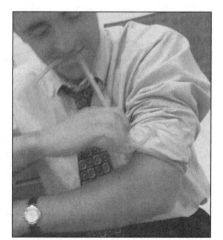

You may need more of the drug to get the same reaction.

(heroin) to get the same relief you got when first taking it. Behavioral tolerance means you may not look drunk with a BAC of .10.

8. Mixing drugs increases the strength of one or both drugs

This is **drug interaction:** A drug gets stronger because another drug is in the body. A fatal dose of a barbiturate is lowered by 50 percent when alcohol is in the body. About half as much of some sleeping medications can be lethal when used with alcohol.

Two depressants more than double the effect of these drugs (*multiplying effect*). One drink and one sedative pill is like taking from three to 10 drinks. Thus, 2 + 2 is not equal to 4. It may be 5. It may be much more.

One drink with cold medicine doubles the effect of each drug. Together, they have a greater effect than either does alone. A stimulant - caffeine pills, coffee, cola, Mountain Dew, cocaine, amphetamines - with alcohol is dangerous. You think you are sober and you are not.

Prescription and over-the-counter drugs used for depression, colds, flu, and relaxing muscles can make you: drowsy, mentally confused, lack coordination, more intoxicated, have problems breathing and even can cause death. Mixed with alcohol they are double-dangerous.

TABLE 1

Five Classes of Drugs: Their Direct and Indirect Effects

DRUG CATEGORY	DIRECT EFFECTS	INDIRECT EFFECTS
Sedatives - suppressors: Alcohol Tranquilizers Barbiturates Sleeping pills Inhalants	Drowsiness, sedated, relaxed, slurred speech, blackouts, poor motor control, depression, confusion, impaired muscle control, impaired judgment, lower blood pressure, impaired vision, work impairment.	Hyper, stimulation, agitation, irritability, hallucinations, delusions, anxiety, fear, shakes, headaches, tremors, seizures, vomiting, insomnia, work impairment.
Narcotics-suppressors: Heroin Oxycodone Codeine Oxycontin Morphine Vicodin Pain killers Percodan Methadone Demerol	Blocks pain, depression, increase sense of pleasure, relax, euphoria, impair judgment, reduce personal care, mental confusion.	Irritability, panic, anxiety, tremors, shakes, chills, sweating, cramps, nausea, loss appetite, runny nose, muscle aches, spasms.
Stimulants-enhancers: Amphetamines Methamphetamine Cocaine Caffeine Ritalin Adderall	Insomnia, euphoric, restless, talkative, weight loss, tremors, hyperactive, panic, agitation, sweating, dry mouth, paranoia, hallucinations, seizures, aggressive actions, inappropriate social behavior, impaired muscle coordination, impaired judgment, overconfident, increased blood pressure, work impairment.	Depression, paranoia, apathy, slow response to stimuli, headaches, fatigue, guilt, cravings, slowing of body functions, over-sleeping, slow responding, indifference.
Hallucinogens-enhancers: LSD Ketamine Mescaline Mushrooms PCP Ecstasy (MDMA)	Excitation, euphoria, hallucinations, insomnia, decrease coordination, confusion, flashbacks, delusions, simulation, increase heart and blood pressure.	Loss of appetite, depression, anxiety, irritability, delirium, paranoia, heavy use can damage brain.
Marijuana - Enhancer and Suppressor	Initially stimulated followed by pleasant feeling, relaxed, well-being, impaired motor coordination, slow reaction time, drowsiness, impairs judgment of speed and distance, impairs short-term memory, sometimes hallucinations, blocks tracking time, impairs ability to concentrate, paranoia.	Anxiety, irritability, paranoia, restlessness, sleeplessness, problems concentrating, stomach pain, vomiting, hostile behavior, increased anger.

ABOUT ALCOHOL

1. Some errors in thinking about alcohol and some facts

Error: Driving with just one drink won't harm.
Fact: One drink can impair your driving skills.

Error: Alcohol increases mental/physical skills.
Fact: Alcohol decreases mental/physical skills.

Error: Alcohol stimulates the body.
Fact: Alcohol slows down and depresses the body.

Error: Beer has less alcohol than whiskey.
Fact: One beer is the same as one shot of whiskey.

Error: Couple drinks warms the body.
Fact: Couple of drinks cools the body.

Error: Black coffee can sober me up faster.
Fact: Nothing will speed up getting sober.

Error: A cold shower can sober me up faster.
Fact: Nothing will speed up getting sober.

Error: Alcohol increases sexual desire/ability.
Fact: Alcohol decreases sexual ability.

Error: People are friendlier when drinking.
Fact: People are more hostile and dangerous.

Error: Alcohol gives you a lift, perks you up.
Fact: It is a sedative-hypnotic drug: it puts you to sleep.

A DRINK
IS A DRINK
IS A DRINK

1 1/4 oz.
mixed drink

5 oz.
wine

12 oz.
beer

ALL EQUAL
1/2 OUNCE PURE
ALCOHOL

A drink is a drink is a drink

2. Different drinks have different alcohol content

Beer: from 3.2 to as high as seven percent alcohol.

Wine: from seven percent to 13 percent.

Mixed drinks: usually 1.25 ounces of 80 proof (40 percent pure alcohol) spirits.

3. Blood Alcohol Concentration (BAC): percent of alcohol in body

A BAC of .10 is one tenth of one percent of alcohol in the body; or ten drops of alcohol to 10,000 drops of blood. For a BAC of .05: five drops of alcohol for 10,000 drops of blood. Each drink (wine, beer, spirits) increases BAC by about .02 percent. Under 140 pounds, the person's BAC increases more. BAC level is set by your weight, number of drinks and length of time drinking.

4. Here is what happens at different BAC levels

.02 -.04: Feel relaxed; judgment impaired; less inhibited; slower reaction time; some motor impairment; mood more intense; bad driving habits become worse.

.05 - .09: Emotions and behaviors magnified; impaired motor skills/judgment; not walk normally; inhibitions lowered; "so what" attitude; poor performance; legally impaired/drunk.

.10 - .14: Don't function normally; lack of muscle and motor control; poor coordination; seriously impairs self-criticism, judgment and emotional control; severe delayed reaction time; clumsiness; serious lack of concern about others and self.

.15 - .19: All the above but more severe; 25 times more likely to have fatal accident; slurred speech; staggering; serious impairment of vision, physical, mental functions; uncoordinated.

.20 - .30: All of the above but more severe; amnesia; blackouts; unable to walk alone; 100 times more likely to have fatal accident.

.30 - .39: Lose consciousness, pass out, stupor, confusion.

.40: Almost all will lose consciousness;

.45-.60: Fatal for most people.

Your risk of getting drunk - losing control over thoughts and behavior - is increased if you weigh less, are female, have little or no food in the body, have had little sleep, drink over a shorter period of time and are relaxed. If you have been drinking for several years, and have had six or seven drinks, you may not look drunk but may have a BAC of .10 - **behavioral tolerance.**

5. Figuring your BAC

Table 2, page 50, gives information for the number of drinks for six time periods which will result in a .05, .10, .15 or .20 BAC for men and women. For each hour beyond six, add one more drink for each BAC level. A 180 lb. man with a BAC of .10 and drank 7 hours would have taken 11 drinks. *Table 3,* page 51, provides approximate information about the number hours from the first drink to a zero BAC based on varying number of drinks for men and women. WARNING: Number of drinks and BACs in *Tables 2 and 3* are not exact. Number of drinks in *Table 2* often puts you above the BAC levels shown. BAC may be higher depending on alcohol content in the drink, food in stomach, body fat, and if person is tired.

Exercise: Using *Tables 2 and 3*, do *Worksheet 9*, page 58, to show your BAC for so many drinks over a period of time and hours it takes for BAC to reach zero. Put down your weight. Take your BAC for four drinks in three hours and read the above effects for that BAC.

6. What about calories?

There are about 80 to 90 calories in an average drink. Four drinks makes up 325 calories.

7. **Absorbing alcohol or taking up the alcohol by the body**

Alcohol begins entering the blood in the stomach. Most alcohol is taken up by the small intestines. It takes only a few minutes before it enters all of your body organs.

8. **Breaking down (metabolizing) alcohol**

The body breaks down one drink per hour: about 98 percent in the digestive system; two percent leaves through breath and urine. *Table 2* shows that a heavier person who drinks the same as a lighter person may have a lower BAC. But, the heavier person with more body fat may have a higher BAC, since body fat slows the breakdown of alcohol. Higher body fat increases risk of alcohol harming the body. Women may be more at risk because of higher body fat.

9. **Health risks and alcohol**

Every organ in the body can be affected by moderate to heavy drinking (three or more drinks). We look at how alcohol affects various parts of the body.

The liver: The liver removes poisons and impurities in the blood. Alcohol is one of these poisons. Six or more drinks a day increases the risk of liver disease. There are three kinds of liver diseases.

▶ **Fatty liver disease:** Fatty tissue builds up with moderate to heavy drinking (three to five drinks a day). Fatty tissue separates the cells and stops the liver from doing its job. This disease is cured through a good diet and no alcohol use.

▶ **Alcoholic hepatitis:** Fatty tissue separates the cells, less blood gets to the cells. The cells die.

▶ **Cirrhosis:** Dead liver cells turn to scar tissue; cannot be cured and can cause death.

Your stomach and digestive organs: Alcohol irritates the throat, stomach lining and digestive system. A burning sensation from straight liquor may be pleasant, but it means mouth, throat and stomach tissue are damaged. Alcohol releases digestive acid which irritates the stomach and can lead to gastritis, ulcers and bleeding in moderate to heavy drinkers. This risk increases if alcohol is used with stomach irritants such as aspirin. Cancers of the digestive system are 40 times greater among heavy drinkers. Heavy drinkers account for a majority of head, neck, mouth, tongue, and throat cancers. Alcohol has "empty calories." Moderate to heavy drinkers may not eat properly. Alcohol prevents vitamins and important food nutrients from going into the blood and body.

The pancreas: The pancreas makes insulin and chemicals that are needed for digesting our food. Alcohol can inflame the pancreas and cause pancreatitis. Acute bleeding of the pancreas occasionally occurs from a single heavy drinking episode.

Your kidneys and lungs: Alcohol can cause fluids to build up in the body. This buildup can increase fluids in the lungs, increasing chances of lung infection.

Your muscles: Muscles are weakened by alcohol - **myopathy.** If you value strong muscles you will want to avoid even moderate drinking.

TABLE 2

BAC BASED ON NUMBER OF DRINKS AND BODY WEIGHT - MEN

Hours drank	120 lbs				140 lbs				160 lbs				180 lbs			
	.05	.10	.15	.20	.05	.10	.15	.20	.05	.10	.15	.20	.05	.10	.15	.20
One	2*	4	5	7	2	4	6	8	3	5	7	9	3	6	8	11
Two	3	4	6	8	3	5	7	9	4	6	8	10	4	7	9	12
Three	3	5	6	8	4	6	8	9	4	7	9	11	5	7	10	12
Four	4	6	7	8	4	7	9	10	5	7	10	12	6	8	11	13
Five	4	7	8	10	5	8	10	11	6	8	11	13	7	9	12	14
Six	5	7	9	11	6	8	10	12	7	9	12	14	8	10	13	16

* refers to the number of drinks

TABLE 2

BAC BASED ON NUMBER OF DRINKS AND BODY WEIGHT - WOMEN

Hours drank	120 lbs				140 lbs				160 lbs				180 lbs			
	.05	.10	.15	.20	.05	.10	.15	.20	.05	.10	.15	.20	.05	.10	.15	.20
One	2*	3	4	6	2	4	5	7	3	4	6	8	3	5	7	9
Two	2	4	5	6	3	4	6	7	3	5	7	9	4	6	8	10
Three	3	4	6	7	3	5	6	8	4	5	7	9	4	6	8	10
Four	3	5	6	7	4	5	7	8	4	6	8	10	5	7	9	11
Five	4	6	7	8	5	6	8	9	5	7	9	11	6	8	10	12
Six	5	7	8	9	6	7	9	10	6	8	10	12	7	9	11	12

* refers to the number of drinks

Note: The number of drinks and BAC are only approximate. The BAC can be higher for the number of drinks depending on how much the person had to eat, how tired the person is and the amount of body fat the person has.

TABLE 3	Approximate Hours from First Drink to Zero BAC levels: FOR MEN						

YOUR WEIGHT IN POUNDS							
Number of drinks	120	140	160	180	200	220	240	260
1	2*	2	2	1.5	1	1	1	1
2	4	3.5	3	3	2.5	2	2	2
3	6	5	4.5	4	3.5	3.5	3	3
4	8	7	6	5.5	5	4.5	4	3.5
5	10	8.5	7.5	6.5	6	5.5	5	4.5
6	11	9.5	9	8	7.5	6.5	6	5.5
7	12	11	10	9	9	8	7	6
8	13	12	11	10	10	9	8	7

* Refers to the number of hours before reaching a BAC of zero

TABLE 3	Approximate Hours from First Drink to Zero BAC levels: FOR WOMEN						

YOUR WEIGHT IN POUNDS							
Number of drinks	120	140	160	180	200	220	240	260
1	3*	2.5	2	2	2	1.5	1.5	1
2	6	5	4	4	3.5	3	3	2.5
3	9	7.5	6.5	5.5	5	4.5	4	4
4	12	9.5	8.5	7.5	6.5	6	5.5	5
5	15	12	10.5	9.5	8	7.5	7	6
6	17	14	12.5	11.5	10	9.5	9	8
7	18	15	14	13	11	11	10	9
8	19	16	15	14	12	12	11	10

* Refers to the number of hours before reaching a BAC of zero

Note: The number of hours is approximate and depends on how much the person has had to eat and the amount of body fat the person has.

Your heart and blood system: Heavy to excessive drinking (five or more drinks) can cause heart problems and increase blood pressure - particularly with smokers. Heavy drinking can weaken and damage heart muscle. Heavy drinking can upset the electrical control pattern causing the heart to beat fast or skip a beat. One to two drinks a day will most likely not increase risk of heart problems or high blood pressure.

Your brain and nerves: Brain damage leading to mental impairment can result from even mild to moderate drinking. Heavy to excessive drinking prevents the brain's ability to do its normal job.

▶ The blood brain barrier blocks alcohol from getting to it if the alcohol amount is small. Several drinks can break this barrier which damages brain cells. Some experts say that brain cells are damaged by the presence of any alcohol in brain. Alcohol damages and destroys brain cells that are responsible for learning, memory and mental functioning.

▶ Heavy drinking can greatly reduce mental power, damage memory and the ability to learn new ideas or new ways to do things. Brains of excessive-chronic alcoholic drinkers are smaller - the outer layer shrinks.

▶ Alcohol and other drugs have a greater negative effect on the adolescent (not fully developed) brain than on the adult.

▶ Some kinds of brain damage from alcohol use cannot be reversed. The good news: most mental impairment due to alcohol use can be reversed.

▶ Excessive drinking can damage nerve cells in the hands, feet and other body extremities noted by tingling of the fingers and feet, weakness of the muscles or numbness.

Figure 6 **shows a picture of the brain and the effects of alcohol on the brain. Look at it carefully.**

Your disease or immune defense system: The immune defense system fights off infections and diseases. Over time, heavy drinking weakens the body and increases the risks of major illnesses such as cancer or minor illnesses such as colds.

The man's reproductive and sexual functioning system: Heavy drinking over time can cause loss of hair, cause fatty tissue to build up in the breasts, and can shrink testicles. Drinking can decrease testosterone levels, damage the ability to perform sexually or cause impotence. Loss of testosterone can increase "female" characteristics of the body. IT MAY TAKE A REAL MAN TO HOLD HIS LIQUOR, BUT THE LIQUOR MAY TAKE AWAY THE REAL MAN.

The woman's reproductive and sexual functioning system: In women, drinking can change sex hormone balances and promote loss of female features of the body. Heavy drinking is linked to sexual, menstrual and gynecological problems. It can decrease ability to get pregnant. Drinking during pregnancy is linked to miscarriage, still births, birth defects and mental deficits in children. It can cause fetal alcohol syndrome (FAS). We will talk about that below.

BRAIN FUNCTIONS AFFECTED BY ALCOHOL

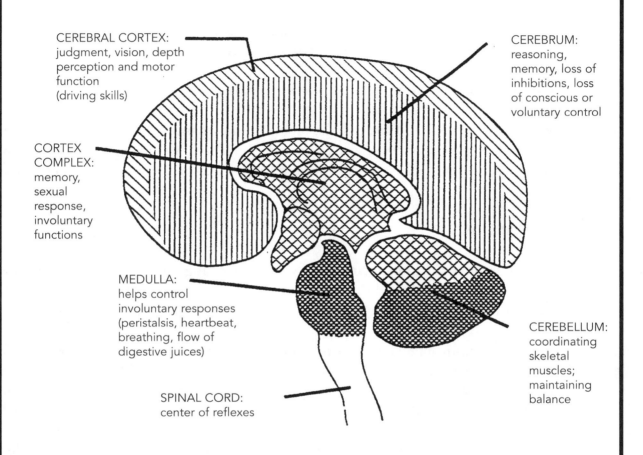

CEREBRAL CORTEX:
judgment, vision, depth
perception and motor
function
(driving skills)

CEREBRUM:
reasoning,
memory, loss of
inhibitions, loss
of conscious or
voluntary control

CORTEX
COMPLEX:
memory,
sexual
response,
involuntary
functions

MEDULLA:
helps control
involuntary responses
(peristalsis, heartbeat,
breathing, flow of
digestive juices)

CEREBELLUM:
coordinating
skeletal
muscles;
maintaining
balance

SPINAL CORD:
center of reflexes

 ONE TO TWO REGULAR DRINKS
(BAC .01 to .04)
reason, caution, intelligence, memory

 FIVE TO SEVEN REGULAR DRINKS
(BAC .09 to .15)
sense, coordination, balance

 THREE TO FOUR REGULAR DRINKS
(BAC .05 to .08)
self-control, judgment

 EIGHT TO TWELVE REGULAR DRINKS
(BAC .16 to .30)
vital centers

one drink = 1 beer or one glass of wine or one mixed drink

11. Loss of tolerance

This takes place because AOD use has damaged the liver and body organs. Loss of tolerance means the effect of alcohol is greater with less amounts of alcohol; and it takes less alcohol to get "high" or drunk; or the same amount of alcohol will have greater impact on the body. If you can't drink as much as "you used to," then you may have tissue damage. This may be true with other drugs.

Exercise: *Worksheet 10,* page 59, helps figure your tolerance or lack of tolerance to alcohol and other drugs you have used. Check whether your tolerance has decreased (takes less of the drug to get high) or has increased (need more of the drug to get high) or stayed the same.

12. Genetic factors - do you inherit AOD addiction and alcoholism?

If you are male and your father had an alcoholic problem, your chances of developing alcoholism is greater. Studies show genetics increase alcoholism risk. There is no specific gene for alcoholism. Psychological, social and cultural factors are powerful influences in developing alcoholism and drug abuse.

WHAT ABOUT MARIJUANA?

The marijuana user often argues that marijuana is not a dangerous drug. Is that really true? It is the most widely used illicit drug in the U.S. The most frequent drug-related visits to emergency rooms for youth 12 to 19 are for marijuana abuse. Physical effects can be severe, especially for adolescents.

Delta-9-THC or tetrahydrocannabinol is the chemical in marijuana that acts on the brain. Marijuana has hundreds of chemicals. More than 60 become active and "storm" the body. THC is stored in body fat and gets trapped in the fatty body parts - the liver, brain, reproductive parts and lungs. It stays in the body for a long time - often 60 days or more.

In *Table 1,* marijuana is described as both an enhancer and suppressor. It can slow down behavior, reaction time, mental reactions and the sense of time. It can increase mental activity, making you more suspicious and paranoid and can cause hallucinations. *Table 4* below provides a summary of the short-term direct effects, long-term direct and indirect effects, and the withdrawal effects.

Marijuana can lead to CRIMINAL CONDUCT. It magnifies the thoughts of "I don't care, so what." AND, if you are drinking alcohol - well, **the picture is clear** (unless you are on alcohol or marijuana)! Your thinking is impaired.

Because marijuana has a much higher level (more than 50 percent) of cancer-causing hydrocarbons than tobacco, it can be damaging to the lungs and cause respiratory problems. Even moderate users may have these kinds of physical problems.

Mixed with other drugs, marijuana can be dangerous. With alcohol and other system supressors, the body can become more depressed and body functions can slow down to a dangerous level.

TABLE 4

Effects of Marijuana

SHORT-TERM DIRECT EFFECTS

Sleepiness and drowsiness
Blocks short-term memory
Blocks ability to learn
Blocks tracking time
Impairs motor coordination
Bloodshot eyes, dry mouth
Less inhibited socially
Paranoia and hallucinations
Blocks messages to brain
Changes how you see and feel
Distorts or twists time
Distorts body parts, space
Causes high rate of accidents

LONG-TERM DIRECT/INDIRECT

Develop tolerance
Develop physical dependence
Increases risk of cancer
Increases testosterone in women
Decreases fertility in women
Reduces sexual pleasure
Reduces motivation to do tasks
Reduces motivation to succeed
May make heart problems worse
Weakens body defense system
Affects memory, learning
Damages lungs
Causes breathing illnesses

WITHDRAWAL OR REBOUND EFFECT WHEN STEADY USER STOPS USING

Restlessness
Aggressiveness
Stomach Pain
Anxiety
Paranoia

Vomiting
Irritability
Increased anger
Hostile behavior

OTHER HEALTH RISKS FROM ALCOHOL AND OTHER DRUGS

1. Harmful mental and physical outcomes of other drugs

Most of the health risks that come from alcohol and marijuana also come from other drugs. All drugs are toxic - they affect the liver, heart, brain and other organs. Here are some examples.

Amphetamines and methamphetamines rapidly increase the pleasure chemicals in the brain - dopamine - that can give euphoria for eight to 24 hours. Excessive and chronic use: causes rapid and irregular heart beat and increased blood pressure that results in damage to small blood vessels in the brain that cannot be reversed and can cause strokes; damages brain cells responsible for memory, judgment and decision-making; and can cause serious mental problems such as depression, anxiety, psychosis, suicidal and violent behaviors.

Cocaine and crack cocaine makes dopamine more available in the brain reward center. Some of the dangers are: rapid addiction, even after one binge exposure; leads to severe depression and intense cravings on withdrawal; seizures; narrows blood vessels that stresses the heart; causes strokes; causes violent behavior; and causes serious long-term mental and behavioral problems for children whose mothers used during pregnancy.

Opiates produce strong addictions and strong drug-seeking behavior, cause serious social adjustment problems; and painful, though not life-threatening, withdrawal.

Ecstasy causes irreversible and long-term damage to nerve cells that bring normal pleasures. Short-term, acute use causes body changes such as dehydration that can lead to heart or kidney failure.

Tobacco's harmful effects are well known. It is responsible for more deaths, money costs and health problems than all other legal and illegal drugs combined.

2. Sexually transmitted diseases (STDs)

Drug use increases risk of STD because drugs reduce judgment and inhibitions, making one less cautious about engaging in unsafe sex. AOD abusers are higher risk for becoming HIV positive and developing the *Acquired Immune Deficiency Syndrome* (AIDS). AIDS is caused by the HIV virus which attacks the body's defenses against diseases. The risk for becoming HIV positive comes from: unprotected and unsafe sex; and from needles used to inject drugs such as heroin.

3. Increased risk of hepatitis B and C

Drug users are at higher risk for getting hepatits B and C because of greater chance to take part in unprotected sex and through intravenous (IV) use of drugs. Hepatitis B and C can also be gotten through getting a tattoo and possibly through nasal (nose) use of cocaine and other drugs. Have a few drinks, lose your inhibitions, get a tattoo and you might get hepatitis C.

4. Fetal Alcohol Syndrome (FAS) and Fetal Drug Effects

Alcohol use during pregnancy can result in the FAS. Alcohol is carried through the baby's blood at the same BAC as with the mother. Even with moderate amounts of alcohol use by the mother, the baby may have slow physical and mental development, mental retardation, poor coordination, behavioral and learning problems, and physical abnormalities of head, face, heart, joints and limbs. FAS is the third leading cause of birth defects. IT CAN BE PREVENTED. DON'T DRINK WHEN YOU ARE PREGNANT.

All drugs in *Table 1,* page 46, may cause damage to the fetus. Stimulants - cocaine, methamphetamines - increase chances of low birth weight, miscarriages, stillbirths and *Sudden Infant Death Syndrome* (SIDS). We are familiar with crack babies. DON'T USE ANY DRUGS WHEN YOU ARE PREGNANT.

Exercise: Using *Worksheet 11,* page 59, decide whether your AOD use has affected your body and mind - caused you health problems.

DRUG USE INCREASES RISK OF CRIMINAL CONDUCT

Table 5 on the next page provides ways that drugs interact with CC. **Exercise:** Using *Worksheet 12,* page 59, write down how AOD use played a part in your past criminal conduct.

SEDATIVE-DEPRESSANTS: ALCOHOL, TRANQUILIZERS, BARBITURATES	MARIJUANA
Impairs judgment Lowers inhibitions Makes mood more intense Impairs the sense of timing Increases impulsive risk taking Unable to predict consequences Makes you not care Causes errors in thinking Weakens moral responsibility	Impairs judgment Lowers inhibitions Impairs memory Causes "so what" attitude Decreases responsible behavior Decreases self-criticism Weakens moral responsibility Blocks awareness of consequences
STIMULANTS: AMPHETAMINES, COCAINE, CAFFEINE	**HALLUCINOGENS: LSD, MESCALINE, PEYOTE, MUSHROOMS**
Impairs judgment Increases edginess Causes overreaction Promotes overconfidence Increases risk-taking Blocks awareness of consequences Causes thinking errors	Impairs judgment Increases unpredictable and dangerous behavior Causes false perceptions Increases erratic behavior Causes errors in thinking

SUMMARY OF SESSION ACTIVITIES, HOMEWORK AND CLOSING GROUP

1. Do *Worksheets 8 through 12.*

2. Update your *Master Skills List, Program Guide 1,* page 291 and MAP, page 295. Continue working on your *Autobiography.* If finished, share this with your provider or counselor. Do your *TAP charting,* page 300, for this week.

3. Using the *SSC Scale* rate your level of understanding of how alcohol and other drugs have affected your mind and body.

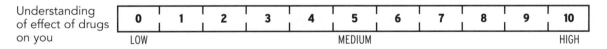

Understanding of effect of drugs on you

0	1	2	3	4	5	6	7	8	9	10
LOW					MEDIUM					HIGH

4. Share with your group the kinds of drugs you have used in your life. What was your drug of choice? Can you live life without using that drug? How attached are you to the drug?

WORKSHEET 8

Drugs that you have used

SPECIFIC SUPRESSOR DRUGS USED	DIRECT (INTOXICATING) EFFECTS	INDIRECT (WITHDRAWAL) EFFECTS
_____	_____	_____
_____	_____	_____
_____	_____	_____
_____	_____	_____

SPECIFIC ENHANCER DRUGS USED	DIRECT (INTOXICATING EFFECTS)	INDIRECT (WITHDRAWAL) EFFECTS
_____	_____	_____
_____	_____	_____
_____	_____	_____
_____	_____	_____

WORKSHEET 9

Your personal BAC level and hours to reach a BAC of zero

YOUR WEIGHT:	NUMBER OF HOURS DRINKING				NUMBER OF HOURS FOR BAC TO "0"
NUMBER OF DRINKS	1 HOUR	2 HOURS	3 HOURS	4 HOURS	
Two drinks	BAC:	BAC:	BAC:	BAC:	
Three drinks	BAC:	BAC:	BAC:	BAC:	
Four drinks	BAC:	BAC:	BAC:	BAC:	
Five drinks	BAC:	BAC:	BAC:	BAC:	
Six drinks	BAC:	BAC:	BAC:	BAC:	
Seven drinks	BAC:	BAC:	BAC:	BAC:	

WORKSHEET 10

Degrees of tolerance

TYPE DRUG	YEARS USED	CHECK COLUMN THAT FITS YOUR CHANGE IN TOLERANCE				
		MUCH DECREASE	SOME DECREASE	SAME	SOME INCREASE	MUCH INCREASE

WORKSHEET 11

Apply what you have learned to your own AOD use: Do you think alcohol or other drugs have affected your mind (brain) and body? If so, how?

DRUG	HAS THIS DRUG AFFECTED YOUR MIND? HOW?	YOUR BODY? HOW?
ALCOHOL		
MARIJUANA		
COCAINE		
AMPHETAMINES		
OTHER DRUGS		

WORKSHEET 12

Your AOD use and criminal conduct (CC): Write down three specific things about your alcohol or other drug use that played a part in your CC.

WHAT ABOUT YOUR AOD USE THAT PLAYED A PART IN YOUR CRIMINAL BEHAVIOR?
1.
2.
3.

SESSION INTRODUCTION AND OBJECTIVES

We look at the different AOD use patterns and see how they fit you. We want you to understand your own use patterns and how you can change them to prevent further AOD problems and criminal conduct.

OBJECTIVES

➡ Share how you see your AOD use patterns.

➡ Look at various AOD use patterns and see how they fit you.

➡ See how AOD use pattern lead to criminal conduct.

GETTING STARTED

▶ *CB Map Exercise.* Share your *Thinking and Action Plan (TAP) Charting, Program Guide 4,* page 300, that you did this week.

▶ For discussion: What is an alcohol or drug problem? Review *Worksheet 8,* page 58, of *Session 5,* Drugs You Have Used.

▶ Key words: quantity, frequency, prediction patterns, benefits from use, solo use, gregarious use.

SESSION CONTENT AND FOCUS

ALCOHOL QUANTITY-FREQUENCY-PREDICTION (QFP) PATTERN

Check the statements below as to how they fit you **before your last arrest and when you were in the community. Quantity** or **amount** per day when you drank.

❑ Light Drinker: one drink.
❑ Moderate drinker: two to three drinks.
❑ Heavy drinker: four to five drinks.
❑ Excessive drinker: six or more.

Frequency or how often: Check the one that fits you.

❑ Infrequent: Less than one time a month.
❑ Occasional: Less than one time a week.
❑ Frequent: One to three days a week.
❑ Consistent: Four to five days a week.
❑ Daily/sustained: six to seven days a week.

Prediction or forecast pattern: Check the one that fits you.

❏ Predictable drinker: Drank at the same time each day, such as only after work.
❏ Unpredictable drinker: Drank at any time, no pattern, one day after work, another after eating.

Describe your QFP pattern. You might be a moderate, frequent and predictable drinker.

OTHER DRUG QUANTITY-FREQUENCY-PREDICTION (QFP) PATTERN

Check the answer under each section below on the basis of **your drug use before your last arrest and when you were in the community. If you did not use drugs other than alcohol, skip rest of page.**

Number of other drugs you have used.

❏ NEVER used any drug other than alcohol.
❏ Mono-drug user: used only one drug besides alcohol.
❏ Polydrug user: used several drugs (besides alcohol).

Frequency or how often.

❏ Infrequent: Less than one day a month.
❏ Occasional: Less than one day a week.
❏ Frequent: One to three days a week.
❏ Consistent: Four to five days a week.
❏ Daily/sustained: Six to seven days a week.

Prediction pattern or how you would forecast your drug use:

❏ Predictable: used same time each day, such as only when get off work.
❏ Unpredictable drug user: Could use drugs at any time.

For each drug in the table below you have used, describe your QFP pattern **before your last arrest.**

```
┌─────────────────────────────────────────────────────────────────────┐
│ MY DRUG QUANTITY-FREQUENCY-PREDICTION PATTERN FOR DRUGS USED          │
│                                                                       │
│ Marijuana _____│
│ Cocaine_____│
│ Amphetamines_____│
│ Hallucinogens _____│
│ Pain Killers _____│
│ Tranquilizers_____│
│ Other Drugs_____│
│                                                                       │
└─────────────────────────────────────────────────────────────────────┘
```

SOCIAL PATTERNS: GREGARIOUS-SOCIAL VERSUS SOLO:

Here are the different social styles of alcohol or other drug use.

▶ **Solo-isolate pattern.** Uses mainly alone, at home, sometimes with others, not at bars and only at parties when necessary.

▶ **Social or gregarious user.** Uses mainly with friends, at bars, at parties, with others.

▶ **Mixed solo and social:** Uses alone at times, and at other times, uses with others.

Exercise: *Worksheet 13: Social-gregarious style,* page 65. Answer the questions as to your past AOD use. Put your score on *Profile 1*, page 67, and mark your score on that line with an "X".

Exercise: Do *Worksheet 14: Solo AOD style,* page 66. Answer the questions as to how you see your past AOD. Put your score on *Profile 1,* page 67.

If you score **high-medium to high** on **Solo** and **low to low-medium** on **Social,** you fit the **Solo** pattern. If you score **high-medium to high Social** and **low** on **Solo,** you fit the **Social** pattern. If you score **high** on both, you are both a **Solo** and **Social** user. Everyone will be either a **Social** or a **Solo** user or both.

BENEFITS OF AOD USE

People can depend on alcohol or other drugs (AOD) to be happy, to handle problems, to perform better and feel less stressed. **Exercise:** Complete *Worksheet 15,* page 67, based on the time when you were involved in AOD use. Put your score for BENEFITS on *Profile 1,* page 67.

For *Worksheets 13* through *15,* you are compared with a group of your peers in the adult judicial system. Look at your percentile scores in *Profile 1.* A 50th percentile score means you score higher than 50 percent of your peers who completed the surveys. How do you compare with your peers on the three scales?

Look at the BENEFITS scale on *Profile 1.* If your score was from eight to 13, you are somewhat AOD dependent as to meeting your social and emotional needs (you score higher than about 70 percent of your peers). If your score is from 14 to 24, you are quite AOD dependent. If your score is above 24, then you may be very dependent on AOD use to meet your social and emotional needs. **Discuss your results.**

SUMMARY OF DIFFERENT PATTERNS OF AOD USE

From what we have learned, we can now identify different patterns of alcohol or other drug use.

▶ **Abstainers - the non-use pattern:** About 25 to 30 percent of adults do not use alcohol.

- **Quantity-frequency-prediction (QFP) use pattern.** If you are a frequent, daily-sustained, heavy AOD user, your AOD use may be a strong part of your CC pattern.

- **Social or Solo:** Some fit one or the other; some fit both.

- **Benefits pattern:** Most people who use alcohol or other drugs do so to relax, deal with stress, overcome depression, deal with physical pain, relate to others better, etc.

How do you see yourself? What is your QFP pattern: "heavy-frequent-unpredictable"? Are you a "solo" user? Are you socially-psychologically AOD dependent? Describe your AOD use patterns in the space below.

DESCRIBE YOUR ALCOHOL OR OTHER DRUG USE PATTERN

_____

_____

_____

_____

AOD USE AND CRIMINAL CONDUCT (CC)

Social style and benefit AOD use patterns are often related to criminal activity.

Exercise: *Worksheet 16,* page 68, gives specific behaviors found among persons who get involved in criminal conduct. Answer the questions as to how the answers best fit you during the time when you were involved in criminal conduct. If your total score is 12 to 16, then your AOD use had a strong relationship with your CC. If your score was 5 to 11, AOD use and CC are related, but not as strongly. If your score is "0" to 2 or 3, then your AOD use has low or no relationship with your CC.

Exercise: Using all of the information you have been given in this session, in the space below, describe your use pattern that led to or was related to your criminal conduct

---

MY AOD USE PATTERN THAT WAS PART OF MY CRIMINAL CONDUCT

_____

_____

_____

_____

CHANGING OUR AOD USE PATTERNS

We change and stop AOD use by changing our thoughts, attitudes and beliefs that are part of our alcohol and other drug use. In *Session 3,* we looked at four types of thought habits or automatic thoughts that lead to emotional and action outcomes. These thought habits also lead to patterns of AOD use that get us into trouble - or relapse. Let's review these. **Expectancies** - "if I take a drink, I'll relax." **Appraisals** - "drinking with my friends is important to me." **Attributions** - "I got caught because the cops were out to get me." **Decisions** - "I decided to have a few drinks to give me courage."

Exercise: *Worksheet 17,* page 68, will help you to see how your past AOD use patterns fit these four thought habits. You change and stop your patterns of use by changing these thought habits or automatic thoughts. You may have already learned some mental skills for changing those thoughts. In group, use these skills for change the thought habits you put on *Worksheet 17.*

SUMMARY OF SESSION ACTIVITIES AND HOMEWORK ASSIGNMENTS

1. Do *Worksheets 13 through 17.*

2. Update your *Master Skills List, Program Guide 1,* page 291 and MAP, page 195.

3. Continue working on your *Autobiography.* If you are finished, share this with your provider or counselor.

4. Do your *TAP charting, Program Guide 4,* page 300, for this week. Look at the *TAP Charting* you have done so far. How do your past patterns of use relate to the pattern you have been charting each week? Share what you see with your group.

5. Using the *SSC Scale,* rate your level of understanding and knowledge of your own alcohol or other drug use pattern.

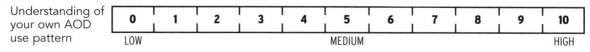

Understanding of your own AOD use pattern	0	1	2	3	4	5	6	7	8	9	10
	LOW					MEDIUM					HIGH

SESSION CLOSURE

Share with your group your AOD use patterns identified in this session. How hard will it be for you to change these patterns? How are these patterns related to problems you have had with AOD use? This is our topic for next session.

Your past *social-gregarious* **AOD** use style: For each question, check the answer in the column that best fits you. Then add up your scores. For every check in the "1" column, give yourself a one, for every check in the "2" column, give yourself a two, and for every check in the "3" column, give yourself a three. Add up each column and put the total score on the bottom row. Then put your score on the *"Social-Gregarious"* row on *Profile 1*, on page 67.

QUESTION	0	1	2	3
1. Do most of your friends drink or use drugs?	No	Yes		
2. Does your social life require you to drink or use drugs?	No	Yes		
3. Do you do most of your drinking at bars?	No	Yes		
4. Do you go to parties where there is drinking or drug use?	No	Once a month	2-3 times a month	4 times or more a month
5. Do you usually drink or use drugs with the same people?	No	Yes		
6. Do you do most of your drinking or drug use with friends and people you know?	No	Yes		
7. Is drinking or drug use an important part of getting together with people?	No	Sometimes	Often	Very often
TOTAL COLUMN SCORES				
TOTAL SCORE				

From K. Wanberg & J. L. Horn, 2004, Alcohol and Other Drug Use Inventory (AOD-UI), Center for Addictions Research and Evaluation, Arvada, CO. Used with permission.

Your past *solo AOD* style: For each question, check the answer in the column that best fits you. Then add up your scores. For every check in the "1" column, give yourself a one, for every check in the "2" column, give yourself a two, and for every check in the "3" column, give yourself a three. Add up each column and put the total score on the bottom row. Then put your score on the "Solo" row on Profile 1, below.

QUESTION	0	1	2	3
1. Do you do most of your drinking or drug use at home?	No	Yes		
2. Do you drink in a bar by yourself?	No	Sometimes	Often	Very Often
3. When drinking or using drugs with others, do you keep to yourself?	No	Sometimes	Usually	Almost always
4. Do you drink or use drugs at home alone?	No	Sometimes	Usually	Almost always
5. Have you stayed in a room by yourself and drank or used drugs?	No	A few times	Many times	Very often
6. Do you drink or use drugs alone?	No	Sometimes	Usually	Almost always
7. When you find yourself alone, do you drink or use drugs?	No	Sometimes	Often	Usually
TOTAL COLUMN SCORES				
TOTAL SCORE				

From K. Wanberg & J. L. Horn, 2004, Alcohol and Other Drug Use Inventory (AOD-UI), Center for Addictions Research and Evaluation, Arvada, CO. Used with permission.

WORKSHEET 15

Benefits you got from drinking or other drug use: Put a check in the column that best fits your answer. For each check in the "sometimes" column, give yourself one point, for each check in the "a lot" column, give yourself two points, for each check in the "almost all the time" column, give yourself three points. Then put your total score in the last line and on Profile 1, below.

I USE ALCOHOL OR OTHER DRUGS TO	0 NO	1 SOMETIMES	2 A LOT	3 ALMOST ALL THE TIME
1. feel less tense or stressed				
2. feel less depressed				
3. forget my problems				
4. bring on good feelings and emotions or to feel happy				
5. have fun with others				
6. be more mentally alert				
7. relax and unwind				
8. change my mood or emotions				
9. calm myself down				
10. get along with others				
TOTAL SCORE: USE THE SCORING GUIDE DESCRIBED ABOVE				

From K. W. Wanberg, 2004, Adult Substance Use Survey - Revised (ASUS-R), Center for Addictions Research and Evaluation, Arvada, CO. Used with permission.

PROFILE 1

AOD Use Profile: Put the score from *Worksheets 13, 14 and 15* under the score column and then find the number on the row and put an X over that number. Where do you fall? In "low," "low-medium," "high- medium" or "high"?

SCALE	SCORE	LOW	LOW-MEDIUM	HIGH-MEDIUM	HIGH
SOCIAL		1	2	3 4	5 7 9 11
SOLO		0	1 2	3	4 8 10 14
BENEFITS		0 1 2 3	4 5 6 7	8 9 11 13	14 18 25 33
PERCENTILE	1	10 20	30 40 50	60 70	80 90 99

WORKSHEET 16

How AOD use is related to criminal conduct: Answer the questions below based on the time that you were involved in criminal conduct. Give yourself a "1" for each check in the "Sometimes true" column, "2" for each check in the "Usually true" column. Put your total score in the last line.

AOD USE AND CRIMINAL CONDUCT	0 NOT TRUE	1 SOMETIMES TRUE	2 USUALLY TRUE
1. Drink with friends who commit crimes			
2. Use other drugs with friends who commit crimes			
3. Used alcohol/drugs before a crime			
4. High on alcohol/drugs when committing a crime			
5. Use alcohol/drugs after committing a crime			
6. AOD use part of daily lifestyle			
7. Drink at bars in neighborhood where criminal associates live			
8. Attitude of "I don't care" when high			
TOTAL SCORE			

WORKSHEET 17

How your thought habits or automatic thoughts are part of your AOD use

THOUGHT HABITS OR AUTOMATIC THOUGHTS	EXAMPLE	EXAMPLES OF HOW THEY APPLY TO YOU
EXPECTANCIES	If I have a couple of beers, I'll relax.	
APPRAISALS	I feel more relaxed now after having a couple.	
ATTRIBUTIONS	I drank because my husband yelled at me.	
DECISIONS	I'm going to have a "couple" before going home.	

SESSION INTRODUCTION AND OBJECTIVES

In *sessions 5* and *6*, you learned about alcohol and other drugs and your own patterns of use. We now look at the AOD impaired control cycles and pathways to AOD problem outcomes and addiction.

> **OBJECTIVES**
>
> ⇒ Understand the pathways to AOD addiction.
>
> ⇒ Learn the AOD impaired control cycles and how you might fit these cycles.

GETTING STARTED

▶ Start with the *CB Map Exercise.* Share your *Thinking and Action Plan (TAP) Charting* for this week. Share one problem you have had from AOD use.

▶ Key words: impaired control cycles, rebound, withdrawal, AOD addiction

SESSION CONTENT AND FOCUS

We look at two pathways to AOD problem outcomes and addiction: 1) the **mental-behavioral** impaired control cycle (MB-ICC); and 2) the **mental-physical** impaired control cycle (MP-ICC).

THE MENTAL-BEHAVIORAL IMPAIRED CONTROL CYCLE - MB-ICC

How AOD use becomes a habit pattern

Remember the two pathways for learning behavior? **First,** when an action **turns on something positive,** it gets strengthened. **Second,** when a behavior **turns off something unpleasant** it gets strengthened. *Figure 7* below shows how these two pathways lead to AOD use becoming a habit pattern. Our thoughts leading to AOD use and our AOD use behavior are strengthened.

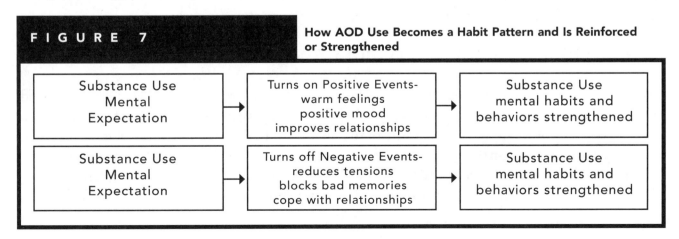

FIGURE 7 — How AOD Use Becomes a Habit Pattern and Is Reinforced or Strengthened

Substance Use Mental Expectation	→	Turns on Positive Events- warm feelings positive mood improves relationships	→	Substance Use mental habits and behaviors strengthened
Substance Use Mental Expectation	→	Turns off Negative Events- reduces tensions blocks bad memories cope with relationships	→	Substance Use mental habits and behaviors strengthened

How Mental-Behavioral Impaired Control Cycle - MB-ICC Works

The first step to AOD problem outcomes is when AOD use becomes a **habit pattern.** This can lead to the MB-ICC, shown in *Figure 8.* We take you step-by-step through this cycle.

▶ **Life situations** (**Point A** in *Figure 8*) lead to a need or desire to feel good (increase pleasure) or not feel bad (decrease discomfort) and we **expect drugs** to do this for us.

▶ **AOD use to increase pleasure or decrease discomfort (Point B)** with the **outcome** that this does happen.

▶ **AOD use expectancies (thoughts) and behaviors are strengthened (Point C).** Many users never go beyond **Point C.** But this path can lead to the problem outcome or impaired-control cycle.

▶ **Negative consequences or problem outcomes** result from AOD use (**Point D**) causing stress. This is called a drug use problem. Many stop here. They think: "I have a problem," (**appraisal**), "It's my problem" (**attribution**), and I'm going to stop to prevent another problem" (**decision**). Such changes in thought lead to changes in action. The person stops AOD use and uses other ways to cope with stress. Continued AOD use sets the stage for the next step.

▶ **Use to cope with stress and discomfort from AOD use (Point E).** If drugs helped cope with the life stresses, then we expect them to help deal with the stress from AOD problems. We drink to handle the problems from drinking. We use drugs to handle the stress we get from AOD use. This leads to the next step.

▶ **Further problems from use (Point F)** to handle the problems from use. At **Point D** it was an AOD *use problem.* Now, it is a pattern of use problems - a *problem user.* Use has also increased stress. Here, many users **decide** to change patterns or stop use. They change thought and action habits to handle life problems in a more adaptive way.

▶ **AOD use to manage life problems and problems from use (Point G).** Now there may be AOD abuse or dependence. Further use leads to more problems. The person uses because he uses. An old proverb: "A man takes the drink. The drink takes the drink. The drink takes the man."

<u>Exercise:</u> Use *Figure 8* as a worksheet to see how you fit the cycle. Write down thoughts you might have at each of the points. Practice changing these thoughts to stop the cycle.

MENTAL-PHYSICAL IMPAIRED CONTROL CYCLE - MP-ICC*

Figure 9 shows an overview of the MP-ICC. The direct effect of drugs may be: feel relaxed, sedated, calm, reduce stress, get excited and stimulated. When the drug wears off, the **indirect** or **withdrawal** effects take over - or **rebound** - the opposite of the direct effect. For **alcohol:** stress, agitation, anxiety and body tension. **Cocaine:** depression, tiredness. What is the quick "cure"? Continue to use, get back the direct effect and "cure" the discomfort. With alcohol: drink to maintain a balance in body tension or stop long enough to work through withdrawal and develop a drug-free state of balance.

FIGURE 8

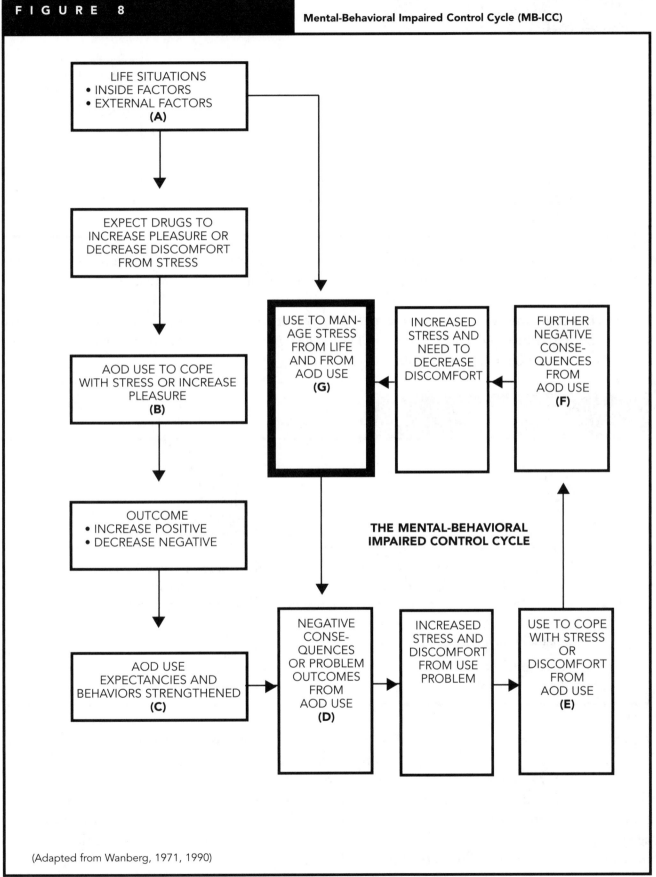

LIFE SITUATIONS
• INSIDE FACTORS
• EXTERNAL FACTORS
(A)

EXPECT DRUGS TO
INCREASE PLEASURE OR
DECREASE DISCOMFORT
FROM STRESS

AOD USE TO COPE
WITH STRESS OR INCREASE
PLEASURE
(B)

OUTCOME
• INCREASE POSITIVE
• DECREASE NEGATIVE

AOD USE
EXPECTANCIES AND
BEHAVIORS STRENGTHENED
(C)

USE TO MAN-
AGE STRESS
FROM LIFE
AND FROM
AOD USE
(G)

INCREASED
STRESS AND
NEED TO
DECREASE
DISCOMFORT

FURTHER
NEGATIVE
CONSE-
QUENCES
FROM
AOD USE
(F)

**THE MENTAL-BEHAVIORAL
IMPAIRED CONTROL CYCLE**

NEGATIVE
CONSE-
QUENCES
OR PROBLEM
OUTCOMES
FROM
AOD USE
(D)

INCREASED
STRESS AND
DISCOMFORT
FROM USE
PROBLEM

USE TO COPE
WITH STRESS
OR
DISCOMFORT
FROM
AOD USE
(E)

(Adapted from Wanberg, 1971, 1990)

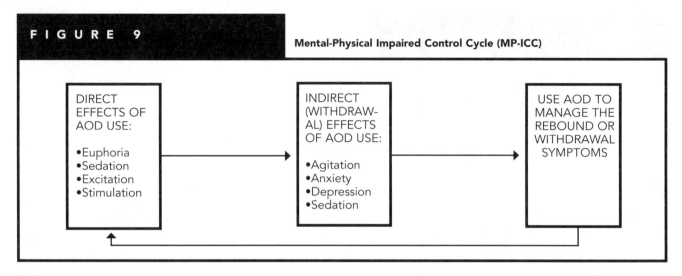

FIGURE 9

Mental-Physical Impaired Control Cycle (MP-ICC)

DIRECT EFFECTS OF AOD USE:

- Euphoria
- Sedation
- Excitation
- Stimulation

INDIRECT (WITHDRAWAL) EFFECTS OF AOD USE:

- Agitation
- Anxiety
- Depression
- Sedation

USE AOD TO MANAGE THE REBOUND OR WITHDRAWAL SYMPTOMS

Figures 10 through 13 show the mental-physical pathways to AOD use impaired control or problem outcomes and addiction. We use the sedative drug alcohol to illustrate the MP-ICC.

Figure 10: **normal or average tension level** (ATL) between lines A and B. Each cycle is around two to three hours. At the high end we could feel good, energetic; or agitated and anxious. The response depends on our mood and physical needs.

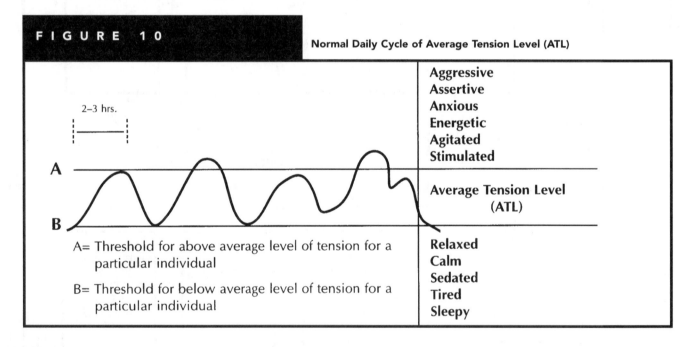

FIGURE 10

Normal Daily Cycle of Average Tension Level (ATL)

2–3 hrs.

A

B

A= Threshold for above average level of tension for a particular individual

B= Threshold for below average level of tension for a particular individual

Aggressive
Assertive
Anxious
Energetic
Agitated
Stimulated

Average Tension Level
(ATL)

Relaxed
Calm
Sedated
Tired
Sleepy

Figure 11 shows that a sedative drug (alcohol) slows down the nervous system and changes the number of ATL cycles. The body's direct reaction to alcohol (suppressor drug) is in the lower right-hand corner of *Figure 11*. When alcohol wears off, we "rebound" into nervous-excitement - withdrawal that lasts longer than sedation. One drink at **D1** causes sedation for up to two hours **followed** by rebound for up to three hours. A second drink taken an hour later at (**D2**) has less sedative effect since it works against rebound from the first drink. A third drink at **D3,** results in little sedation since that drink has to work against the rebound from the first two drinks.

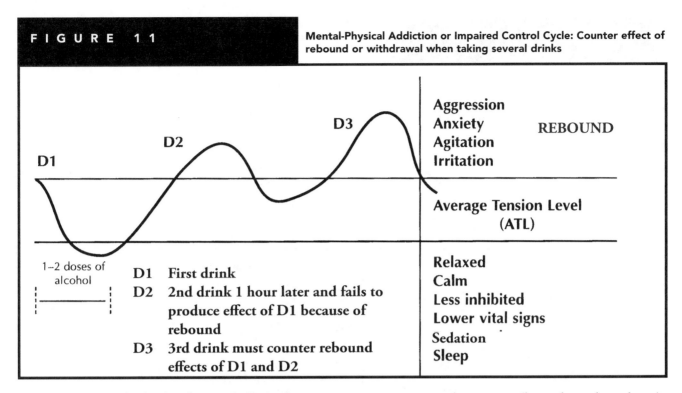

FIGURE   11

Mental-Physical Addiction or Impaired Control Cycle: Counter effect of rebound or withdrawal when taking several drinks

Aggression
Anxiety   REBOUND
Agitation
Irritation

Average Tension Level (ATL)

D3

D2

D1

1–2 doses of alcohol

D1   **First drink**
D2   **2nd drink 1 hour later and fails to produce effect of D1 because of rebound**
D3   **3rd drink must counter rebound effects of D1 and D2**

Relaxed
Calm
Less inhibited
Lower vital signs
Sedation
Sleep

Rebound keeps the body chemicals from slowing or stopping normal activities (heart beat, breathing). During deep sleep, natural stimulant chemicals are produced to keep all activities from stopping - or death. The body's reaction to alcohol is the same - producing the natural stimulants to prevent sedation. But alcohol is so strong, it blocks this natural chemical. When alcohol wears off, the natural stimulant-like drugs that have been blocked are released and take over. The body rebounds into a state of stimulation and agitation.

Figure 12 on the next page shows rebound or withdrawal when the sedative (alcohol) leaves the body and the natural stimulants are released. The length of rebound depends on how long and how much we drink. It may continue for several weeks or even months after drinking is stopped.

Several days after alcohol leaves the body, rebound is less intense, but there is ongoing, low level stress. Add this to normal daily stress, and the need and urge to drink is increased. This risk of relapse can last several months after quitting drinking. Taking a drink can relieve the stress and stop the withdrawal symptoms. A drink or more at *D2* in *Figure 12* "takes off the edge" - "the hair of the dog that bit you." It is one of the bases of addiction to alcohol.

Figure 13 on the next page shows a pattern of daily, steady drinking and a need to drink every one or two hours during non-sleep to avoid withdrawal — the "strung out" user. Doses are closer together and work against the rebound of prior doses. Rebound reduces the strength of each dose. The body demands more of the drug to maintain the body balance. Steady use may be only to relieve the pain of withdrawal. If the drug is stopped, minor symptoms such as inability to sleep or shakes may occur within 24 hours. More serious symptoms may occur within 72 hours. These symptoms, upper right hand column of *Figure 13,* may be life-threatening.

*The Mental-Physical impaired control cycle and graphs are based on the work of: Stanley Gitlow (1966, 1970, 1982, 1988); Stuart Gitlow (2001); Glenn & Hochman, 1977; Glenn & Warner, 1975; Glenn, Warner & Hockman, 1977; Peyser, 1988; Grilly, 1989; Fromme & D'Amico, 1999; Wanberg, 1990; Wanberg & Milkman, 1998). Sources are in the Provider's Guide.

FIGURE 12

Mental-Physical Addiction or Impaired Control Cycle: Longer periods of rebound and withdrawal from a longer time of heavy to excessive alcohol use.

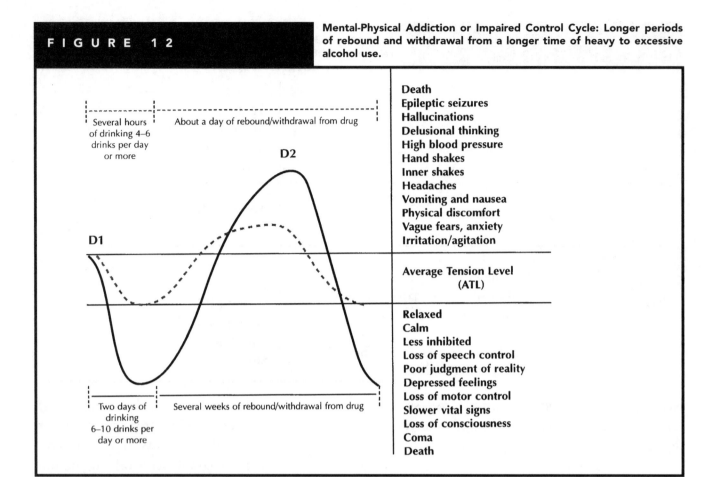

Several hours of drinking 4–6 drinks per day or more

About a day of rebound/withdrawal from drug

D2

D1

Two days of drinking 6–10 drinks per day or more

Several weeks of rebound/withdrawal from drug

Death
Epileptic seizures
Hallucinations
Delusional thinking
High blood pressure
Hand shakes
Inner shakes
Headaches
Vomiting and nausea
Physical discomfort
Vague fears, anxiety
Irritation/agitation

Average Tension Level (ATL)

Relaxed
Calm
Less inhibited
Loss of speech control
Poor judgment of reality
Depressed feelings
Loss of motor control
Slower vital signs
Loss of consciousness
Coma
Death

FIGURE 13

Mental-Physical Addiction or Impaired Control Cycle: The "strung out user"

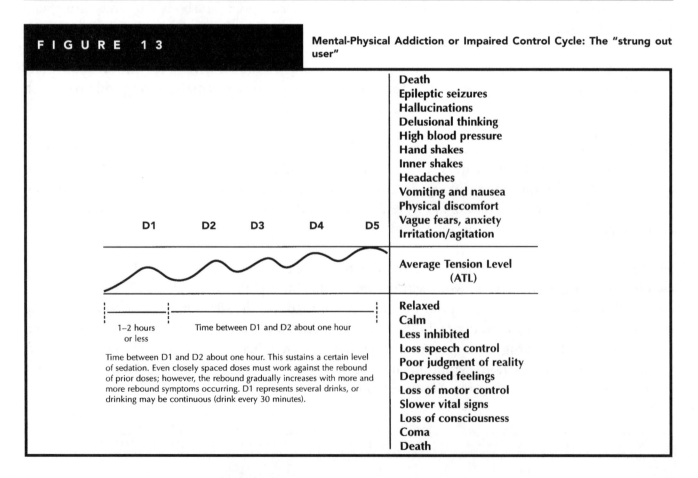

D1   D2   D3   D4   D5

1–2 hours or less

Time between D1 and D2 about one hour

Time between D1 and D2 about one hour. This sustains a certain level of sedation. Even closely spaced doses must work against the rebound of prior doses; however, the rebound gradually increases with more and more rebound symptoms occurring. D1 represents several drinks, or drinking may be continuous (drink every 30 minutes).

Death
Epileptic seizures
Hallucinations
Delusional thinking
High blood pressure
Hand shakes
Inner shakes
Headaches
Vomiting and nausea
Physical discomfort
Vague fears, anxiety
Irritation/agitation

Average Tension Level (ATL)

Relaxed
Calm
Less inhibited
Loss speech control
Poor judgment of reality
Depressed feelings
Loss of motor control
Slower vital signs
Loss of consciousness
Coma
Death

This MP-ICC applies to other drugs. The direct effects of a stimulant (amphetamines, cocaine) are physical and mental stimulation or agitation. When the drug starts to leave the body, rebound or withdrawal begins and is the opposite of that for sedative drugs or system supressors. This rebound causes depression, tiredness, and a "crashing" effect. Relief for the rebound is to use the drug. The cocaine-addict uses cocaine to stop the cocaine withdrawal symptoms. **Mental-physical addiction or dependence is using the drug to stop the rebound or withdrawal from the drug. A continuous AOD user is avoiding the mental and physical discomfort of withdrawal.**

Exercise: Using *Figure 9,* page 72, write down the direct results you get from alcohol (first Block in *Figure 9*). What are withdrawal or indirect results (second Block) that you might have had? Now, look at how *Figures 10* through *13* apply to you. **Exercise:** Discuss this in group. Relate how you have used alcohol or other drugs to cope with rebound or withdrawel effects.

SUMMARY OF SESSION ACTIVITIES OR HOMEWORK

1. Using *Worksheet 18,* page 75, do a Thinking Report on an event that made you think you wanted a drink. Describe the event, your thoughts, attitudes, beliefs, feelings and outcome.

2. Update your *Master Skills List, Program Guide 1,* page 291 and MAP, page 195. Continue working on your Autobiography. If finished, share this with your provider or counselor. Do your *TAP charting, Program Guide 4,* page 300 for this week.

SESSION CLOSURE

Share with your group how you fit the *mental-behavioral impaired control cycle* (MB-ICC) and the *mental physical-impaired control cycle* (MP-ICC) for drugs you have used in your life.

WORKSHEET 18	**Thinking Report:** Use an event that happened to you when you thought you wanted a drink.

DESCRIBE THE EVENT:
YOUR THOUGHTS:
YOUR FEELINGS:
YOUR ATTITUDES AND BELIEFS:
THE OUTCOME:

SESSION INTRODUCTION AND OBJECTIVES

In *Session 7,* we learned that AOD use can result in two impaired controlled cycles: the Mental-Behavioral and Mental-Physical. Now, we will look at how those cycles lead to AOD problem outcomes and specific patterns of AOD misuse and abuse.

OBJECTIVES

➡ Identify the specific symptoms and negative outcomes you have experienced from AOD use.

➡ Look at specific AOD problem outcome and misuse patterns and see how they fit you.

GETTING STARTED

▶ Start with the *CB Map Exercise.* Share your *Thinking Report* on *Worksheet 18,* page 75 and your *Thinking and Action Plan (TAP) Charting* that you did this week.

▶ Review the patterns of AOD use in *Session 6* and Impaired Control Cycles in *Session 7.*

▶ Key words: AOD problem outcomes, AOD problem, problem user, *Substance Abuse, Substance Dependence.*

SESSION CONTENT AND FOCUS

PROBLEM OUTCOMES AND SYMPTOMS FOR DIFFERENT DRUGS

In *Session 5, Table 1,* page 46, we look at the direct and indirect effects of the five classes of drugs. Many of these effects are actual problem outcomes or symptoms of drug use.

Exercise: Put a circle around each drug in *Table 1* that you have used. Then, put a check by each direct and indirect effect that has been a symptom or problem outcome of your drug use.

FOUR TYPES OF AOD PROBLEM OUTCOMES

Type 1 problem outcome: AOD use problem

If you have had a problem from AOD use, then you have had an **AOD problem.** Many AOD users will have gotten an AOD problem at least once in their lifetime. A hangover, saying something that offended another person or being arrested for DWI. You can fit this pattern even though you are not addicted or do not fit the rules for *Substance Abuse* or *Substance Dependence* described below.

Type 2 problem outcome: *Problem drinker or AOD problem user*

The *problem drinker or problem user* has developed a pattern of problems from AOD use. This is the person who has continued to points F and G in *Figure 8,* page 71.

Exercise: *Worksheet 19,* page 79, is a measure of problem outcomes or negative consequences resulting from AOD use **during your lifetime.** BE HONEST. It is only for your use. Put your score in the AOD PROBLEMS score box on *Profile 2,* page 80, and find your score on that row. Where do you fall? A score between 3 and 6 indicates problems from your use. A score between 7 and 23 indicates a **problem drinker** or **problem user** and maybe **Substance Abuse.** A score between 24 and 43 indicates **Substance Abuse.** A score higher than 44 suggests **Substance Abuse** or even **Substance Dependence.** The higher the score, the greater the chances of having further AOD problems in the future.

The percentile score allows you to compare your score with clients in the adult justice system. **Example:** A score of 15, would mean that you score higher than 50 percent of a sample of clients in the adult justice system. If you have done Session 13, then you have already done Worksheet 19. Go ahead and do it again. Then put your total score in the 2nd column on the table on page 107. Compare your scores. Is the one you just took higher? Lower?

Type 3 Problem Outcome: *Problem user - Substance Abuse*

From 10 to 15 percent or more of adults will fit a diagnosis of *Substance Abuse* or *Substance Dependence* disorder. These diagnoses are based on guidelines developed by the *American Psychiatric Association.* *Substance Abuse* **(SA) is a maladaptive pattern of substance use that leads to a condition of impairment or distress revealed or shown by one of the conditions found in** *Worksheet 20.*

Exercise: *Worksheet 20, page 80,* gives the rules for *Substance Abuse* (SA). Check if any of the four statements fit you within any 12 month period. If you checked one of the four statements, you might fit the SA diagnosis. At the bottom of *Worksheet 20,* write down two or three of the AOD use outcomes that have been most upsetting to your life.

Type 4 Problem Outcome: *Problem user - Substance Dependence*

As many as 10 percent or more of adults will fit the *Substance Dependence* (SD) diagnosis. *Substance Dependence* **is a maladaptive pattern of substance use that leads to a condition of impairment or distress revealed or showed by three or more of the conditions found in** *Worksheet 21.*

Exercise: *Worksheet 21,* page 81, gives the guidelines for *Substance Dependence* (SD). Check whether any of the seven statements fit you within any 12 month period. If you checked 3 or more, then you might fit the SD disorder. At the bottom of *Worksheet 21,* write two or three of the AOD use outcomes that have been the most upsetting to your life.

Only a qualified professional can make a diagnosis of *Substance Abuse* or *Substance Dependence.* *Worksheets 20 and 21* give you guidelines as to whether you might fit these two AOD use problem outcomes.

PUTTING IT TOGETHER

Put your scores for GREGARIOUS, SOLO and BENEFITS from *Profile 1,* page 67, on *Profile 2,* page 80. You will use *Profile 2* to describe your AOD use and outcome pattern. How do you see your AOD use problem outcome pattern? Have you had a **drinking problem?** Were you a **problem drinker?** Do you fit the *Substance Abuse or Substance Dependence* categories? **Exercise:** Use *Worksheet 22,* page 82, and check all that apply to you. If you check *Substance Dependence,* then you will check yes to all of the other three categories. It could be that you only checked number 1, "Have had a drinking problem."

Exercise: Using the work space at the bottom of *Worksheet 22,* page 82, describe your AOD use pattern. Describe your style (daily, weekends, solo, gregarious), degree of disruption (low, medium, high), and the type of problem outcome pattern: use problem, problem user, problem user-*Substance Abuse* or problem user-*Substance Dependence.* Share your findings with group. What skills can you use to change these patterns.

SUMMARY OF SESSION ACTIVITIES OR HOMEWORK

1. Do *Worksheets 19* through *22.* Update your *Master Skills List, Program Guide 1,* page 291. Do some work on your *Master Assessment Plan* (MAP), page 295. Continue working on your *Autobiography.* If you are finished, share this with your provider or counselor.

2. Do your *TAP charting, Program Guide 4,* page 300, for this week. How do your past patterns of use relate to the pattern you have been charting each week. Share what you see with your group.

3. Using the *SSC Scale,* rate your level of understanding and skills for what you learned in *Sessions 7 and 8.*

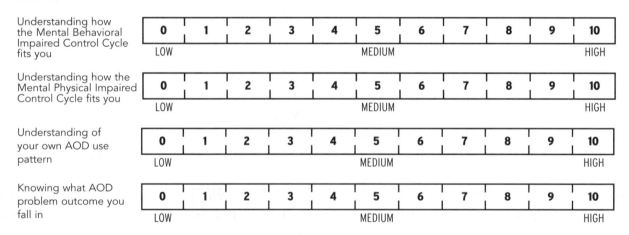

SESSION CLOSURE

Share your AOD use patterns that you identified in this session. Do you fit either the *Substance Abuse or Substance Dependence* diagnosis? How serious do you think your AOD problem is?

Negative outcomes from alcohol or other drug use: Put a check in the column that best fits your answer. For each check in the "1" column, give yourself a one; for each check in the "2" column, give yourself a two; for each check in the "3" column, give yourself a three; for each check in the "4" column, give yourself a four. Put your total score in the last row.

NEGATIVE OR UNPLEASANT SYMPTOMS RESULTING FROM YOUR ALCOHOL OR OTHER DRUG USE	0 NEVER	1 1-3 TIMES	2 4-6 TIMES	3 7-10 TIMES	4 MORE THAN 10 TIMES
1. Had blackout when using (forgot what you did but still awake)					
2. Became physically violent					
3. Staggered and stumbled around					
4. Passed out (became unconscious)					
5. Tried to take your own life					
6. Saw or heard things not there					
7. Became mentally confused					
8. Thought people out to get you					
9. Had physical shakes or tremors					
10. Became physically sick or nauseated					
11. Had a seizure or a convulsion					
12. Had a rapid or fast heart beat					
13. Became very anxious, nervous or tense					
14. Was very feverish, hot, sweaty					
15. Did not eat or sleep					
16. Caused money problems					
17. Unable to go to work or school					
18. Neglected your family					
19. Broke the law or committed a crime					
20. Could not pay your bills					
TOTAL SCORE (USE THE INSTRUCTIONS AT TOP OF CHART FOR SCORING)					

From K. W. Wanberg, 2004, Adult Substance Use Survey - Revised (ASUS-R), Center for Addictions Research and Evaluation, Arvada, CO. Used with permission.

AOD Use Summary Profile: Put the scores from *Profile 1, page 67, in the Score boxes of the profile below.* Then find the number on the row and put an X over that number. Where do you fall? In "low," "low-medium," "high-medium" or "high"?

SCALE	SCORE	LOW		LOW-MEDIUM		HIGH-MEDIUM		HIGH	
SOCIAL		0	1	2		3	4	5 - 11	
SOLO		0		1	2	3		4 - 14	
BENEFITS		0 1 2 3		4 5 6 7		8 10 12 13		14 20 25 33	
AOD PROBLEMS		0 1 2 3		4 5 7 8 9 14		15 20 21 28 30		37 49 50 80	
PERCENTILE		10 20	30 40 50	60 70	80 90 99

Risk of Substance Abuse: Put a check in the right column of these patterns if they happened to you within any 12-month period.

GUIDELINES FOR SUBSTANCE ABUSE	CHECK
1. Repeated substance use making you unable to do your duties at work, school, or home (such as repeatedly missing work or poor work output, being late to work, being suspended or expelled from school, neglecting your household duties or children).	
2. Repeated substance use in situations where it is physically hazardous (such as driving or operating a vehicle under the influence of a substance).	
3. Repeated substance-related legal problems (such as several DWIs, subsance-related disorderly conduct, charges related to domestic violence).	
4. Continued substance use knowing that you have had repeated social or relationship problems caused by or made worse by the effects of substance use (such as conflicts with spouse about your substance use, arguments and physical fights, etc.).	
YOUR TOTAL SCORE (ADD UP YOUR CHECK MARKS)	

WRITE DOWN 2 OR 3 OF THE AOD USE OUTCOMES THAT HAVE BEEN MOST UPSETTING TO YOUR LIFE.

_____

_____

_____

Based on criteria for Substance Dependence as defined by the American Psychiatric Association (2000). *Diagnostic Statistical Manual of Mental Disorders* (4th ed., text revision). Washington, DC, Author

Risk for Substance Dependence: Put a check in the right column of these patterns if they happened to you within the same 12 month period.

GUIDELINES FOR SUBSTANCE DEPENDENCE	CHECK

1. Your tolerance has changed in either of the following ways:
  a) you need a lot more of the substance to get the desired outcome or intoxication; or
  b) you get a lower effect with use of the same amount of substance.	

2. You have had signs or symptoms of withdrawal from AOD use as shown by one or both at the following:
  a) when stopping the use of a substance you have symptoms such as: sweating, increased pulse rate, shakes, unable to sleep, sick to stomach, seeing, hearing or feeling things not there, feeling anxious, having a convulsion or seizure;
  b) you take the substance to relieve or avoid the symptoms of withdrawal.	

3. You have taken the substance in larger amounts over a longer period of time than you really meant to.	
4. When you won't cut down or control the use or you have been unable to cut down, control or stop using the substance.	
5. You have spent a lot of time trying to get substances (such as driving to get liquor late at night, driving long distances to a bar or liquor store, making sure you would always have your afternoon drinks), or a lot of time trying to recover from its use.	
6. You have given up important and fun social, work or recreational activities or cut down on these activities because of substance abuse.	
7. You continue to use the substance even though you know its use has caused you ongoing problems (such as: continue to drive even though you know you can get or have gotten a DWI; continue to drink even though you know it will upset your spouse or cause you to get into conflicts with your spouse; continue to use cocaine even though you know it causes depression on withdrawal).	
TOTAL SCORE (ADD ALL OF THE CHECKS)	

WRITE DOWN 2 OR 3 OF THE AOD USE OUTCOMES THAT HAVE BEEN MOST UPSETTING TO YOUR LIFE.

_____

_____

_____

_____

_____

_____

Based on criteria for Substance Dependence as defined by the American Psychiatric Association (2000). *Diagnostic Statistical Manual of Mental Disorders* (4th ed., text revision). Washington, DC, Author

Your AOD classification: Rate yourself as to what classes of AOD use problems you fit into **when you were drinking or using other drugs.** Check all that apply.

AOD USE PROBLEM CLASSES: CHECK ALL THAT FIT YOU	NO	YES
1. **Drinking or Other Drug Use Problem:** If you have ever had a problem from AOD use, then check "yes." If you had a DWI arrest and see it as being a problem, then you have an AOD use problem. If you checked any symptom in *Worksheet 19*, you may have had an AOD problem.		
2. **Problem Drinker or Problem Drug User:** If you have had several AOD use problems for a period of time or during your lifetime, then you have been into a pattern of alcohol or other drug misuse. We call this *problem drinking* or *problem drugging.* If you checked several symptoms in *Worksheet 19, or reached point F in Figure 8, page 71,* you are probably a *problem drinker or problem user.*		
3. **Problem Drinker or User - Substance Abuse:** You probably fit this category if you have had several AOD use problems for a period of time or during your life and you checked one or more of the statements in *Worksheet 20, page 80.*		
4. **Problem Drinker or User - Substance Dependence:** You probably fit this category if you have had repeated problems from AOD use and if you checked three or more of the statements in *Worksheet 21, page 81.* IF YOU FIT THIS CATEGORY, YOU FIT THE ABOVE THREE CATEGORIES.		
YOUR TOTAL SCORE (ADD UP YOUR CHECK MARKS)		

PUTTING IT TOGETHER: MAKE A SUMMARY OF YOUR AOD USE PATTERNS
1. Your style of use (what drugs, how often, how much):
2. Your style of use (social, solo):
3. Your level of seriousness of your AOD use problem:
4. Type of outcome or classification:

MODULE 4

OVERVIEW

Understanding and Changing Criminal Thinking and Behavior

The most important goal of this program is to prevent backsliding into criminal thinking and conduct - *to prevent recidivism.* Knowledge about criminal conduct, antisocial behavior and prosocial and responsible living provides us with the basis for changing our patterns of criminal thinking and behavior. In this Module, we look at some basic ideas about criminal conduct, what it means to live a prosocial life and the cycles of criminal conduct. We see how this knowledge applies to our own personal situation. On completion of *Module 4,* you will have a good idea of your antisocial and criminal pattern, how you can avoid recidivism, what you can do to **live a prosocial** and **responsible life** and your prosocial strengths.

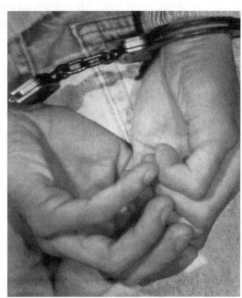

Here are the specific goals of this module.

◆ Understand criminal conduct and prosocial thinking and behaviors.

◆ Do a personal evaluation of your antisocial attitudes and behaviors and understand your risk for future criminal behavior - recidivism.

◆ Understand how thinking errors lead to criminal conduct and the criminal conduct cycles.

Module 4 has two sessions.

Session 9: Prosocial, Antisocial and Criminal Thinking and Behavior

Session 10: Thinking Errors and the *Criminal Conduct Cycle*

SESSION INTRODUCTION AND OBJECTIVES

> ### OBJECTIVES
>
> ➡ Learn about prosocial, antisocial and criminal thinking and behavior.
>
> ➡ Look at your antisocial attitudes and behaviors and understand your risk for future criminal behavior - recidivism.

GETTING STARTED

▶ *CB Map Exercise* and share your *Thinking and Action Plan (TAP) Charting, Program Guide 4,* that you did this week. Start with talking about what criminal conduct or behavior means to you.

▶ Key words: antisocial, criminal conduct, risk factors.

SESSION CONTENT AND FOCUS

GUIDES FOR RESPONSIBLE LIVING

Responsible living is based on personal values, strength of character or moral strength, and prosocial relationships with people. **Prosocial values and moral responsibility** involve:

▶ Respecting the rights of others;

▶ Being accountable to the laws and rules of our community and society;

▶ Living in harmony with the community;

▶ Having positive regard for and caring about the welfare and safety of others; and

▶ Contributing to the good of the community and society.

ANTISOCIAL ATTITUDES AND BEHAVIORS

This involves a pattern of disregarding and violating the rights of others, doing harm to others and going against the norms, rules and laws of society. **Exercise:** Complete *Worksheet 23,* page 86, which describes antisocial attitudes and behavior. The higher the scores, or the more "sometimes" and "much of the time" responses you have, the more likely you are to be antisocial and have a higher risk for criminal conduct unless you **change thinking and actions.** Scores above 20 to 25 suggest **higher** risk for future antisocial behavior.

From the results of *Worksheet 23,* rate yourself as to the need to change antisocial behaviors and strengthen prosocial attitudes and behaviors by checking one of the following.

❑ I need to make a lot of changes in becoming more prosocial.

❑ I need to make some changes in becoming more prosocial.

❑ I need to make just a few changes.

❑ I do not need to make any changes and see myself as prosocial.

Exercise: Make a prosocial statement out of each statement in *Worksheet 23.*

WHAT IS CRIMINAL CONDUCT?

Criminal conduct is actions that break the law and becomes a focus of the adult criminal justice system. Here are four views of criminal conduct. **Exercise:** Check the ones that fit you as to your past actions. If you did not check all of them, share with the group why.

❑ **Legal:** an act not allowed by a city, state or nation, punishable by law.

❑ **Moral:** an act against the standards or principles that you see as right or wrong;

❑ **Social:** an act against the customs and traditions of the community and punishable by the community.

❑ **Psychological:** an antisocial act that brings pain and loss to others but may be rewarding to the offender.

WHAT LEADS TO CRIMINAL THINKING AND CONDUCT (CTC)

There are many influences that lead to criminal conduct. We call these risk and need factors.

Past Risk Factors or Influences

Exercise: Using the first part of *Worksheet 24,* page 87, check the **past** risk factors that fit you. If you checked most or all as "moderate" or "high," or have a score of 12 to 21, you are at **higher** risk for recidivism. You can't change these past factors, but you can stop them from influencing your life if you understand and change your thoughts, attitudes and beliefs about them. For each that applies to you, write one thought to stop it from influencing your present and future.

Present Risk Factors or Influences

Exercise: *Worksheet 24* also gives present or active (dynamic) risk factors that make you more at risk of criminal conduct and recidivism. Complete the worksheet based on your life before your last arrest. Scores from 15 to 25 indicate a high risk of recidivism. Scores higher than 25 increases that risk. **You can change these risk and need factors to stop recidivism.** For each that you check, write down how you will change your thinking and actions. Add other influences or factors that apply to you and are not on the list. Share your findings in group.

SUMMARY OF SESSION ACTIVITIES, HOMEWORK AND SESSION CLOSURE

1. Do *Worksheets 23* through *24*.

2. Update your *Master Skills List, Program Guide 1*, page 291. Continue working on your *Autobiography*. Do your *TAP charting, Program Guide 4*, page 300, for this week.

3. Share with your group how you see your pattern of criminal conduct. What thoughts will you need to change to prevent recidivism?

Antisocial behavior and attitudes: Rate yourself on these attitudes and behaviors that are seen as antisocial. For every "Fits me sometimes" check, give yourself a "1." For every "Fits me much of the time" check, give yourself a "2."

WORKSHEET 23

ANTISOCIAL BEHAVIORS AND ATTITUDES	**0** USUALLY DOES NOT FIT ME	**1** FITS ME SOMETIMES	**2** FITS ME MUCH OF THE TIME
1. Am impulsive and fail to plan ahead.			
2. Get aggressive and into physical fights.			
3. Get frustrated easily.			
4. Poor problem solving skills in relationships.			
5. Lack guilt and remorse when hurting others.			
6. Do not follow the rules.			
7. Do things that can get arrested for.			
8. Do not follow social norms.			
9. Lie or don't tell the truth.			
10. Con others for personal gain.			
11. Am reckless and not careful about my safety or safety of others.			
12. Not responsible with money/finances.			
13. Not responsible in relationships.			
14. Hard to put off a need when I have it.			
15. Not responsible in work or job.			
16. Deny responsibility for own mistakes.			
17. Blame others for my mistakes.			
18. Have friends who take part in illegal actions or behaviors.			
19. Violate the rights of others.			
20. Lack understanding (empathy) for others.			
TOTAL SCORE			

WORKSHEET 24

PAST RISK FACTORS AND INFLUENCES	DEGREE THEY FIT YOU			WRITE A THOUGHT OR ACTION THAT REDUCES RISK
	1 LOW	2 MODERATE	3 HIGH	
1. Was a juvenile delinquent				
2. Family has a criminal history				
3. School failure				
4. Child/teen AOD abuse				
5. Friends were delinquent				
6. Rejected by average peers				
7. Past criminal acts/conduct				
YOUR TOTAL SCORE				

PRESENT RISK FACTORS AND INFLUENCES	DEGREE THEY FIT YOU			WRITE A THOUGHT OR ACTION THAT REDUCES RISK
	1 LOW	2 MODERATE	3 HIGH	
1. Antisocial/criminal peers				
2. Have criminal role models				
3. Criminal thinking/attitudes				
4. Spend time with criminal peers				
5. Lack family closeness				
6. Get rewards through crime				
7. Live in high crime communities				
8. Poor relationship skills				
9. Lack emotional support				
10. Rebel against authority				
11. Poor problem solving skills				
12. Need to manipulate others				
13. Lack moral reasoning				
14. Angry and hostile attitude				
15. Act on spur of moment				
16. Alcohol/drug abuse				
YOUR TOTAL SCORE				

SESSION INTRODUCTION AND OBJECTIVES

OBJECTIVES

➡ See how thinking errors lead to criminal conduct.

➡ Understand the cycle of criminal conduct.

➡ Understand how AOD use relates to criminal conduct and your prosocial strengths.

GETTING STARTED

▶ Start with the *CB Map Exercise* and then share your *TAP Charting, Program Guide 4,* that you did this week. Share with your group changes you are making to prevent recidivism.

▶ Key words: criminal thinking and conduct (CTC) cycle, prosocial thinking.

SESSION CONTENT AND FOCUS

THINKING ERRORS THAT CAN LEAD TO CRIMINAL CONDUCT (CC)

Go back over *Worksheet 5,* page 35, in *Session 3* and see which of the thinking errors you checked as being part of your criminal conduct. Some thinking errors can lead to and support criminal conduct. **Exercise:** *Worksheet 25,* page 92, gives a list of thinking errors that support criminal conduct. Practice replacing those thinking errors with thoughts that lead to prosocial outcomes. We will work more on these later in another session. You may want to review the meaning of prosocial, page 84.

THE CRIMINAL CONDUCT CYCLE

Review of the AOD Mental-Behavioral Impaired Control Cycle (MB-ICC)

AOD use and abuse are learned. We expect AOD use to turn on pleasure or to turn off pain (help cope with life problems). When this happens, our AOD thinking and behaviors get strengthened. But, AOD use can cause problems in living. The AOD addiction cycle begins when the individual engages in AOD use to cope with problems that come from AOD use.

The Criminal Thinking and Conduct (CTC) Correction Cycle

Criminal thinking and conduct (CTC) are also learned. CTC are ways to handle events of our outside and inside world. CTC can turn on positive feelings and events or they can turn off stress and unpleasant events. When this happens, CTC get strengthened. They become **criminal thought habits** and **criminal action habits.** CTC lead to irresponsible actions and bad outcomes, for you and for the community. The result: you now engage in CTC to handle the problems that come from CTC.

Punishment resulting from criminal conduct can weaken or even stop the behavior. But, it may strengthen this behavior because it may strengthen criminal thinking. Being punished for a crime may just reinforce the person's belief that "nothing is fair," or "the world is out to get me." Just as with AOD use, the individual will engage in criminal conduct to cope with the bad outcomes that come from criminal conduct itself.

As with AOD use and abuse, there is a *Criminal Thinking and Conduct (CTC) Cycle, Figure 14,* page 90. By taking part in criminal activities, the cycle gets reinforced. Thought habits and action habits form around this cycle. Even though people differ as to particular thinking and action responses, the CTC cycle applies to most who engage in criminal conduct. Here is what can happen.

▶ There are three **events** that can set off the CTC cycle: 1) mental reactions to our outside world; 2) the world inside our minds; and 3) what we call criminal needs.

▶ These events can lead to **mental choices** involving **criminal thinking.**

▶ There are **emotional outcomes** to these choices and these can lead to criminal actions.

▶ Once a criminal act takes place, it sets off new mental reactions which **strengthen CTC.**

You change or correct this cycle by changing your mental reactions to the inside or outside events or to your criminal needs. You can replace your criminal thinking with **prosocial thinking.** This thinking says "I want to follow the laws of society. I want to be a positive part of my community."

You can also change the events or things outside of you that set off the CTC cycle. For example, avoid situations that are high risk for being involved in criminal conduct. However, we are not able to shelter ourselves from all outside and inside events that lead to criminal conduct. True change and self-correction comes when you handle the mental reactions and change your thinking and beliefs. Change comes when you learn the skills that will help you to choose prosocial actions.

Exercise: Use *Worksheet 26,* page 93, to show your criminal conduct cycle and how you correct that cycle.

RELATIONSHIP BETWEEN AOD ABUSE AND CRIMINAL CONDUCT

Look at *Worksheet 16,* page 68. Alcohol and other drug use feeds into and makes stronger the criminal behavior and the CTC cycle. It can do this in these ways:

▶ AOD use may be part of the events that set off criminal thinking. AOD intoxication lowers self-control, stops good judgment and gets us into irrational beliefs and errors of thinking;

▶ Drugs are often part of situations of high risk for criminal activity;

▶ AOD use can block the use of skills to make self-correction;

▶ AOD use and intoxication can strengthen thinking errors that excuse criminal conduct. It blocks fear and guilt that can stop criminal acts or fear and guilt that should follow a criminal act.

FIGURE 14   The Criminal Thinking and Conduct Correction Cycle

EVENTS THAT SET OFF CRIMINAL CONDUCT CYCLE

EXTERNAL EVENTS
- Risk Factors
- Relationship problems
- Opportunities to offend

CRIMINAL NEEDS
- Antisocial associates
- Antisocial attitudes/beliefs
- AOD Abuse

INTERNAL EVENTS
- Memories
- Anger and rage
- Anxiety/stress

MENTAL CHOICES

CRIMINAL THINKING

ERRORS IN THINKING AND LOGIC
- I deserve more than this
- People have more than me
- I feel screwed, treated badly

IRRATIONAL THINKING
- I won't get caught
- Only way I can feel powerful

THINKING ABOUT/PLANNING A CRIME
CHOOSING A VICTIM OR CRIME TARGET
THINKING ABOUT GETTING REVENGE

THINKING ABOUT AND DESIRE FOR AOD
- Lowers controls/impairs thinking

SUPPORTED BY CRIMINAL CORE BELIEFS
- Life has never been fair
- People and life owe me

PROSOCIAL THINKING

CORRECT/CHANGE CRIMINAL THINKING
- Change errors in thinking
- Change irrational thoughts

ALTERNATIVES TO PLANNING CRIMES
- Think of healthy activities
- Think of prosocial activities
- Imagine doing positive acts

CHOOSE DIFFERENT ENERGY OUTLETS
- Think of someone you can help
- Decide not to victimize

THINK OF FORGIVING AND PRAISING
FOCUS ON ALTERNATIVES TO AOD USE

SUPPORTED BY PROSOCIAL CORE BELIEFS
- Life is fair and good to me
- I am a responsible, caring person

EMOTIONAL AND FEELING OUTCOMES

FEEL MORE POWERFUL
EXCITEMENT AND EMOTIONAL HIGH
FEEL REVENGEFUL
ANGER AND RESENTMENT
FEEL COURAGEOUS AND BOLD
EMOTIONAL HIGH FROM CRIMINAL THINKING

EMOTIONAL AND FEELING OUTCOMES

FEELING GOOD BEING CRIME FREE
SELF-ASSURED AND CONFIDENT
FEEL FORGIVING
FEEL KINDNESS AND LOVE
FEEL PROUD AND HUMBLE
FEEL EMOTIONAL HIGH BEING AOD FREE

CRIMINAL BEHAVIOR AND ACTIONS

MORE TIME WITH CRIMINAL PEERS
ISOLATING FROM FAMILY MEMBERS
INCREASE IN AOD USE
PRE-CRIME ACTS - CRUISING TOWN
MISDEMEANORS SUCH AS STEALING
BRAGGING AND BRAVADO WITH FRIENDS
SCOPING OUT CRIMINAL TARGETS
COMMIT LARGER CRIMINAL ACTS

PROSOCIAL BEHAVIOR AND ACTIONS

MORE TIME WITH PROSOCIAL PEERS
INCLUDE SELF IN FAMILY ACTIVITIES
CHANGE AOD USE PATTERN OR STOP USE
COMMIT PROSOCIAL/RESPONSIBLE ACTS
- Volunteer work in community
- Attend support/religious groups
SEEK/ENGAGE IN HEALTHY ACTIVITIES
ROLE MODEL/MENTOR OTHER OFFENDERS

CRIMINAL OUTCOMES AND CONSEQUENCES

GET ARRESTED AND JAILED
GET BY WITH IT - DON'T GET CAUGHT
MORE RESPECT FROM CRIMINAL PEERS

**THOUGHTS AND BEHAVIORS
STRENGTHENED**

PROSOCIAL OUTCOMES AND CONSEQUENCES

RESPECT RIGHTS OF OTHERS
OBEY LAWS AND KEEP FREEDOM
MORE RESPECT FROM FAMILY AND FRIENDS

**THOUGHTS AND BEHAVIORS
STRENGTHENED**

EVALUATING YOUR PROSOCIAL VALUES AND STRENGTHS

All of us have prosocial values and strengths. The problem is that the antisocial and pro-criminal needs and values overpower the pro-social values and strengths. What we want to do is to **strengthen the prosocial values** to overpower the procriminal values and needs. **Exercise:** *Worksheet 27,* page 94, gives a list of prosocial values and strengths. Check if you think you have these values and strengths. Then, add your own values and strengths not in the list, using spaces 20 through 25.

Sharing is being prosocial.

SUMMARY OF SESSION ACTIVITIES AND HOMEWORK

---

1. Do *Worksheets 25 through 27.*

2. Update your *Master Skills List,* page 291 and MAP, page 295. Continue working on your *Autobiography.* Do your *TAP charting, Program Guide 4,* page 300, for this week.

3. Using the *SSC Scale,* rate your level of understanding and skills for what you learned in *Sessions 9* and *10.*

Understanding of my antisocial thinking and behaviors	0	1	2	3	4	5	6	7	8	9	10
	LOW					MEDIUM					HIGH

Understanding of my past and present risk for further criminal conduct	0	1	2	3	4	5	6	7	8	9	10
	LOW					MEDIUM					HIGH

Understanding of the criminal conduct cycle	0	1	2	3	4	5	6	7	8	9	10
	LOW					MEDIUM					HIGH

My ability to think and act in a proscoial way	0	1	2	3	4	5	6	7	8	9	10
	LOW					MEDIUM					HIGH

SESSION CLOSURE

Talk about your procriminal thinking and values and how these compare with prosocial values and strengths that you have. Share with the group whether you truly want to give up your criminal patterns.

Changing antisocial thinking errors and social relationships that can lead to antisocial behaviors and criminal conduct. Practice replacing these with thoughts and relationships that can lead to prosocial behaviors and outcomes.

ERRORS IN THINKING OR SOCIAL RELATIONSHIPS THAT COULD LEAD TO ANTISOCIAL BEHAVIOR AND OUTCOMES.	REPLACE WITH PROSOCIAL THOUGHTS OR RELATIONSHIPS THAT LEAD TO PROSOCIAL BEHAVIORS/OUTCOMES.
POWER THRUST: "I'm better than others." "Don't mess with me." "He's weak."	
INNOCENT: "I didn't know I was breaking the law." "I didn't do it."	
BLAMING STANCE: "It's your fault this happened to me." "No one got hurt."	
IRRESPONSIBLE: "It's ok if it doesn't hurt anybody." "Just as well get wasted."	
VICTIM STANCE: "Somebody's always blaming me." "If you grew up where I did, you'd commit crimes."	
CARELESS: "I don't care how it affects somebody else." "Not my problem."	
JUST DESSERTS: "They had it coming." "They're stupid and left their house unlocked."	
DISTRUST: "You can't trust anybody." "The system really sucks."	
CHEATED: "I never get what's coming to me." "I deserve more than this."	
SCREWED: "I'm always getting screwed." "This only happens to me."	
SOCIAL: Spending a lot of time with antisocial friends or with criminal peers.	
SOCIAL: Most friends are angry at society and laws of society.	
SOCIAL: Always critical or angry at people, putting them down.	
SOCIAL: Spending all free time in bar drinking or getting high with friends.	
RELATIONSHIP: Rejecting family or friends who are supportive.	

The Criminal Thinking and Conduct Correction Cycle

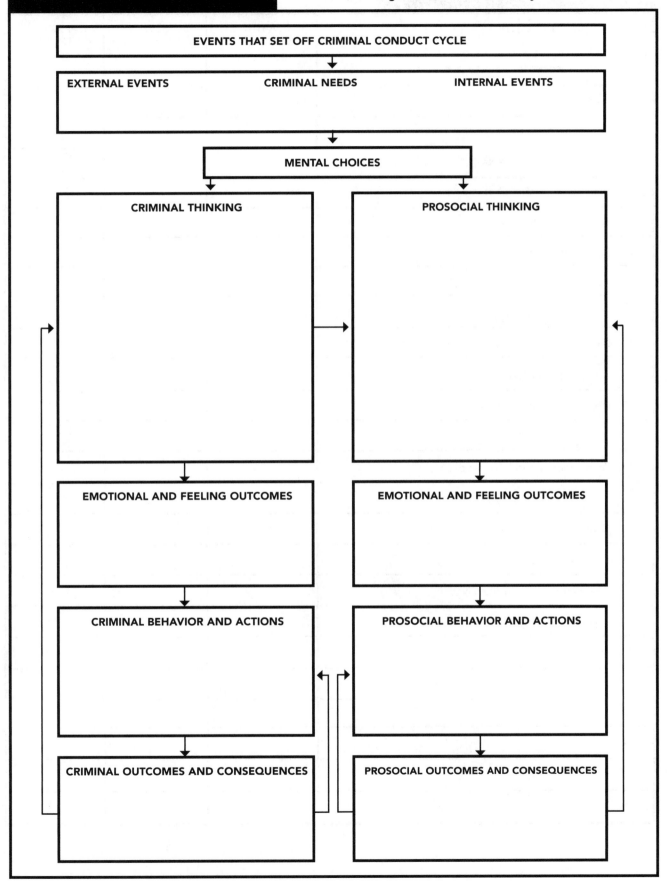

EVENTS THAT SET OFF CRIMINAL CONDUCT CYCLE

EXTERNAL EVENTS   CRIMINAL NEEDS   INTERNAL EVENTS

MENTAL CHOICES

CRIMINAL THINKING

PROSOCIAL THINKING

EMOTIONAL AND FEELING OUTCOMES

EMOTIONAL AND FEELING OUTCOMES

CRIMINAL BEHAVIOR AND ACTIONS

PROSOCIAL BEHAVIOR AND ACTIONS

CRIMINAL OUTCOMES AND CONSEQUENCES

PROSOCIAL OUTCOMES AND CONSEQUENCES

Your prosocial strengths: For each of the prosocial strenghts, check the response that best fits you. Then, add other prosocial strengths that you have.

PROSOCIAL STRENGTHS	NOT A STRENGTH	SOMEWHAT A STRENGTH	DEFINITELY A STRENGTH
1. Have prosocial friends and peers			
2. Care about my family			
3. Am polite and courteous to others			
4. Follow the rules at work			
5. Respect the rights of others			
6. Am honest with others			
7. Follow the laws of society			
8. Give compliments and praise			
9. Help others in trouble			
10. Enter another's personal space only with permission			
11. Am friendly and social			
12. Don't take what belongs to others			
13. Have good manners			
14. Try to understand how people feel			
15. Follow through with promises			
16. Give to worthy causes			
17. Drive with care			
18. Settle arguments peacefully			
19. Support my family and friends			
20.			
21.			
22.			
23.			
24.			
25.			

MODULE 5

Sharing and
Listening:
Communication
Pathways to
Self-Awareness
and Other-
Awareness

OVERVIEW

Self-awareness is a key to opening the door to change. Self-awareness comes through effective communication. The communication pathway to self-awareness is **active sharing.** We do this through **self-disclosure** - sharing how we see ourselves - and through **receiving feedback** - inviting others to share how they see us.

Other-awareness opens the door to responsible relationships. The communication pathway to other-awareness is **active listening.** Active listening involves inviting others to share and giving them feedback. Active listening increases our understanding of others and leads to responsible and positive relationship outcomes. Here are the goals of this Module.

◆ Learn and practice active sharing and active listening skills.

◆ To be challenged to take a deeper look at your history of substance use problems and criminal conduct.

Module 5 **has four sessions.**

Session 11: Pathways to Self-Awareness: The Skills of *Active Sharing*

Session 12: Pathways to Other-Awareness: The Skills of *Active Listening*

Session 13: A Deeper Sharing of Your AOD Use Problems and Your Emotions.

Session 14: A Deeper Sharing of Your Criminal Conduct History

Self-disclosure leads to self-awareness. Self-awareness leads to change.

SESSION INTRODUCTION AND OBJECTIVES

Self-awareness is an important part of the puzzle of change. The communication pathway to self-awareness is the skill of **active sharing,** our focus for this session.

OBJECTIVES

⟹ Understand verbal and nonverbal communication.

⟹ Learn the process and use the tools of self-directed communication - *Active Sharing.*

GETTING STARTED

▶ *CB Map Exercise* and share your *(TAP) Charting.*

▶ Key words: nonverbal communication, verbal communication, self-oriented communication (active sharing), defensive, receiving feedback, self-awareness, *Johari Window.*

SESSION CONTENT AND FOCUS

WHAT KEEPS US FROM SELF-DISCLOSURE?

During much of our lives we were told to not talk about our feelings and problems. If we did express our emotions, we often were put down or even punished. Often we were told not to get angry or to be happy when we were sad. When we did show feelings, it was after we stored them and then they came out by "blowing up" or pouting. **The main problem** is we did not learn healthy ways to tell our thoughts or show our feelings. We were often taught to blame others as a way to solve frustrations and problems. Or, we learned to solve problems by someone being right and someone being wrong. We still hold on to the old ways of showing our feelings and thoughts - by losing our temper or, getting depressed when we don't get our way.

Being **open to feedback** from others **is difficult.** What we often get is not feedback but a reaction to what we have done. It is usually a judgment or telling us we are wrong. Feedback is most helpful when people make it clear that this is how they see us - it is only their view or opinion of us. We listen to feedback when people relate to us and don't just react to what we say or do - when we think the other person understands us. When this happens, we learn about ourselves and are more aware of who we are. By entering this program you are saying "give me feedback about me. Tell me about me so that I can change." Our goal is to give feedback in a non-blaming manner and help you become more aware of yourself.

TWO KINDS OF COMMUNICATION

Nonverbal communication

This is **"talking" without words.** We show it through our face, body, hands, the tone of our voice. In this way we tell people what we think and feel. "Talking" without words is often not the same as our talking with words (verbal communication). If we are to have people understand us, we must say the same thing with words that we say without words.

Good communication means that we say the same thing with words that we say without words.

Exercise: Show the following emotions without words. What are your thoughts when you show these feelings?

ANGER FEAR SHAME JOY LOVE SURPRISE

Verbal communication

This is **talking with words.** Clear and honest verbal communication helps other people understand us and helps us better understand our own thoughts, feelings and behaviors. Then we can change those thoughts and behaviors that hurt us and others.

Communication breaks down when we confuse opinion and fact. Opinions are based on how each of us sees the world. Opinions can have different meanings. Facts are what the picture shows - they are camera-checkable. Opinions are what the picture means to you. **Most opinions are not right or wrong.** We can solve problems if we stick to the facts and hear the opinions of others. Verbal communication is also difficult because words mean different things to different people, like "music," or "food." Sometimes different words have the same meaning, like "young man," "boy," "lad."

Exercise: Group members will share one meaning of the words "fly," and "light." If these words have different meanings, think how we can differ around words that are less clear, such as "love."

TWO PATHWAYS TO COMMUNICATION

There are two ways that we direct our communicating: **self-oriented communication** and **other-oriented communication.** Both are important if you want to understand and be understood. Both are basic to positive and successful relationships with others. Both are necessary for responsible living. In this session, we will focus on the pathways and skills of self-directed communication - *Active Sharing.*

ACTIVE SHARING OR SELF-ORIENTED COMMUNICATION

This is communication about you. It is an important pathway to self-awareness. There are two skills to active sharing - **self-disclosure** and **receiving feedback.**

First Active Sharing Skill: Self-disclosure

This is telling others about you. It involves talking about yourself and not the other person. It is sharing with someone - how you see your past and your current feelings, thoughts and actions. It is using the "I" message in communication. There are four basic parts to this communication.

▶ I think!   ▶ I feel!   ▶ I need!   ▶ I do or act!

Using the word "I" is **unselfish**. It is one way to share yourself. Sharing yourself is unselfish. Active sharing is about you, not about the other person. It's not bragging. It's just being honest about you. Self-disclosure does three things. **These are keys to change.**

▶ It tells you about yourself. It is "you talking to yourself." It makes you more self-aware.

▶ It allows others to see who you are and give you honest feedback on how they see you.

▶ It helps others to self-disclose to you.

We use the word "I" and not "you" in this kind of communication. When we start with the word "you" we are talking about the other person, and not ourselves. When we are mad at someone, we use the word "you." Practice talking with others without using the word "you."

Active sharing may involve telling someone you are upset or bothered by that person's actions. Here are some tips on how to make active sharing have positive outcomes.

▶ **Use "I" messages.** Avoid "you" messages or blaming statements.

▶ **Use self-talk** to stay in control: "I need to be calm."

▶ **Focus on the problem** and not the person.

▶ **Make it clear it is about you,** and what is acceptable to you.

▶ **Listen to the other person.** This is the topic for next session.

▶ **Get closure.** Don't go on and on. Finish on a positive note.

<u>Exercise:</u> Role play telling someone you are upset with them. Have someone role play that person. Use the above tips. Make the outcome positive. Do not use the word "you." Use the word "I."

Second Active Sharing Skill: Receiving Feedback

Receiving feedback helps you hear yourself through others. This is hard to do. But you give people permission to talk to you **about you. The key: Don't get defensive** or push away. This stops feedback. If the feedback is critical or negative, we get defensive. When feelings and emotions are high between two people, they get defensive. The feedback becomes blaming. But we even tend to push away feedback that is a compliment or positive. Feedback is less threatening if the other person makes it clear that this is only his or her opinion. Or, if you think, "that's only his opinion."

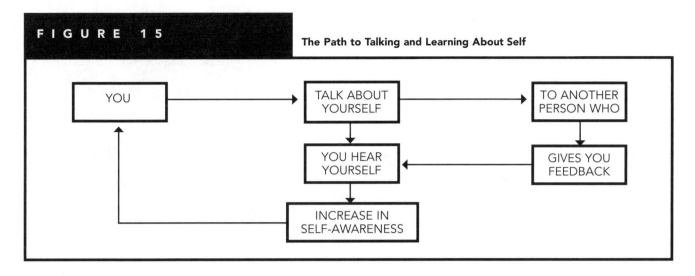

FIGURE 15   The Path to Talking and Learning About Self

Exercise: Do *Worksheet 28,* page 101, *Thinking Report* on a time when you got defensive.

Figure 15 above provides a picture of self-oriented communication or active sharing.

THE ACTIVE SHARING WINDOW

We can use the *Johari Window,* Figure 16, to look at four parts to ourselves.   First, what we know about ourselves that others do not know - the **Hidden Area.** What others see about ourselves and we don't see - the **Blind Area.** What we don't and others don't know about ourselves - **Unknown Area.** What we see and know and that other people see and know - the **Free Area** or **Open Area.** It is healthy to increase the **open area.** The goal of this program is to make the **Free Area** larger and to shrink the **Blind** and **Hidden** areas. This is done through self-disclosure and receiving feedback.

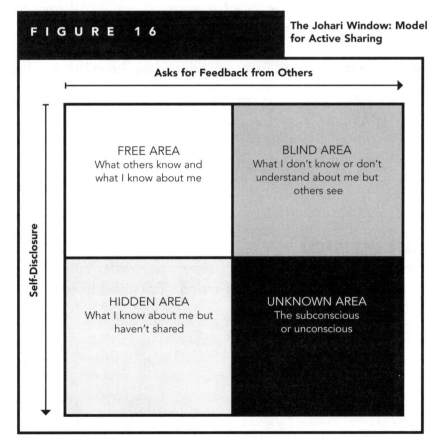

In SSC, we self-disclose through session worksheets, questionnaires, surveys, tests, group exercises and group discussion. We receive feedback from group members and counselors who share their views of us. Self-disclosure and receiving feedback lead to self-awareness and to change.

From Joseph Luft, Of Human Interaction, National Press Books, Palo Alto, CA, 1969.

PRACTICING ACTIVE SHARING

Exercise: In groups of three, one person shares using "I" messages. The second person listens. The third person listens and gives feedback on how well the "active sharing" person is doing. Then change roles. PRACTICE...PRACTICE.

Exercise: Role play a situation where one person is telling another person about a problem he/she is having at work. How did the person do on the skills of active sharing?

Exercise: As homework, do *Worksheet 29,* page 101, *Active Sharing.*

SUMMARY OF SESSION ACTIVITIES AND HOMEWORK

1. Do *Worksheet 28* in group and *Worksheet 29* for homework.

2   Try to use only "I" messages for the coming week. See if you use "you" messages more than the "I" messages. Keep track of the number of times you get defensive this week.

3. Update your *Master Skills List,* page 291, and MAP, page 295. Continue working on your *Autobiography.* Do your *TAP charting,* page 300.

4. Using the *SSC Scale,* rate yourself on your knowledge and use of the *Active Sharing Skill.*

Active sharing skill knowledge

0	1	2	3	4	5	6	7	8	9	10
LOW					MEDIUM					HIGH

Active sharing skill level

0	1	2	3	4	5	6	7	8	9	10
LOW					MEDIUM					HIGH

SESSION CLOSURE

Share the work you did in this session. Talk about how you get defensive with people close to you.

Thinking Report about a time when you got defensive: How could you have made it better by using the above communication skills?

1. DESCRIBE THE EVENT:

2. YOUR THOUGHTS:

3. YOUR ATTITUDES AND BELIEFS:

4. YOUR FEELINGS:

5. THE OUTCOME:

Active sharing: Take one situation when you used active sharing this week.

1. DESCRIBE THE SITUATION:

2. WHO WAS INVOLVED?

3. WHAT SPECIFIC ACTIVE SHARING SKILLS DID YOU USE?

4. HOW DID THEY WORK? DID THE OTHER PERSON LISTEN? DID YOU RECEIVE FEEDBACK? DID YOU GET DEFENSIVE?

SESSION 12: Pathways to Other-Awareness: The Skills of Active Listening

SESSION INTRODUCTION AND OBJECTIVES

Awareness of the thoughts and feelings of others is also an important part of the puzzle of change. The communication pathway to other-awareness is the skill of *active listening*, our focus for this session. **There is power in what we are learning and practicing. It is the power of communication. It is the power of sharing and the power of listening.**

OBJECTIVES

⟶ Review the active sharing skills.

⟶ Learn the process and use the skills of other-directed communication - *Active Listening*.

GETTING STARTED

▶ *CB Map Exercise* and share your *TAP Charting*.

▶ Review *Worksheet 29,* page 101, you did for homework.

▶ Keywords: other-oriented communication (active listening), inviting others to share, giving feedback, body language, thinking filters, open channel, listening, other awareness.

SESSION CONTENT AND FOCUS

REVIEWING YOUR WORK ON ACTIVE SHARING

The skills of active sharing are the first step of increasing self-awareness which leads to change. Recall the two important parts of active sharing: 1) Self-disclosure; and 2) Receiving Feedback.

We self-disclose and receive feedback through verbal communication and through nonverbal communication. **Exercise:** Using *Worksheet 30,* page 105, list some nonverbal way you self-disclosed this past week and some nonverbal feedback you received from other people.

WHAT IS ACTIVE LISTENING OR OTHER-ORIENTED COMMUNICATION?

This skill opens other people up to you. It **increases your awareness of others** and the world - which also increases self-awareness. Active listening leads to positive relationship outcomes. There are **two active listening skills.**

First Active Listening Skill: Inviting others to share or self-disclose

▶ **Open stance.** Keeping your hands and arms open, as a basket, for people to put their message in.

▶ **Open questions:** "What happened to you?" "How did your day go?" Avoid closed questions that get a "yes" or "no" response. "Did you go to work?"

▶ **Open statement:** This is more powerful. "Tell me how you feel!" "Give me your ideas."

Second Active Listening Skill: Feedback or reflective listening skill

This skill lets the person know you hear them. It reflects or mirrors back what the person says. "You're not very happy today." It communicates that you understand the person. "This is how I see you," or "I see you as upset." *Reflective listening* is a powerful skill.

HOW TO MAKE ACTIVE LISTENING WORK

Bypass your thinking filters - Choose an open channel

Our "thinking filters" are the screens that we run through what other people say. These thinking filters are our beliefs and values. We don't have to give up these beliefs and values to listen. We can have an open "listening channel." Our responses can come from that channel and not our "thinking filters." When we run what we hear through our "thinking filter," we stop listening.

"Listen" to the person's body language

Failing to "listen" to body talk keeps us from hearing the other person, and prevents us from knowing what to reflect back. Some body talk that we can listen to and learn from:

▶ facial expressions   ▶ voice tone   ▶ eye contact   ▶ touch

▶ posture and gestures   ▶ personal space   ▶ dress and clothing   ▶ timing

Clear and accurate reflections or feedback

No matter how close you listen, if you don't use talk that reflects back what the person is saying, that person will not know you have heard them. This is critical - reflecting what is said.

Here are some tips for active listening

▶ **Look at the person** you are talking with. Make comfortable eye contact.

▶ **Watch the person's body language.**

▶ **Pay attention** to what is being said. If you don't understand, ask an open question.

▶ When you do understand, nod your head to **encourage the speaker.**

▶ **Reflect** or mirror back what you hear; this tells the other person you are listening.

▶ **Do some active sharing.** Share with the other person who you are and what you feel and think.

PRACTICING ACTIVE LISTENING

Exercise: Break up into groups of three. One person practices **active sharing** skills, one practices **active listening** and the third person watches and gives feedback on how well the other two are doing in their roles. Change roles. PRACTICE...PRACTICE.

Exercise: Role play a situation where one person is telling another person a problem he/she is having communicating with his/her spouse. How did the person do in active sharing and listening?

Be open to have people tell you about how they see you. Acitive listening builds good relationship outcomes.

SUMMARY OF SESSION ACTIVITIES AND HOMEWORK

1. Do *Worksheet 30.* Update your *Master Skills List,* page 291 and MAP, page 295. Continue working on your *Autobiography.*

2. Do your *TAP Charting* for this week, page 300.

3. Practice the **active listening** skills this week. Do as much reflecting as you can. Look for the results. Also, keep track of the number of times you get defensive this week.

   Exercise: Use *Worksheet 31,* page 105, for your homework this week. Take an event where you used **active listening.**

4. Using the *SSC Scale,* rate yourself on your knowledge and use of the active listening skills.

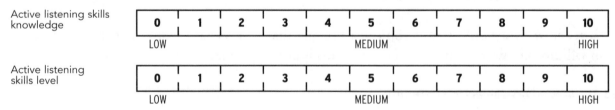

Active listening skills knowledge

0	1	2	3	4	5	6	7	8	9	10

LOW   MEDIUM   HIGH

Active listening skills level

0	1	2	3	4	5	6	7	8	9	10

LOW   MEDIUM   HIGH

SESSION CLOSURE

Share the work you did in this session. Talk about how you get defensive with people close to you. Practice **active listening** skills in your group.

WORKSHEET 30	Nonverbal ways you self-disclosed and some nonverbal feedback you received this past week.

NONVERBAL WAYS YOU SELF-DISCLOSED	NONVERBAL FEEDBACK YOU RECEIVED FROM OTHERS

WORKSHEET 31	Active listening: Take one situation where you used active listening this week.

1. DESCRIBE THE SITUATION:

2. WHO WAS INVOLVED?

3. WHAT SPECIFIC ACTIVE LISTENING SKILLS DID YOU USE?

4. HOW DID THEY WORK? DID THE OTHER PERSON LISTEN? DID YOU RECEIVE FEEDBACK? DID YOU GET DEFENSIVE?

SESSION INTRODUCTION AND OBJECTIVES

As part of the **Challenge** phase of change, you look deeper into the negative outcomes of your AOD use and the impact of that use on the lives of other people. Another part of this challenge looks at experiences in your life that have been difficult and helps you to develop a better mental outcome around these experiences. This session focuses on the HIDDEN part of the *Johari Window,* parts of our lives we have avoided. This session may be difficult for you. There are some experiences that you may not want to share in group, but rather with your individual counselor. That's OK.

OBJECTIVES

➡ Share in a deeper way, your past AOD use problems and consequences.

➡ See whether you have changed as to sharing your AOD problem outcomes.

➡ Share feelings about a personal-emotional experience in your life.

GETTING STARTED

▶ *CB Map Exercise* and share your *TAP Charting.*

▶ Talk about *Worksheet 31,* page 105, which you did for homework this week.

▶ Key words: deeper sharing, AOD use history.

SESSION CONTENT AND FOCUS

A DEEPER SHARING OF YOUR AOD USE HISTORY

Now, we want you to take an honest look at the problem outcomes of your AOD use. You already did (or will do) some of this in *Sessions 7 and 8.*

Retesting of your AOD surveys or tests

How have you changed as to your willingness to share the bad outcomes of your AOD use? We will look at this in several ways.

▶ **Exercise:** Complete *Worksheet 32,* page 109, *Client Self-Assessment Scale (CSAS).* Put your score under the 2nd score in the table below. Then go to page 18, *Worksheet 3,* and put the score on the CSAS you took at *Orientation* under the 1st score column in the table below.

▶ In *Session 8,* you completed *Worksheet 19,* page 79, *Negative outcomes of AOD use.* Go back and complete the survey again. Use a different mark for your answers. Add your new score. Put your first and second scores in the table below. How do they compare? If you have not completed *Session 8,* you are asked to complete *Worksheet 19* at this time and put your score in the 1st SCORE column.

▶ You may have taken the *Adult Substance Use Survey - R (ASUS-R)* or another survey like that when you started the program. You are asked to retake it. Use the table below to put your 1st and 2nd scores of the *ASUS-R* GLOBAL SCALE (or the total scores from the other survey you took).

▶ Compare your scores. If you were very open on the first time you took these surveys, your scores probably didn't change. If you were defensive the first time, your scores probably increased.

TEST OR SURVEY	1ST SCORE	2ND SCORE
CSAS (WORKSHEET 3 AND WORKSHEET 32)		
WORKSHEET 19 - NEGATIVE OUTCOMES OF AOD USE		
ASUS-R GLOBAL SCALE		
OTHER SURVEY		

Your specific AOD problem outcomes and how these affected others

Exercise: Using *Worksheet 33,* page 110, write down the specific problem outcomes resulting from your alcohol or other drug use. Be honest. This is only for your use. Share your findings in group. Change your thinking around these AOD outcomes so that you have a more positive emotional outcome.

Exercise: Using *Worksheet 34,* page 110, identify persons in your life who were upset or hurt or negatively affected by your alcohol or other drug use. Again, you can't change other people's reactions to these outcomes, but you can change your thinking to have better emotional outcomes around them.

SHARING DEEPER FEELINGS

You may have been carrying around some deep emotions about past experiences such as hurt, disappointment, resentment, sadness or grief.

Exercise: You are asked to write down your emotions about one of these experiences. Use the space on the next page. If you are uncomfortable in self-disclosing, share some of this with your group. This exercise is hard for some people. Take your time. You may find you have some feelings you still have to work on. If this is true, set up some time with your counselor to talk about them.

You cannot change these experiences, but you can change your thinking about them so that you can have better emotional outcomes around them.

MY DEEPER EMOTIONS ABOUT AN IMPORTANT EMOTIONAL EXPERIENCE

SUMMARY OF SESSION ACTIVITIES

1. Do *Worksheets 32* through *34.*

2. Update your *Master Skills List,* page 291 and MAP, page 295. Have you finished your *Autobiography?* Do your *TAP Charting* for this week, page 300.

3. Using the *SSC Scale,* rate yourself on your ability to be open and share the negative or bad outcomes of your AOD use and your deeper emotions.

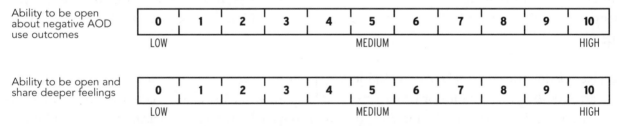

SESSION CLOSURE

Some of the work you did in this session may have been difficult for you. You may want to work more on these issues with your counselor. Be sure that your sharing in group is within your comfort level.

Client Self-Assessment Scale (CSAS): Rate yourself on each question. For every check in the "1" column, give yourself a 1, for every check in the "2" column, give yourself a 2, for every check in the "3" column, give yourself a 3, and for every check in the "4" column, give yourself a 4. Total your score.

Rate yourself on each of the following questions	0 None	1 Low	2 Moderate	3 High	4 Very High
1. Degree of problems you have had with the use of alcohol?					
2. Degree of problems you have had with drugs other than alcohol?					
3. Degree of problems you have had with criminal conduct in the past?					
4. Degree of help you need to keep from having further problems with alcohol or other drug use?					
5. Degree of help you need to keep you from being involved in criminal behavior?					
6. To what degree do you want to make changes in your life?					
7. To what degree do you think that you have made changes in your life?					
YOUR SCORE FOR EACH COLUMN					
YOUR TOTAL SCORE					

WORKSHEET 33

Recording problem outcomes from your AOD use

YOUR AGE	DESCRIBE THE AOD PROBLEM OUTCOME OR NEGATIVE CONSEQUENCE

WORKSHEET 34

Persons who have been upset, hurt or negatively affected by your alcohol and other drug use

SPECIFIC PERSONS WHO WERE HURT, UPSET OR NEGATIVELY AFFECTED BY YOUR AOD USE	WAS THIS PERSON HURT OR UPSET?		WAS IT HARD TO ADMIT: WERE YOU DEFENSIVE?		EXPLAIN HOW YOUR AOD USE AND ABUSE HURT, UPSET OR AFFECTED THESE PERSONS
	YES	NO	YES	NO	
Your parent(s)					
Brother or Sister					
Spouse/intimate partner					
Your child/children					
Close friend(s)					
Someone in community					
Other:					
Other:					

SESSION INTRODUCTION AND OBJECTIVES

We all think that we are people who want to do good. Even persons with a long history of criminal offenses have a hard time seeing and accepting their past criminal conduct and seeing themselves as "bad." Most offenders are aware of their past criminal history. But many have not taken a clear and honest look at that history and how their criminal past related to their AOD use.

OBJECTIVES

➥ Increase awareness of your past criminal conduct and offenses.

➥ Understand how your AOD use and abuse relates to your past criminal conduct.

GETTING STARTED

▶ *CB Map Exercise* and share your *TAP Charting*.

▶ Reflect on last week's session.

▶ Key words: deeper sharing, criminal conduct history.

SESSION CONTENT AND FOCUS

As part of the **Challenge** phase of change, you are asked to look deeper into your criminal history and what this history has cost you. Be as honest as you can in doing this session's exercises.

DEEPER SHARING OF YOUR CRIMINAL CONDUCT

In *Sessions 9 and 10,* we looked at antisocial attitudes and behaviors and how you might fit these. We also looked at your risk for recidivism. Now, we want you to look at your specific criminal conduct and record and its cost to you.

We look at how our criminal past is related to alcohol or drug use.

Retesting on the CSAS

Have you changed in your openness to share how you see your past criminal conduct? **Exercise:** In *Session 13* you redid the *Client Self-Assessment Scale (CSAS), Worksheet 32,* page 109. Compare your responses to questions 3 and 5 on *Worksheet 32* with those in *Worksheet 3,* page 18. Were you more open on these questions on the second testing?

Your Criminal Conduct Log

Exercise: Using *Worksheet 35,* put together your *Criminal Conduct History Log.* Take time to complete it as exact as you can. **Do only columns** 1 through 5: 1) list all of your arrests you can recall by year; 2) type of charge; 3) months on probation; 4) months in jail or in prison; 5) months on parole. If the arrest did not result in probation or jail/prison or parole, put NA in each column that does not apply.

Exercise: If you have your actual official record, compare that record or your official legal history with the *Criminal Conduct Log* you just completed. How do they compare. Did you put more in your log than is in your official record? Or did you put less?

HOW ARE YOUR AOD USE AND CRIMINAL CONDUCT RELATED?

Exercise: Do the last column of *Worksheet 35,* page 113. For each arrest, write (**B**) if you used AOD (alcohol or other drugs) **before** the offense; write (**D**) if you used AOD **during** the offense; write (**A**) if you used AOD **after** the offense. If all three apply, write BDA. If none of these apply, write NA.

WHAT HAS YOUR CRIMINAL CONDUCT HISTORY COST YOU?

Most offenders never take time to figure out what their history of criminal conduct has cost them in time, money and effort. **Exercise:** Use *Worksheet 36,* page 114, to summarize the cost of all of your lifetime legal problems in money and time. You may want to do this as homework, or in group.

SESSION ACTIVITIES AND CLOSURE GROUP

1. Update your *Master Skills List, Program Guide 1,* page 291 and *MAP, Program Guide 3,* page 295. Have you finished your *Autobiography?* Do your *TAP Charting* for the coming week, page 300.

2. **Exercise:** Group members are asked to do a thinking report on one event or time when the use of alcohol or other drugs led to committing a crime. Then go back and do a re-thinking report making changes that would have led to a prosocial outcome. The thinking report steps are: EVENT, THOUGHTS, BELIEFS, FEELINGS, OUTCOMES.

3. Rate yourself on your ability to be open about your criminal conduct history.

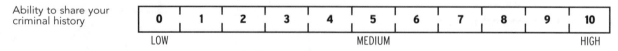

Ability to share your criminal history

| 0 | 1 | 2 | 3 | 4 | 5 | 6 | 7 | 8 | 9 | 10 |
| LOW | | | | | MEDIUM | | | | | HIGH |

4. Closure group: talk about whether you were able to be open and honest in doing the exercises in this session.

Your Criminal Conduct History Log. List all of your arrests. If an arrest did not lead to probation or jail/prison or parole, then put NA in each column that does not apply.

ARREST YEAR	TYPE OF CHARGE	MONTHS ON PROBATION	MONTHS IN JAIL/PRISON	MONTHS ON PAROLE	RELATED TO AOD USE

In the last column for each arrest, put a:
B if you drank or used other drugs before the offense
D if you drank or used other drugs during the offense
A if you drank or used drugs after the offense
BDA if you drank or used drugs before, during and after the offense
NA if AOD not involved in any way.

Cost of your criminal conduct and legal problems in money and time during your lifetime.

SPECIFIC AREAS OF COSTS	PUT COST IN DOLLARS
1. Your conviction fines	
2. Court costs	
3. Increases in insurance rates	
4. Attorney fees and expenses	
5. Lost salary and wages	
6. Cost of treatment programs	
7. Other cost in dollars	
8. Other:	
9. Other:	
10. Other:	
Total cost of your criminal conduct in dollars	

SPECIFIC AREAS OF COST IN TIME	TIME COST IN MONTHS
1. Time spent planning crimes	
2. Time spent committing crimes	
3. Time spent with attorneys and legal counsel	
4. Time spent waiting for court and in court	
5. Time spent looking for job	
6. Time spent away from job	
7. Time in treatment programs	
8. Time spent with probation workers	
9. Time spent in jail or prison	
10. Time spent with parole workers	
11. Other:	
12. Other:	
13: Other	
Total time in months lost due to criminal conduct	

MODULE 6

OVERVIEW

Understanding and Preventing Relapse and Recidivism

Preventing relapse and recidivism are two primary goals of SSC. **Full relapse** is going back to a pattern of use that results in negative outcomes and problems. Relapse begins long before AOD use problems once again occur. It begins in our thinking, attitudes and beliefs. Recidivism also begins long before we commit a criminal act. It starts in our thinking, attitudes and beliefs. We want you to learn the pathways, maps and skills for understanding and preventing relapse and recidivism. We look at cravings, urges and refusal skills. Here are the goals for this module.

◆ Understand the pathways to relapse and recidivism (R&R).

◆ Understand the pathways and learn skills to prevent R&R.

◆ Identify and develop skills to manage high risk exposure that are setups for R&R.

◆ Learn about cravings and urges and refusal skills.

Module 6 **has three sessions.**

Session 15: Pathways to Relapse and Recidivism

Session 16: Pathways, Skills and Plan for Preventing Relapse and Recidivism

Session 17: Managing Urges and Cravings and Learning Refusal Skills

SESSION INTRODUCTION AND OBJECTIVES

Criminal conduct and substance use and abuse have related pathways. From 70 to 90 percent of persons who have committed a crime have a history of AOD problems. As many as 80 percent who are incarcerated for robbery, burglary or assault committed these crimes when using alcohol or other drugs. AOD use can lead to criminal conduct and criminal conduct can lead to substance use. Many offenders *use* before committing a crime; many are *high* when committing crimes; many use substances after a crime. Relapse into AOD abuse is high risk for recidivism. Recidivism often leads to relapse. Both involve an erosion process. They are triggered by exposures to high-risk thinking and situations.

Yet, relapse and recidivism are different. They have different outcomes. AOD relapse may not lead to jail. You can go back to criminal conduct - recidivism - without relapsing. Many relapse without going back to committing crimes. However, one of the highest risk patterns for recidivism is relapse.

OBJECTIVES

➡ Understanding the process of relapse and recidivism (R&R).

➡ Look at the pathways to R&R and define high-risk exposures that lead to R&R.

➡ Defining your risk for R&R.

GETTING STARTED

▸ *CB Map Exercise* and *TAP Charting sharing.* Share the work you did last session on the cost of your criminal conduct, Worksheet 36, page 114.

▸ Key words: recidivism and relapse (R&R), erosion, high risk exposures, pathways to R&R, lapse, full relapse, recidivism, full recidivism, R&R risk, triggers.

SESSION CONTENT AND FOCUS

RELAPSE AND RECIDIVISM - A PROCESS OF EROSION

Relapse is a process of erosion. Soil erosion is a gradual wearing away of the top soil that produces rich and healthy crops. It is difficult to see and takes a long time. With relapse and recidivism, there is a gradual wearing away of the rich resources of the mind that were developed to live an AOD-free and crime-free life. The erosion starts with risk-exposures - high-risk thinking or high-risk situations. A return to problem use or criminal conduct may appear to be the result of a spur-of-the-moment act, but the erosion of the skills and strengths of prevention occur over a long period of time. *Figure 17* gives a picture of this erosion process.

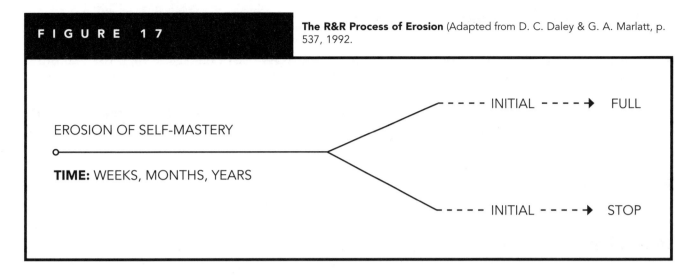

FIGURE 17   **The R&R Process of Erosion** (Adapted from D. C. Daley & G. A. Marlatt, p. 537, 1992.

EROSION OF SELF-MASTERY

TIME: WEEKS, MONTHS, YEARS

INITIAL ----➔ FULL

INITIAL ----➔ STOP

Example: Here is a story showing the process of erosion told by a judicial client.

I drank when stressed. When a kid, my dad would yell at me, and I'd go with my friends and get high. We'd break car radio aerials, and break into garages, stuff like that. Got caught a few times. Even put in the "Hall." I decided to go to the army, but got drunk and smoked pot. Had hangovers and even blackouts. Passed out a lot. I stole some equipment and got caught. Got an honorable. But drinking and smoking pot got worse. Mainly when I felt down, or tense. One night, three of us broke into a store. The alarm went off and the cops swarmed. Got arrested, and because of my record, got three years. Did well. Finished high school and two years of tech - computers. Got into treatment and made the decision - a promise - to stop using. Came out knowing computers and got a good job. Got married, and it went well, but had some job problems. Started thinking about drinking and pot. Started thinking about my old buddies. Even started seeing a couple. One just heisted a liquor store. Started making plans to even join him on one. One day I stopped off to see him and had a couple. He started putting pressure. The program I was in flashed back: I'm into relapse and recidivism. I had lapsed (I learned this stuff in treatment). My P.O. was wise. He said, "you're going back to prison or to more treatment." Was a "no-brainer." I went through six more months of therapy. I learned that change was in my head. Change your thinking and what you believe and great things happen. That was four years ago. Never did go into a full relapse. Haven't even thought about that crime stuff. But it was close. Even today, I have to use all those skills - change my thinking when I get bummed or stressed. But it works. My wife is a big help. I'm never going back to crime or to using. But every once in a while, I find myself in relapse thinking and situations. I deal with them.

UNDERSTANDING RELAPSE

The meaning of relapse

Relapse means going back to a pattern of AOD use that you have decided to change. There are two goals you can set around relapse.

▶ Living an AOD-free life - abstaining from all use. This is the abstinence goal. SSC recommends this since being here probably means you have had serious AOD use problems.

▶ Living an alcohol-problem free life and abstaining from the use of all illegal drugs and from the misuse of prescription drugs.

For these two goals, we use these three definitions.

▶ **Process of relapse:** Being involved in thinking about AOD use or engage in high risk exposures (defined below) that put you at risk of a lapse or lead to a full relapse.

▶ **Lapse:** Any use of alcohol that can lead to a problem use pattern **after you have committed yourself** to a non-harmful pattern of alcohol use; **or,** for the goal of total abstinence, any use of alcohol or illegal drugs.

▶ **Full relapse:** Returning to a pattern of drinking or other drug use that causes problems, is harmful and is upsetting to you and to others. This applies to both relapse prevention goals.

What defines relapse for you?

▶ If your goal is to never use alcohol or illegal drugs and you go **back to a pattern of use that will lead** to problems, you are **into relapse.**

▶ If your goal is to never allow alcohol to cause another problem and you go **back to a pattern of use that will lead** to problems, you are **into relapse.**

▶ If your goal is to never use alcohol or illegal drugs **or** never again have alcohol use problems and your AOD use **is causing problems for yourself or others,** you **have relapsed.**

WHAT DOES RELAPSE MEAN TO YOU?

_____

_____

Understanding high-risk exposures

Relapse erosion starts when you experience high-risk exposures that have led to AOD problems or abuse in the past. These are the **high risk exposures.**

▶ **High risk thinking** is thought habits (automatic thinking) that lead to problem substance use. **Examples:** "If I have a drink, I'll relax," or "I may as well get high, no one gives a damn."

▶ **High risk situations** are events that trigger thoughts and feelings that you need to use alcohol or other drugs. **Example:** conflict with significant other.

▶ **High-risk feelings** are emotions that trigger thoughts that you need to use alcohol or other drugs. **Example:** Being angry at a spouse, boss, girlfriend, boyfriend; feeling down or depressed; feeling lonely, sad; happy over getting a better job.

▶ **High-risk attitudes and beliefs. Attitude:** "Nobody's telling me how much I can drink." **Belief:** "A good time means you drink."

Exercise: Using *Worksheet 37,* page 122, list high-risk exposures that could lead to relapse for you.

UNDERSTANDING RECIDIVISM

Recidivism is a gradual erosion process. You are **into recidivism** when you take part in high-risk exposures that lead to criminal conduct. **Full recidivism** is committing another criminal act.

High-risk (HR) exposures for recidivism

High-risk thinking: Thought habits that lead to criminal conduct. **Examples:** Thinking about robbing and stealing; that you can get by with it; that you "deserve better" or "they have it coming."

High-risk situations: People, places or events that trigger criminal thinking. **Examples:** Relationship conflicts that produce stress; hanging around peers involved in crime; going into high-crime neighborhoods; looking for a place to rip-off.

High-risk feelings: Emotions that trigger thoughts about committing a crime. **Examples:** Being angry at a spouse, boss, girlfriend, boyfriend; feeling depressed; feeling powerful when with criminal friends.

High-risk attitudes and beliefs that lead to criminal conduct. Attitudes: "They have it coming." "My P.O. ain't telling me what to do." **Beliefs:** "Life's not been fair." "I always get the short end."

Exercise: Using *Worksheet 37,* page 122, list high-risk exposures that could lead to recidivism.

Using Illegal Drugs

Using illegal drugs is a violation of the law and puts you in the process of recidivism. Say that you choose the relapse prevention goal of using, but preventing problem outcomes from use. But if such use involves illegal and illicit drugs, is this being AOD-problem free? Doesn't this put you into recidivism? Does using illegal drugs put you at risk of **full recidivism? Exercise:** Discuss this in group.

TRIGGERS FOR RELAPSE AND RECIDIVISM

Here are some high-risk exposures that are triggers for R&R.

▶ Conflict with another person, especially someone close.

▶ Social or peer pressure to use drugs or commit a crime.

▶ Unpleasant feelings and emotions - sadness, depression or anger.

▶ A change in your self-image: seeing yourself as clean and sober, and then you use drugs, and say "I've failed, just as well do it again." Or, getting out of lockup and thinking, "I'm going to go out and cut loose."

Exercise: For each R&R trigger in *Worksheet 38,* page 123, write specific thoughts, feelings, and actions that apply to you. Did the action lead to or stop R&R?

YOUR RISK OF RELAPSE OR RECIDIVISM - REVIEW

You worked on the negative outcomes of AOD use in *Session 8, Worksheets 19* through *22,* pages 79 to 82. High scores on these worksheets increase your risk of relapse. In *Session 9, Worksheets 23 and 24,* pages 86 and 87, you worked on your risk of being involved in antisocial behavior and criminal conduct. The higher your scores on these worksheets, the greater your risk of recidivism.

PATHWAYS TO RELAPSE AND RECIDIVISM

Figure 18 (next page) shows a map of the pathways to relapse and recidivism. The two have their own separate pathways, but they are also linked together. Study the map and then discuss how it fits you. This map also provides the keys for preventing recidivism and relapse. **Exercise:** Use *Worksheet 39,* page 124, to map possible pathways to relapse and recidivism for you.

RELAPSE AND RECIDIVISM (R&R) LOG

The *R&R Calendar, Worksheet 40,* page 125, will help you understand how your AOD and legal problems are related. Do this for homework or in group. Use a two to three year time period. Start with the date of your first serious attempt to stop AOD abuse and criminal conduct. Use a straight line to indicate periods of being drug-free and crime-free. Use a wavy line to indicate periods of relapse or recidivism. You will be asked to share your findings next session.

SESSION ACTIVITIES AND CLOSURE GROUP

---

1. Update your *Master Skills List,* page 291 and MAP, page 295. Have you finished your *Autobiography?* Do your *TAP charting,* page 300.

2. Do *Worksheets 37 through 39* in group. Do *Worksheet 40* either in group or as homework.

3. Using the *SSC Scale,* rate yourself on your understanding of the process of relapse and recidivism.

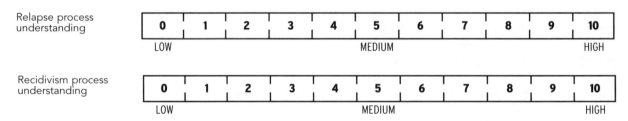

4. Closure group: discuss whether your R&R prevention goals include **not** using illegal drugs. Be open and honest about this issue.

FIGURE 18

Cognitive-Behavioral Pathways for Relapse and Recidivism.

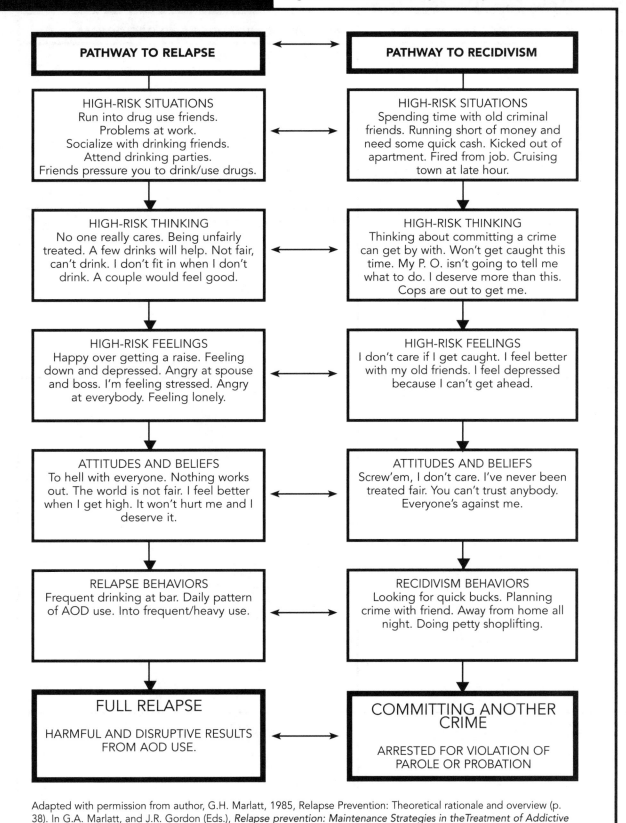

PATHWAY TO RELAPSE

PATHWAY TO RECIDIVISM

HIGH-RISK SITUATIONS
Run into drug use friends.
Problems at work.
Socialize with drinking friends.
Attend drinking parties.
Friends pressure you to drink/use drugs.

HIGH-RISK SITUATIONS
Spending time with old criminal friends. Running short of money and need some quick cash. Kicked out of apartment. Fired from job. Cruising town at late hour.

HIGH-RISK THINKING
No one really cares. Being unfairly treated. A few drinks will help. Not fair, can't drink. I don't fit in when I don't drink. A couple would feel good.

HIGH-RISK THINKING
Thinking about committing a crime can get by with. Won't get caught this time. My P. O. isn't going to tell me what to do. I deserve more than this. Cops are out to get me.

HIGH-RISK FEELINGS
Happy over getting a raise. Feeling down and depressed. Angry at spouse and boss. I'm feeling stressed. Angry at everybody. Feeling lonely.

HIGH-RISK FEELINGS
I don't care if I get caught. I feel better with my old friends. I feel depressed because I can't get ahead.

ATTITUDES AND BELIEFS
To hell with everyone. Nothing works out. The world is not fair. I feel better when I get high. It won't hurt me and I deserve it.

ATTITUDES AND BELIEFS
Screw'em, I don't care. I've never been treated fair. You can't trust anybody. Everyone's against me.

RELAPSE BEHAVIORS
Frequent drinking at bar. Daily pattern of AOD use. Into frequent/heavy use.

RECIDIVISM BEHAVIORS
Looking for quick bucks. Planning crime with friend. Away from home all night. Doing petty shoplifting.

FULL RELAPSE
HARMFUL AND DISRUPTIVE RESULTS FROM AOD USE.

COMMITTING ANOTHER CRIME
ARRESTED FOR VIOLATION OF PAROLE OR PROBATION

Adapted with permission from author, G.H. Marlatt, 1985, Relapse Prevention: Theoretical rationale and overview (p. 38). In G.A. Marlatt, and J.R. Gordon (Eds.), *Relapse prevention: Maintenance Strategies in the Treatment of Addictive Behaviors* (p. 38), Guilford Press.

Give examples for each high-risk exposure that could lead to relapse and recidivism for you.

HIGH RISK EXPOSURES FOR RELAPSE	HIGH RISK EXPOSURES FOR RECIDIVISM
HIGH-RISK THINKING:	HIGH-RISK THINKING:
HIGH-RISK SITUATIONS:	HIGH-RISK SITUATIONS:
HIGH-RISK FEELINGS AND EMOTIONS:	HIGH-RISK FEELINGS AND EMOTIONS:
HIGH-RISK ATTITUDES:	HIGH-RISK ATTITUDES:
HIGH-RISK BELIEFS:	HIGH-RISK BELIEFS:

WORKSHEET 38

Triggers for relapse and recidivism: For each trigger write one past situation that applies to you. Write your thoughts and feelings. What was your action? Did it prevent R&R? Did it lead to R&R? Relapse example: Situation: You had a fight with your boss. Thought, "screw the job." Feelings, angry. Action, you went to talk with a friend, a positive coping behavior, rather than drinking. Use positive thoughts.

TRIGGERS FOR RELAPSE	THOUGHTS	FEELINGS	ACTION: + OR -
Unpleasant or negative feelings and emotions:			
Conflict with another person:			
Social or peer pressure to drink or use drugs:			
A change in self-image:			
TRIGGERS FOR RECIDIVISM	**THOUGHTS**	**FEELINGS**	**ACTION: + OR -**
Unpleasant or negative feelings and emotions:			
Conflict with another person:			
Social or peer pressure to drink or use drugs:			
A change in self-image:			

WORKSHEET 39

Map what you think might be a relapse-recidivism path for yourself.

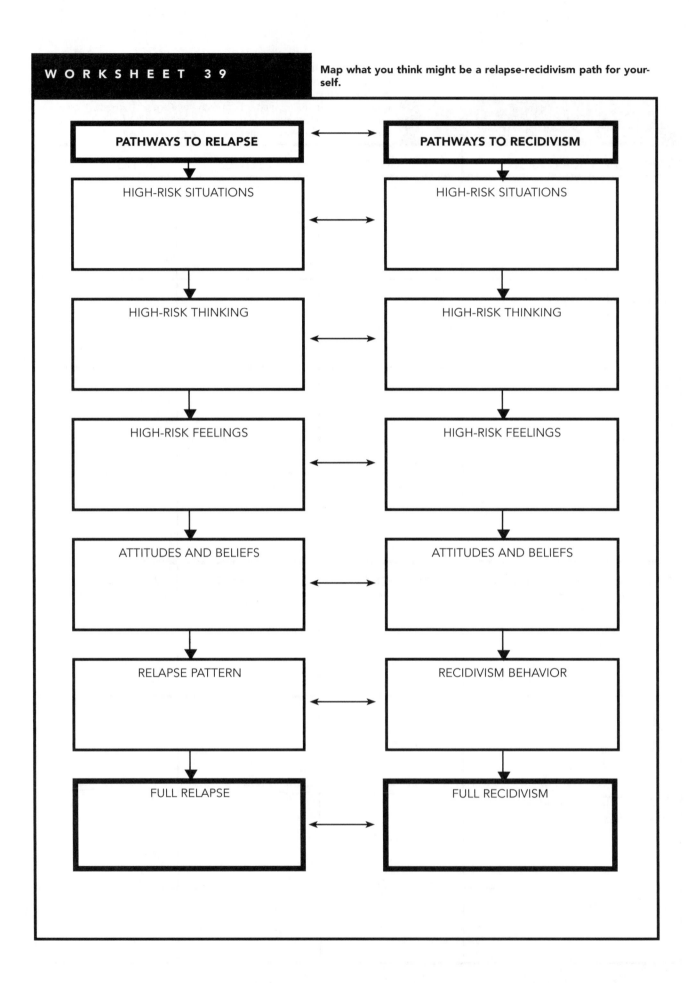

| PATHWAYS TO RELAPSE | ⟷ | PATHWAYS TO RECIDIVISM |

HIGH-RISK SITUATIONS ⟷ HIGH-RISK SITUATIONS

HIGH-RISK THINKING ⟷ HIGH-RISK THINKING

HIGH-RISK FEELINGS ⟷ HIGH-RISK FEELINGS

ATTITUDES AND BELIEFS ⟷ ATTITUDES AND BELIEFS

RELAPSE PATTERN ⟷ RECIDIVISM BEHAVIOR

FULL RELAPSE ⟷ FULL RECIDIVISM

The Relapse and Recidivism Log. Use this log to look at your relapse and recidivism pattern. It will help you see how your AOD use and criminal conduct are related. Start with a year that you made your first serious attempt to stop AOD abuse and criminal behaviors. Use a straight line to indicate periods of no AOD use and no criminal behavior. Use a wavy line to indicate periods of AOD use and criminal activity.

YEAR	JAN	FEB	MAR	APR	MAY	JUN	JUL	AUG	SEP	OCT	NOV	DEC
AOD												
CRIME												

YEAR	JAN	FEB	MAR	APR	MAY	JUN	JUL	AUG	SEP	OCT	NOV	DEC
AOD												
CRIME												

YEAR	JAN	FEB	MAR	APR	MAY	JUN	JUL	AUG	SEP	OCT	NOV	DEC
AOD												
CRIME												

YEAR	JAN	FEB	MAR	APR	MAY	JUN	JUL	AUG	SEP	OCT	NOV	DEC
AOD												
CRIME												

Adapted from Gorski, 1993 and Wanberg and Milkman, 1998.

SESSION INTRODUCTION AND OBJECTIVES

Recidivism prevention **always** involves your personal goal and the goal of society. Society **and** your community expects you to never commit another crime. **It is your choice and society's choice.** Relapse prevention involves your personal goals around AOD use. **It is mainly your choice.** And, you decide what relapse means to you.

OBJECTIVES

➠ Understand the process of relapse and recidivism prevention.

➠ Learn the skills to prevent relapse and recidivism.

➠ Look at the pathways to R&R prevention.

➠ Develop a recidivism and relapse prevention plan.

GETTING STARTED

▶ *CB Map Exercise* and *TAP Charting* sharing. Share your R&R log you did for homework.

▶ Key words: R&R prevention, prevention skills, R&R prevention plan.

SESSION CONTENT AND FOCUS

SETTING YOUR R&R PREVENTION GOAL - OUR GOALS GUIDE OUR ACTIONS.

In the orientation sessions, you stated your recidivism prevention goal, page 9. Now we ask you to restate your recidivism prevention goal.

MY RECIDIVISM PREVENTION GOAL

_____

_____

_____

In the orientation sessions, you stated your relapse prevention goal, page 10. In *Session 15,* page 118, you said what relapse means to you. Using these statements, restate your relapse prevention goal.

```
┌─────────────────────────────────────────────────────────────────┐
│  MY RELAPSE PREVENTION GOAL                                       │
│                                                                   │
│  _____     │
│                                                                   │
│  _____     │
│                                                                   │
└─────────────────────────────────────────────────────────────────┘
```

RELAPSE AND RECIDIVISM (R&R) PREVENTION

In *Session 15,* page 121, *Figure 18* showed the pathways to R&R and how high-risk exposures lead to R&R. Now, we look at another map, *Figure 19,* page 129, to understand the process of R&R **prevention.** We prevent R&R through the use of strong coping skills. We will discuss each part of *Figure 19.*

▶ **High-Risk Exposures.** Situations, thoughts, feelings, attitudes and beliefs that increase the risk of R&R.

▶ **Weak or strong coping skills.** Weak coping skills decrease self-mastery and self-control. Strong coping skills increase self-mastery and self-control.

▶ **Decreased or increased self-mastery** in coping with high-risk exposures.

▶ **Expected Outcome:** Expect drugs will help you handle stress; committing a crime solves the need for money. **Or,** you expect your use of skills will prevent R&R.

▶ **Initial lapse and recidivism or preventing lapse and recidivism.** Having a couple after deciding to be AOD-free; deciding to "do one more crime" after deciding to be crime-free. **Or,** you stick with your prevention goals and rules and your self-control and self-mastery are strengthened.

▶ **Rule Violation-Effect:** Going against your promise of living AOD and crime-free causes conflict inside you. Do you see yourself as living without drugs and crime? Or, with drugs and crime? You lapse, and you say, "hell with it, I might just as well get drunk now that I've gone this far." You steal something and say, "just as well continue stealing now that I started again, just take my chances." This solves your conflict. You go back to old patterns and old views of yourself - acceptance of using drugs and crime. You make excuses: "And anyway, I like to drink; and its easier to get what I want when I steal." Or, you could use self-talk and say, "I'm going to stick by my rules and goals." You could argue against the R&R thoughts and say, "do I want to go through all the problems of another arrest?"

▶ **Decrease or increase of self-control:** You lose control over AOD use and criminal conduct and see it as a "weakness." **Or,** you increase self-control over these behaviors.

▶ **Increase or decrease your chances of full relapse and full recidivism.**

SKILLS IN PREVENTING RELAPSE AND RECIDIVISM

Figure 20, page 130, gives the pathways to preventing R&R. The steps are based on cognitive-behavioral skills to manage high-risk exposures that lead to R&R. *Figure 20* shows you have choices. If you are on the path to R&R, you can shift to the right and get on the path to prevention at any point. You have a choice of self-control and avoiding high-risk exposures. This program is about learning skills and developing self-mastery to cope with and manage the high-risk exposures. Here is a summary of the skills as given in *Figure 20,* page 130.

▶ **Manage high-risk situations.** Change or better manage your situation by using good relationship skills. These could be refusal skills; skills to handle conflicts with others.

▶ **Manage high-risk thinking.** Skills to change thoughts, attitudes and beliefs (Session 19).

▶ **Manage high-risk feelings and emotions.** Use skills to manage stress, depression and guilt.

▶ **Manage high-risk attitudes and beliefs.** Change core beliefs. Get feedback on your attitudes.

▶ **Relapse and recidivism prevention and control** is strengthened by remembering bad outcomes of AOD use and CC. Self-control and self-mastery increase.

▶ Look at *Worksheet 36.* page 114, your CC cost. DO YOU WANT THAT AGAIN?

Exercise: Use *Figure 20,* page 130, and write down in the margin, on the right-hand side of the page, a skill or action that you use or would use to manage each of the high risk exposures.

YOUR RELAPSE AND RECIDIVISM PREVENTION PLANS

Exercise: Use *Worksheet 41,* page 131, to develop **your relapse prevention plan.** Base this on your relapse prevention goal.

Exercise: Use *Work Sheet 42,* page 132, in developing **your recidivism prevention plan.**

SESSION ACTIVITIES AND CLOSURE GROUP

---

1. Do *Worksheet 41* and *42.* Update your *Master Skills List,* page 291 and MAP, page 295. Have you finished your *Autobiography?* Do your *TAP charting,* page 300.

2. Use the *SSC Scale* to rate yourself as to the degree of self-control over relapsing and recidivism.

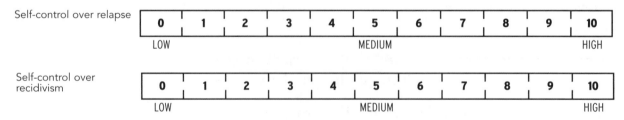

3. Closure group: Talk about your R&R prevention plan. **Exercise** for closure group: Have someone read the example of John's R&R on page 32. Have someone play the role of John and then have group members help John develop a R&R prevention plan.

The Process of Relapse and Recidivism Prevention: How it works.

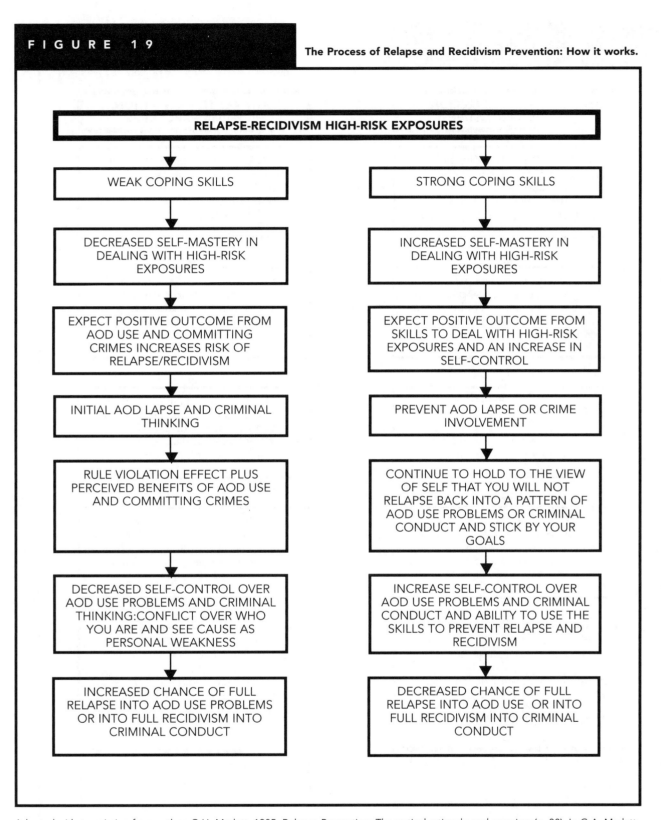

Adapted with permission from author, G.H. Marlatt, 1985, Relapse Prevention: Theoretical rationale and overview (p. 38). In G.A. Marlatt, and J.R. Gordon (Eds.), *Relapse Prevention: Maintenance Strategies in the Treatment of Addictive Behaviors* (p. 38), Guilford Press.

Pathways for Relapse and Recidivism Prevention

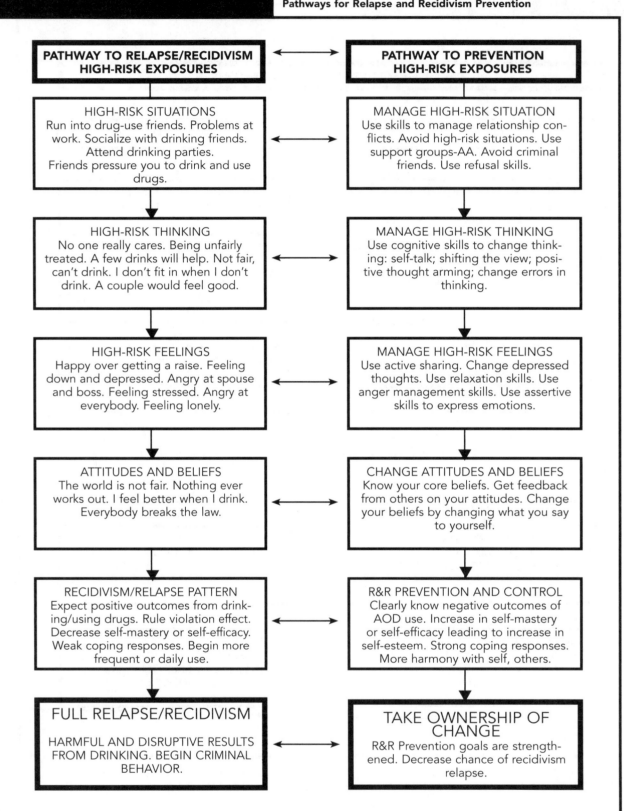

PATHWAY TO RELAPSE/RECIDIVISM HIGH-RISK EXPOSURES	PATHWAY TO PREVENTION HIGH-RISK EXPOSURES

HIGH-RISK SITUATIONS
Run into drug-use friends. Problems at work. Socialize with drinking friends. Attend drinking parties. Friends pressure you to drink and use drugs.

MANAGE HIGH-RISK SITUATION
Use skills to manage relationship conflicts. Avoid high-risk situations. Use support groups-AA. Avoid criminal friends. Use refusal skills.

HIGH-RISK THINKING
No one really cares. Being unfairly treated. A few drinks will help. Not fair, can't drink. I don't fit in when I don't drink. A couple would feel good.

MANAGE HIGH-RISK THINKING
Use cognitive skills to change thinking: self-talk; shifting the view; positive thought arming; change errors in thinking.

HIGH-RISK FEELINGS
Happy over getting a raise. Feeling down and depressed. Angry at spouse and boss. Feeling stressed. Angry at everybody. Feeling lonely.

MANAGE HIGH-RISK FEELINGS
Use active sharing. Change depressed thoughts. Use relaxation skills. Use anger management skills. Use assertive skills to express emotions.

ATTITUDES AND BELIEFS
The world is not fair. Nothing ever works out. I feel better when I drink. Everybody breaks the law.

CHANGE ATTITUDES AND BELIEFS
Know your core beliefs. Get feedback from others on your attitudes. Change your beliefs by changing what you say to yourself.

RECIDIVISM/RELAPSE PATTERN
Expect positive outcomes from drinking/using drugs. Rule violation effect. Decrease self-mastery or self-efficacy. Weak coping responses. Begin more frequent or daily use.

R&R PREVENTION AND CONTROL
Clearly know negative outcomes of AOD use. Increase in self-mastery or self-efficacy leading to increase in self-esteem. Strong coping responses. More harmony with self, others.

FULL RELAPSE/RECIDIVISM

HARMFUL AND DISRUPTIVE RESULTS FROM DRINKING. BEGIN CRIMINAL BEHAVIOR.

TAKE OWNERSHIP OF CHANGE
R&R Prevention goals are strengthened. Decrease chance of recidivism relapse.

Adapted with permission from author, G.H. Marlatt, 1985, Relapse Prevention: Theoretical rationale and overview (p. 38). In G.A. Marlatt, and J.R. Gordon (Eds.), *Relapse prevention: Maintenance Strategies in the Treatment of Addictive Behaviors* (p. 38), Guilford Press.

Your relapse prevention plan: Use all of the skills and ideas you have learned in this program.

IDENTIFY THE HIGH-RISK THINKING, ACTION AND SITUATION PATTERNS THAT COULD LEAD TO YOUR RELAPSE	PLAN: REPLACE THOSE HIGH-RISK THINKING, ACTION AND SITUATION PATTERNS TO PREVENT RELAPSE
List the negative outcomes for you if you continue the same AOD use pattern:	List the positive outcomes if never returning to that AOD use pattern:
List high-risk thoughts that could lead to relapse:	Replace those with thoughts that will prevent relapse:
List high-risk behaviors that could lead to relapse:	Replace those high-risk actions that will prevent relapse:
High-risk situations that could lead to relapse:	Substitute those high-risk situations with low-risk, safe situations that prevent relapse:
List some desires, needs and cravings that can lead to relapse:	What are some things you can do to replace those needs, desires and cravings that cause relapse?
What are the imbalances in your daily lifestyle that could lead to relapse:	List involvements that will give you a more balanced lifestyle:

Your recidivism prevention plan: Use all of the skills and ideas you have learned to prevent backsliding into criminal thinking and behavior.

IDENTIFY THE HIGH-RISK THINKING, ACTION AND SITUATION PATTERNS THAT COULD LEAD BACK TO CRIMINAL BEHAVIOR	PLAN: REPLACE THOSE HIGH-RISK THINKING, ACTION AND SITUATION PATTERNS TO PREVENT RECIDIVISM
List the negative outcomes for you if you return to criminal behavior:	List the positive outcomes for you if you never again engage in criminal activity:
List high-risk thoughts that could lead to committing aother crime:	Replace those with thoughts that will prevent recidivism:
List high-risk behaviors that could lead to another crime:	Now, list specific things you will do (actions) to never again become involved in criminal behavior:
High-risk situations you get into that could lead to another crime:	Your plan to prevent being in those situations:
List some desires, needs that could lead to further criminal conduct:	What can replace those needs, desires and cravings that cause recidivism?
What are the imbalances in your daily lifestyle that could lead back to criminal conduct?	List your involvements that will give you a more balanced lifestyle.

SESSION INTRODUCTION AND OBJECTIVES

Cravings and urges can lead to AOD addiction and relapse. They are an important part of criminal conduct and recidivism. Managing cravings and urges is part of preventing relapse and recidivism.

> **OBJECTIVES**
>
> ➡ Understanding and managing cravings and urges.
>
> ➡ Learn and practice refusal skills.

GETTING STARTED

▶ *CB Map Exercise* and *TAP Charting* sharing. Share how you are doing in SSC.

▶ Key words: cravings, urges, refusal skills.

SESSION CONTENT AND FOCUS

URGES AND CRAVINGS

Cravings are *drug-wanting* and *crime-wanting thoughts and feelings.* **Urges** are *drug-seeking* and *crime-seeking actions.* They are the actions towards fulfilling the craving. Cravings and urges are high-risk thoughts, feelings and behaviors. They may increase when you commit to not using or not being involved in criminal conduct. But, the rewards of being AOD problem and crime-free will replace those cravings. Look at this **example:**

Harry gets a call from an old drinking buddy who is still doing crimes and says, "meet me at Joe's" (bar). Harry has a strong sentiment (feeling) about the "good old times," and has a flash of excitement of doing another crime (cravings - crime-wanting). He gets in the car and drives to Joe's Bar, pulls in the parking lot (urges). Then, he remembered that his 9-year-old son has a baseball game in two hours. He yells (STOP), remembering his class on "stop-thinking." He relaxes, and calmly drives to the ball park. He has thoughts of self-confidence, self-control and self-mastery.

Triggers for cravings and urges for substances

Cravings for substances may be triggered by high-risk exposures or events: being around people who are using drugs, certain emotions, including fatigue, stress, self doubt, nostalgia, anger, frustration, excitement or accomplishment. Often, the basis of cravings is anxiety. Something is bothering us. Rather than looking at what is bothering us, we give in to the cravings and begin substance-seeking - the urge. Urges may cause physical symptoms, nervousness, tightness in the stomach.

Triggers for cravings and urges for criminal involvement

You may find yourself craving - desiring - to do a crime. This could be triggered by being with people who are doing crimes, anxiety about money, boredom, an angry attitude. We stop crime-wanting thinking by using mental change skills and by figuring out what's bothering us. When we seek out old criminal friends, go into high-risk neighborhoods, look for a victim, we are into crime-seeking urges. These urges may cause physical symptoms - nervousness, tightness in the stomach.

Steps in coping with cravings and urges

▶ **Stop and think** about your cravings - they are thoughts. Change those thoughts. Ask, "What are the feelings related to my cravings?"

▶ **Decide if it is still a craving. Or is it now an urge?** If you feel it in your body and you are taking action to fulfill the craving - like going to the liquor store, or calling an old friend you did crimes with - **it is an urge.** Cravings are mental; urges move you to action.

▶ **"Tough it out" or "urge surf" and get control.** Focus on your body where you feel the urge. "Talk down" the urge."

▶ Talk with a non-using friend. Go for a walk. Go to the gym. The urge will go away. **TURN THE CORNER.**

▶ **Remember the bad things** that can happen if you start using and the bad things that have happened in the past when you broke the law. Make a list of these bad outcomes.

▶ **Make a list of the rewards and positive outcomes of being drug-free and crime-free.**

▶ **Ask, "What are the joys and pleasures you would lose** by backsliding into AOD abuse and criminal behavior?" <u>**Exercise:**</u> Now do *Worksheet 43,* page 137.

Practice managing cravings and urges

Choose an episode where you had a craving - for drugs, food, gambling, criminal activity. Follow the above steps to cope with this episode. What were the thoughts and feelings behind the craving? "Stop the thought." "Shift the view" to "I'm going to crave for a talk with a good friend." Use "self-talk." "I'll get past it." Is it an urge? Change direction. Go to the gym or talk with a friend.

<u>Exercise:</u> Use *Worksheet 44,* page 137 - *Dealing with Cravings and Urges.* The plan you make for this exercise will deal with cravings and urges you get down the road.

REFUSAL SKILLS AND STEPS TO HANDLE PRESSURE TO USE DRUGS OR DO A CRIME

▶ **First, what are your thoughts?** If your thoughts are leaning to a "yes," get firm and make it a "no" thought.

▸ **Quickly follow the "no"** thought with a "no" statement without hesitation. Be clear and firm, but kind. Tell the person your risk. Use "I" messages. "I can't afford to take the risk."

▸ **Give choices and make them clear:** "I'll go to a movie, not the bar. I'm not talking about doing crimes but let's talk about the game. I'll shoot pool but not rob someone."

▸ **Don't feel guilty about refusing.** FEEL GUILTY IF YOU DON'T.

▸ **Don't let your self-image get in the way.** You may think "I can handle my drinks," or "I'm not afraid of the street," or "I'm not afraid to do a crime." Don't be cocky. Sitting in a jail cell isn't anything to be "cocky" about. **Being responsible.** That's something to be "cocky" about.

Exercise: Group members will be asked to role-play refusal skills starting with Harry and his buddy (page 133). You may be asked to put pressure on someone to use drugs, to do a crime. How does it feel to play that role?

THOUGHT SOLUTIONS IN PREVENTING RELAPSE AND RECIDIVISM

From what we learned about R&R prevention, cravings and urges, and refusal skills, we practice using **thought solutions** in managing specific situations. **Exercise: Thought solutions.** Imagine you are the person in each example in *Work Sheet 45*, page 138. Put thought solutions for each situation. Use the last row in *Worksheet 45* to describe AOD use situations that led to your last arrest.

YOUR HIGHWAY TO RESPONSIBLE LIVING OR COLLAPSE

The R&R prevention plans (*Session 16*, pages 131 and 132) are maps for responsible living. *Figure 21,* page 136, is the highway for this map. You have been on this highway many times. You have resisted relapse and recidivism. You are set on staying on *Responsible Living Road 101* to *Responsibility City.* Keep this highway in mind. But whichever direction you take - *Collapse City* or *Responsibility City,* remember - **IT IS YOUR CHOICE. YOU ARE IN THE DRIVER'S SEAT.**

SESSION ACTIVITIES AND CLOSURE GROUP

1. Do *Worksheet 43* through *45*. Update your *Master Skills List,* page 291 and MAP, page 295. Have you finished your *Autobiography?* Do your *TAP charting* for the coming week, page 300.

2. Using the *SSC Scale*, rate yourself as to your level of skills in handling cravings and urges and your level of refusal skills. Do you need more work in these areas?

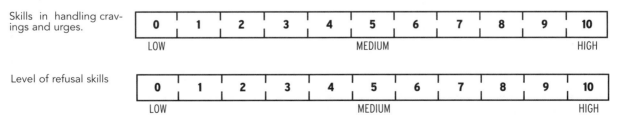

Skills in handling cravings and urges.

| 0 | 1 | 2 | 3 | 4 | 5 | 6 | 7 | 8 | 9 | 10 |
| LOW | | | | | MEDIUM | | | | | HIGH |

Level of refusal skills

| 0 | 1 | 2 | 3 | 4 | 5 | 6 | 7 | 8 | 9 | 10 |
| LOW | | | | | MEDIUM | | | | | HIGH |

4. Use the closing group to talk about your concerns at this point in the program.

FIGURE 21

Highway to Responsible Living and Change

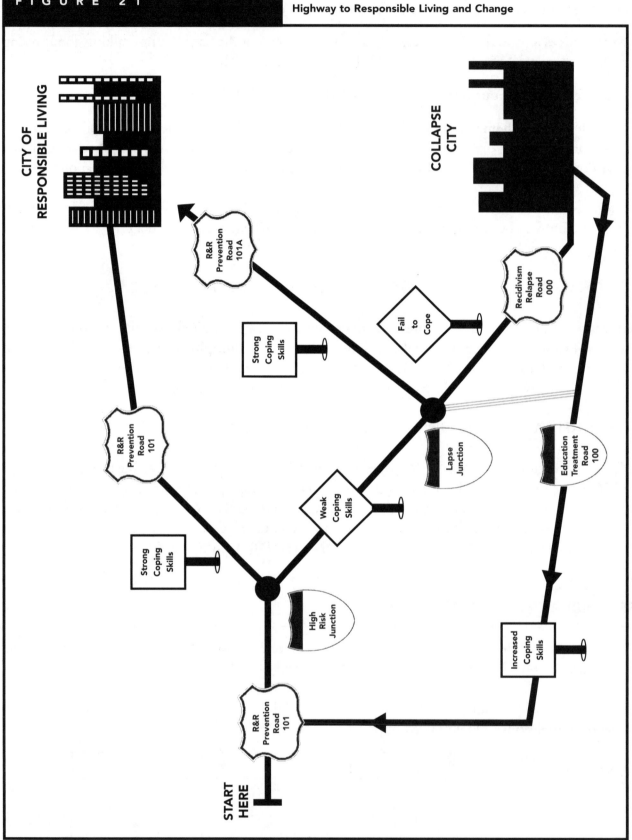

Adapted with permission from authors G.A. Parks and G.H. Marlatt, 1999, Relapse Prevention Therapy for Substance Abusing Offenders: A Cognitive-Behavioral Approach. In E. Latessa (Ed.), *What Works - Strategic Solutions: The International Community Corrections Association Examines Substance Abuse,* American Correctional Association.

Loss of joys and pleasures: What are your joys and pleasures and would you lose them if you backslid into AOD problem use or got put in jail?

PLEASURES AND JOYS THAT YOU HAVE IN YOUR LIFE. MAKE THESE YOUR TOP PLEASURES AND JOYS:	WOULD YOU LOSE THEM IF YOU RELAPSED/RECIDIVATED?	
	YES	NO

Dealing with cravings and urges: Make a plan to deal with an episode of craving. Pick two or three of the strategies suggested and show how you would use them to handle strong cravings or urges to drink, use drugs or take part in criminal conduct.

Describe your episode of a strong desire to have a drink.

What mental skills could you use? Thought stopping? Shifting the view?

What social skills could you use? Active sharing? Call a friend?

What physical skills could you use? Go for a walk? Go to the gym and work out?

Thought solutions: Read each problem situation and then write a thought solution that will prevent relapse or recidivism.

PROBLEM SITUATION	YOUR THOUGHT SOLUTION TO THE PROBLEM
You are at a party and your favorite music is on. You've been drug-free and crime-free for a year. You think: "It'd be nice to have a couple. Won't hurt, I can handle it. I deserve it, been doing good."	
You recently broke up with your partner. You have lonely and depressed thoughts. You remember thinking this before and that's when you used drugs. "It'd help now."	
You were just promoted to a better job - more pay. You have thoughts of being proud and satisfied with yourself. You think, "I've always had a few to celebrate. Why not now?"	
You stopped by to see a friend who is still dealing. He wants you back helping. You've been clean and straight for a year. Thoughts: "Need the dough, I can handle it a couple of times."	
You're angry with your spouse. You're being controlled, told what to do again. No breathing room. Last time this happened you were arrested for domestic violence. You think, "If I keep getting pushed...I don't know what I'll do."	
A friend called. She's on the streets. You'd hustled with her before, but got busted. Just got out of women's minimum. You think: "I won't get caught. Need the money."	
DESCRIBE THE SPECIFIC DRINKING SITUATION YOU WERE IN THE LAST TIME YOU WERE ARRESTED. THEN WRITE THE THOUGHTS THAT WOULD HAVE PREVENTED YOU FROM BREAKING THE LAW.	

MODULE 7

OVERVIEW

Do you want to change? What do you need to change? Are you still wavering - still ambivalent - about changing? We have learned that self-improvement and change takes place in steps and stages. We tend to resist and put up roadblocks to change. Change does not just happen - it takes knowledge and skills and putting those skills to work. But most important, change is based on awareness of our problems and strengths, and a plan to guide us in making changes. These are the topics of this module. Here are its goals.

◆ Have a better understanding of the steps and stages of change and to evaluate the steps we are in.

◆ Identify and see how to get through the barriers and roadblocks to change.

◆ Learn and use specific skills in making mental and action changes.

◆ See the problem areas for change and develop a plan for change for those areas.

◆ Identify strengths that support change.

Module 7 **has three sessions.**

Session 18: Stages, Steps and Roadblocks to Change

Session 19: Skills for Changing Thinking and Beliefs

Session 20: Plan for Change: Your *Master Profile* (MP) and *Master Assessment Plan* (MAP)

Steps, Stages and Skills for Self-Improvement and Change

Change starts with a challenge.

SESSION INTRODUCTION AND OBJECTIVES

Congratulations. You are working hard in this program. You are taking risks in sharing your past and present problems. This sharing brings you to a better understanding of the problems you have had with AOD use and criminal conduct. The sessions you are completing prepare you for the **Commitment** stage of change. Now we want you to take a look at where you are in making change.

OBJECTIVES

➡ Reviewing the process for changing thinking, feelings and behavior.

➡ Understand the stages of change.

➡ Spot the barriers that keep us from changing.

GETTING STARTED

▶ Share *TAP Charting.* Discuss your work in *Worksheet 45,* page 138.

▶ Key terms: stages of change, barriers to change.

SESSION CONTENT AND FOCUS

REVIEW THE KEY TO CHANGE - THE *CB MAP, FIGURE 2,* PAGE 14

We are doing the *CB Map Exercise* almost every session. Daily use of this map gives you self-control and better outcomes. We take time to review it in this session.

Exercise: Each group member is asked to share a past event that led to a bad or negative AOD use outcome. Then, share thoughts, attitudes, beliefs, feelings and actions that would have led to a positive outcome from that same event.

STAGES OF CHANGE: WHERE ARE YOU NOW?

We have learned that change takes place in steps or stages. These stages are like a spiral. We may slip back to an earlier stage of change, but never back to where we started. The stage you are in for changing AOD problems may be different than where you are in changing criminal thinking. These are our main targets. But we look at other areas of change such as **our relationships, managing emotions and being more responsible to the community.** We now look again at the stages of change.

Challenge to Change: This stage involves taking risks in disclosing your problems, receiving feedback about yourself, and sharing your past AOD and criminal conduct (CC) history. You are in **challenge** when you seriously think about making changes in your AOD use and CC thinking and behavior. You have met the **challenge** when you are willing to commit to more treatment and a desire to learn the skills to be free of AOD use problems and avoid criminal conduct. You have met the challenge when you and your counselor have agreed on your Master Profile (MP) and Master Assessement Plan (MAP).

Commitment to Change: In this stage, you are much more open to talking about your problems and the changes that need to be made. You have committed - made a pledge or promised - to stop AOD use problems and CC. You learned and use skills to change automatic thoughts, attitudes and beliefs, and these changes keep you from AOD use problems and criminal thinking and conduct. You have less desire for AOD use and CC. **You are replacing AOD use with other activities.**

Ownership of Change: In this stage, you make changes because you want to and not because others - the court, family, probation officer, counselor - want you to. You have been free of AOD problems and criminal thinking and conduct for longer periods of time. You replace drug use and criminal needs and activities with alternative activities. You are not bugged by thoughts of doing drugs or crimes. You have confidence in handling high-risk exposures that could lead to relapse or recidivism.

<u>Exercise:</u> Where are you in these stages for AOD use and Criminal Conduct? Use *Worksheet 46* for AOD abuse and *Worksheet 47* for your criminal thinking and conduct. For each statement, circle the number for the rating that fits you. Your counselor is doing the same. Compare yours with his/hers. Add your score for each part of each worksheet. Your CHALLENGE score should be higher than your COMMITMENT and OWNERSHIP. If your score on any stage is less than 30, you are still in that stage and have more work to do in that stage. Your counselor will give you guidelines for what various scores mean.

BARRIERS OR ROADBLOCKS TO CHANGE

Most often, these involve thinking barriers - refusal to change thinking, or letting our thinking errors take over. A big job in the **challenge** stage is to remove these thinking roadblocks. **Here are some thinking and behaving roadblocks or barriers to change. Check the ones that fit you. Are there others?**

☐ Everybody does it, why shouldn't I?

☐ I've tried that and it didn't wotk.

☐ I've always done it this way.

☐ I have to do it this way, there is no alternative.

☐ I'm not wrong. It's everybody else that's screwed up.

☐ I'm not talking. Nobody's finding out what I think or feel.

What are your roadblocks to change?

❏ My thoughts don't need changing because I'm right.

❏ Not listening or attending.

❏ Clamming up and being silent in group.

❏ Attacking others.

Commitment to change is replacing drug use with other activities.

The biggest roadblock is not making the effort. We may block change because it is too uncomfortable or just too much work. Or, you "get tired of pleasing people," and "throw in the towel." **Here is the clue.** When we change one thought and behavior, and that keeps us out of trouble, life gets better. Then we look for another thought to change to make it even better. Now, you are "practicing change" and, with practice, you overcome not making the effort.

We may find that feeling good about what we are doing and doing what most of the world finds "right" pays off. It is better than any payoff we found when we were abusing drugs and doing crimes. But, be honest if you are **not really trying** to change. Admit it. That often "kicks you out of the rut" - and you start changing.

SESSION ACTIVITIES

1. Update your *Master Skills List*, page 291. Share some of your Autobiography? Do this week's *TAP charting*, page 300.

2. Do *Worksheets 46* and *47*.

3. Using the SSC Scale, rate the degree to which you are blocking change.

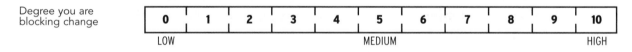

Degree you are blocking change	**0**	**1**	**2**	**3**	**4**	**5**	**6**	**7**	**8**	**9**	**10**
	LOW					MEDIUM					HIGH

CLOSURE GROUP

4. Use the closure group to talk about your stage of AOD use and CC change. Discuss the barriers you are putting up to change.

CHALLENGE TO CHANGE IN AREA OF AOD USE

SELF-UNDERSTANDING STATEMENTS	NOT TRUE		MAYBE TRUE		QUITE TRUE		VERY TRUE	
I understand my AOD use problem	0	1	2	3	4	5	6	7
It's easy for me to stop AOD use	0	1	2	3	4	5	6	7
I have tried to stop AOD use	0	1	2	3	4	5	6	7
I need help with AOD problems	0	1	2	3	4	5	6	7
It's easier to share about my AOD problems	0	1	2	3	4	5	6	7
I think about making changes	0	1	2	3	4	5	6	7
I want to learn about AOD problems	0	1	2	3	4	5	6	7
I want to know about my problems	0	1	2	3	4	5	6	7
I want to stop all AOD use	0	1	2	3	4	5	6	7
I want more AOD treatment	0	1	2	3	4	5	6	7

MY TOTAL SCORE FOR THIS STAGE

COMMITMENT TO CHANGE IN AREA OF AOD USE

SELF-UNDERSTANDING STATEMENTS	NOT TRUE		MAYBE TRUE		QUITE TRUE		VERY TRUE	
I want to know more about my AOD use	0	1	2	3	4	5	6	7
I see value of getting AOD help	0	1	2	3	4	5	6	7
I am more open to sharing problems	0	1	2	3	4	5	6	7
I made a promise to stop AOD use	0	1	2	3	4	5	6	7
I told others I'm stopping AOD use	0	1	2	3	4	5	6	7
I want to be AOD problem free	0	1	2	3	4	5	6	7
I am able to stop AOD use thinking	0	1	2	3	4	5	6	7
I can avoid high-risk AOD situations	0	1	2	3	4	5	6	7
I have a relapse prevention plan	0	1	2	3	4	5	6	7
I have been AOD free for several months	0	1	2	3	4	5	6	7

MY TOTAL SCORE FOR THIS STAGE

OWNERSHIP OF CHANGE IN AREA OF AOD USE

SELF-UNDERSTANDING STATEMENTS	NOT TRUE		MAYBE TRUE		QUITE TRUE		VERY TRUE	
I have no desire for AOD use	0	1	2	3	4	5	6	7
I seldom if ever think about using	0	1	2	3	4	5	6	7
I seldom have urges or cravings	0	1	2	3	4	5	6	7
I have replaced AOD with other interests	0	1	2	3	4	5	6	7
I am sure I can avoid relapsing	0	1	2	3	4	5	6	7
I handle high-risk AOD situations	0	1	2	3	4	5	6	7
I feel no pressure to be in treatment	0	1	2	3	4	5	6	7
I want to be in AOD treatment	0	1	2	3	4	5	6	7
I have been AOD free more than 3 months	0	1	2	3	4	5	6	7
I am getting great rewards not using	0	1	2	3	4	5	6	7

MY TOTAL SCORE FOR THIS STAGE

Self-rating on criminal thinking and conduct (CTC)

CHALLENGE TO CHANGE CRIMINAL THINKING AND CONDUCT

SELF-UNDERSTANDING STATEMENTS	NOT TRUE		MAYBE TRUE		QUITE TRUE		VERY TRUE	
I fully admit to my CTC past	0	1	2	3	4	5	6	7
It's easy for me to stop CTC	0	1	2	3	4	5	6	7
I have tried to stop CTC involvement	0	1	2	3	4	5	6	7
I am sure I need help with my CTC	0	1	2	3	4	5	6	7
I feel no pressure to get CTC help	0	1	2	3	4	5	6	7
It's easier to share CTC problems	0	1	2	3	4	5	6	7
I think about making changes in my CTC	0	1	2	3	4	5	6	7
I want to learn about CTC problems	0	1	2	3	4	5	6	7
I want to know about my CTC problems	0	1	2	3	4	5	6	7
I want to stop CTC	0	1	2	3	4	5	6	7

MY TOTAL SCORE FOR THIS STAGE

COMMITMENT TO CHANGE CRIMINAL THINKING AND CONDUCT

SELF-UNDERSTANDING STATEMENTS	NOT TRUE		MAYBE TRUE		QUITE TRUE		VERY TRUE	
I want know more about my CTC	0	1	2	3	4	5	6	7
I see value of getting CTC Help	0	1	2	3	4	5	6	7
I am open to sharing CTC problems	0	1	2	3	4	5	6	7
I have made a promise to stop CTC	0	1	2	3	4	5	6	7
I have told others I'm stopping CTC	0	1	2	3	4	5	6	7
I want to be free of CTC problems	0	1	2	3	4	5	6	7
I am able to stop CTC thinking	0	1	2	3	4	5	6	7
I avoid high-risk CTC situations	0	1	2	3	4	5	6	7
I have a recidivism prevention plan	0	1	2	3	4	5	6	7
CTC thought-free for few months	0	1	2	3	4	5	6	7

MY TOTAL SCORE FOR THIS STAGE

OWNERSHIP OF CHANGE OF CRIMINAL THINKING AND CONDUCT

SELF-UNDERSTANDING STATEMENTS	NOT TRUE		MAYBE TRUE		QUITE TRUE		VERY TRUE	
I have no desire for CC involvement	0	1	2	3	4	5	6	7
I seldom think about CC involvement	0	1	2	3	4	5	6	7
No urges or cravings for CC	0	1	2	3	4	5	6	7
I replaced CC with other interests	0	1	2	3	4	5	6	7
I am sure I can avoid recidivism	0	1	2	3	4	5	6	7
I handle high-risk CC situations	0	1	2	3	4	5	6	7
No pressure to be in CC treatment	0	1	2	3	4	5	6	7
I want to be in CC treatment	0	1	2	3	4	5	6	7
CC thought free for many months	0	1	2	3	4	5	6	7
I see rewards to be CC free	0	1	2	3	4	5	6	7

MY TOTAL SCORE FOR THIS STAGE

SESSION 19: Skills for Changing Thinking and Beliefs

SESSION INTRODUCTION AND OBJECTIVES

This session is about learning and practicing specific skills to get better outcomes in our lives.

> **OBJECTIVES**
>
> ⇒ See what specific thoughts produce feelings and behaviors.
>
> ⇒ See what specific beliefs lead to thoughts.
>
> ⇒ Learn and practice specific mental skills to control emotional and behavioral outcomes.

GETTING STARTED

▶ Start with the *CB Map Exercise.* Then share your *TAP Charting.*

▶ Key words: core beliefs, self-talk, mental change skills.

SESSION CONTENT AND FOCUS

SPECIFIC THOUGHTS THAT PRODUCE EMOTIONS AND BEHAVIORS

An important part of SSC is learning the specific thoughts that produce emotions and behaviors.

Example: John was working extra-hard expecting to be promoted to lead plumber in his company. Another person was given the job. He keeps thinking, "I was betrayed - I was cheated, wasn't right." He decides "I'll get back." He starts coming to work late and leaving early. He also steals some supplies from the company "to make things even."

Exercise: Discuss John's specific thoughts that lead to his antisocial behavior. **Role-play:** One group member plays John and another helps John see how he can change his thinking.

Exercise: *Worksheet 48,* page 148, connects thoughts with feeling and behavior outcomes. Fill in the missing thoughts, feelings or behaviors. For each thought, write down whether it is an **expectancy, appraisal, attribution or decision.**

SEEING HOW SPECIFIC BELIEFS PRODUCE SPECIFIC AUTOMATIC THOUGHTS

Changing thoughts is not enough to get ongoing positive outcomes. We must change our core beliefs. Sometimes, these beliefs are so deep we are not aware of them - like the air we breathe. But when they are challenged, it is like having the air cut off - we gasp for breath and even panic. They are the hidden, blind or unconscious panes of the *Johari Window, Figure 16,* page 99. Usually, there are several core beliefs that lead to our AOD use and CC. What are John's core beliefs? **Exercise:** *Worksheet 49,* page 149, has examples of core beliefs. Write in two thoughts that could come from each belief.

YOUR CORE BELIEFS AND LIFE THEMES

What are the core beliefs that led to your AOD abuse and criminal conduct. **<u>Exercise:</u>** Use *Worksheet 50* to put together a *Master List of Core Beliefs* that lead to AOD abuse and criminal conduct. You may want to add to the list later.

MENTAL-COGNITIVE SKILLS FOR SELF-CONTROL AND GOOD OUTCOMES

Knowing our thoughts and beliefs that lead to negative or bad outcomes is also not enough. We need skills to change our thinking - what we say to ourselves - our **self-talk.**

Thought stopping or thought braking: Do this by "shouting" to yourself "STOP." Or, by imagining a big STOP sign, or "slamming on the brakes."

Countering or arguing against a thought: Thought: "Can't trust anybody." **Counter:** "That's stupid, I have some friends I trust." **Thought: "**I'm always screwing up." **Counter:** "We all make mistakes." Babe Ruth struck out 1,330 times but hit 714 home runs.

Shifting the view is looking at situations in more than one way. **View:** "I must do what my friends want." **Shift:** "Are they friends if they get me in trouble?" **View:** "Only way to get dough to pay my bills is to steal." **Shift:** "Almost everyone works to pay bills." **View:** "He cheated me." **Shift:** "Maybe he made a mistake?" In *Figure 22*, we can see either an old woman or young woman by shifting our view. These often are errors in how we see things. The brain can shift its view.

Thinking "their position": What if I were in their position? This is prosocial thinking.

Thinking "taking responsibility": You see your part in both good and bad outcomes. "It's my fault." This is prosocial thinking.

Planting a positive thought: Replacing a negative with a positive thought. Negative thinking leads to negative outcomes. **But make your positive thoughts realistic.**

Exaggerating or overstating the thought - flooding: Victor Frankl, a famous psychiatrist, when in a German concentration camp, would say to people wanting to give up: "Go ahead and give up." This forced the person back to reality and doing the opposite. When you worry in an irrational (nonsense) way, say, "OK, I'm going to worry myself sick about this for 20 hours." This forces us to look at the thinking error. **There is power in realistic thinking.**

FIGURE 22

Old woman or young woman? What we perceive is often due to our expectations. When looking at this famous ambiguous figure, do you see a young woman or an old woman?

Figure 22 was drawn by cartoonist W.E. Hill and was originally published in *Puck*, November 6, 1915, later published be E.G. Boring, 1930.

Thought conditioning: Making thoughts weaker or stronger: Reward positive thoughts. Punish negative thoughts. When wanting to use drugs, think of all of the bad things that happened when you did. Imagine the bad outcomes. When thinking about doing a crime, imagine being put in jail and the door slamming. When you stop thoughts of wanting to use drugs or do a crime, reward yourself.

Logical (sensible) study - going to court with your thought: This is fighting errors in thinking. You think about stealing. Go to court: "Does this make sense? In the long run, is it logical?" It has three steps: State your thought; get your evidence; make your verdict. This gives time to think it through.

Coping statement is self-talk to increase self-mastery and confidence. "I can handle this." "I've overcome bigger problems."

Relaxation skills: Under stress, our automatic thoughts or thought habits take over. We get tired, fatigued and lose mental control. Relaxing gives you control. Here are some relaxation skills your counselor will guide you through. We learn more about these in *Phase II, Session 26*.

- ▶ **Muscle relaxation:** Tensing and relaxing your muscles one at a time.

- ▶ **Imagining calm scenes:** Mentally putting yourself in a calm and relaxing place - by the ocean or a mountain stream.

- ▶ **Body focus:** Closing your eyes and saying to yourself over and over - "my arms are heavy and relaxed; my forehead is cool."

- ▶ **Deep breathing:** Sit with your eyes closed. Take in a deep breath and let it out through your mouth. Do this only three or four times. Then relax.

Feel the power of these skills in changing thoughts and beliefs.

SESSION ACTIVITIES AND CLOSURE GROUP

1. Do *Worksheets 48 through 50*. Update your *Master Skills List,* page 291, and your MAP, page 295. Do this week's *TAP charting*.

2. Rate yourself as to your being able to clearly identify your core beliefs that lead to AOD use and criminal conduct (CC).

Able to see my beliefs that lead to AOD use	0	1	2	3	4	5	6	7	8	9	10
	LOW					MEDIUM					HIGH

Able to see my beliefs that lead to CC	0	1	2	3	4	5	6	7	8	9	10
	LOW					MEDIUM					HIGH

3. Talk about your core beliefs. Do you have more work to do on these so that you have a clear understanding of what they are?

Connecting specific thoughts, feelings and behaviors: Fill in thoughts, feelings and behaviors where there are blank spaces.

THOUGHTS	FEELINGS OR EMOTIONS	BEHAVIOR/ACTION OUTCOME
He's cheating on me	Rejection and anger	Goes into a rage when he gets home late
My boss is always on my back	Anger and resentment	
I'm not happy in my marriage		Gets depressed, avoids relating to spouse
I can have one or two drinks with no problem		
I won't get caught this time		
It's my friends who get me in trouble		
		Gets high and verbally abusive
		Stealing some parts from the supply room
I'm starting to panic about paying my bills		
I can get high and be in control		
I'm going to work as hard as I can to change		
I'm going home and not stopping for a few drinks		
If I work out, I'll feel better		
		Going to AA and getting support
		Attending all therapy sessions
		Being open and honest with my P.O.

WORKSHEET 49

Hooking specific core beliefs to thoughts: Write two thoughts for each core belief.

CORE BELIEFS	THOUGHTS THAT COME FROM EACH BELIEF
1. AOD addiction/dependence: I have a right to use drugs - It's my only pleasure.	
2. AOD addiction/dependence: I've been using drugs all my life and I'm not stopping.	
3. AOD addiction/dependence: I have a drug problem and I'm going to take care of it.	
4. Criminal conduct: I deserve more than what I have and I'm going to get it.	
5. Criminal conduct: I've been a victim of a lot of people - so they deserve it.	
6. Criminal conduct: I can be a responsible person to others and society.	

WORKSHEET 50

Master list of your core beliefs that lead to your AOD use problems and CC: You will have a chance to add to the list later. You may even change some of your core beliefs.

CORE BELIEFS THAT UNDERLIE AND SUPPORT MY AOD USE AND ADDICTION	CORE BELIEFS THAT UNDERLIE AND SUPPORT MY CRIMINAL CONDUCT

SESSION INTRODUCTION AND OBJECTIVES

In *Orientation,* you were introduced to two tools for change: *The Master Profile (MP)* and the *Master Assessment Plan (MAP).* You also made of list of problems to work on, *Worksheet 4,* page 19. You may have completed an inventory with a profile to summarize your life-situation problems. You use these tools to take a closer look at your past and present problems to develop a plan for change.

> **OBJECTIVES**
>
> ➡ Look at your profiles from in-depth self-report inventories you took when you entered SSC.
>
> ➡ Review the *Problem List* you did in *Orientation.*
>
> ➡ Complete the MP and MAP.
>
> ➡ Key terms: targets for change, plan for change, *Master Profile, Master Assessment Plan.*

SESSION CONTENT AND FOCUS

THE JOHARI WINDOW AS A GUIDE FOR SELF-ASSESSMENT

The *Johari Window, Figure 16,* page 99, shows how self-assessment works. The goal is to bring information from the hidden area through self-disclosure and from the blind area through receiving feedback into the free area.

YOUR TARGETS AND STEPS FOR CHANGE

The first step of change is awareness of the thinking and actions that cause our problems. The next step is to decide what you want to change. These are the **target thoughts and target actions.** In *Session 19,* we worked on the thought and belief targets that lead to problem behavior. Here are the **four** steps in making changes in target thoughts, beliefs and problem areas in your life.

▶ **Pick the target** - thought, belief or problem areas.

▶ **Set a goal.** What changes do you need to make?

▶ **Choose a method or methods to change thinking or acting.** These are interventions - specific skills and resources you use such as mental change skills, counseling in specific problem areas, your judicial supervision, etc.

▶ **Look at the results.** Step back and see if it is working. Are you changing? Do other people notice the difference? Date the results.

YOUR MASTER PROFILE

You have competed or are completing the *MP, Program Guide 2,* page 292. Now go back over the *MP* and rate yourself again. Use your worksheets and surveys you completed, *Worksheet 4, Problem List,* page 19, *Autobiography* and counselor and group feedback. The *MP* gives you the targets for change. Your counselor also completed the *MP* on you. Compare the two *MPs.* When you met with your counselor did you come up with an *MP* on which you both agree? **Exercise:** Share your *MP* with the group. Ask for feedback.

YOUR PLAN FOR CHANGE - *THE MASTER ASSESSMENT PROFILE (MAP)*

With the help of your counselor, you should have completed your *MAP, Program Guide 3,* page 295. Now, update your *MAP.* The *MAP* follows the above steps for changing target thoughts and actions. Identify as many problems as you want. They can be thoughts, beliefs, behaviors, life adjustment areas. The *MAP* is your *plan for change.* You add new problems as you continue in *SSC.* Here are the areas that you will look at as targets for change.

▶ Thoughts and beliefs about your childhood.

▶ Alcohol and other drug use and abuse thinking, beliefs and behaviors.

▶ Criminal and antisocial thinking and conduct.

▶ Current life-situation problems: includes employment and job; living stability; social-interpersonal relations; marital-family relationships; health; psychological-emotional.

▶ Your core beliefs.

▶ Interest and readiness for treatment and your stage of change.

Exercise: Share the most important parts of your *MAP* with the group.

SESSION ACTIVITIES AND CLOSURE GROUP

1. Update *Worksheet 4,* page 19, your *Problem List.*

2. Look over the profiles of the questionnaires you took when you entered the program. Update your *MP* and *MAP.*

3. Update your *Master Skills List,* page 291. Do this week's *TAP charting* for the week

4. Use the *SSC Scale* to rate yourself as to your being able to clearly identify your targets for change.

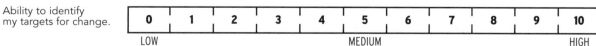

Ability to identify my targets for change.

0	1	2	3	4	5	6	7	8	9	10

LOW   MEDIUM   HIGH

5. Use the closure group to talk about your targets for change and your *MAP.* Share your most important targets and your plan for change.

PHASE I CLOSURE: LOOKING FORWARD AND MAKING A COMMITMENT

You have now come to a fork in the road in your treatment journey. You have experienced and learned a lot. You have worked hard. You have grown and matured. You have gained knowledge and skills for change. The question is: do you want to go into *Phase II* of SSC?

You may be saying: "I've taken action. I've changed. I'm OK," and stop here. Some of you may have to continue because that is the condition of probation, parole or your sentencing. Even so, share your thoughts and feelings. We want you to take a honest look at how open you are to continuing this treatment path.

If you have been in a closed group setup, you do this closure group together. If in an open SSC group, time will be set aside in your last *Phase I* group to bring a close to your *Phase I* journey.

Closing Reflections and Sharing

▶ Share the progress and important changes you have made and changes you still need to make.

▶ Share some of the most important parts of your Autobiography.

▶ Receive feedback from other members as to how they see your progress and change.

Evaluation of Your Progress and Change

Both you and your counselor filled out questionnaires to evaluate your progress and change. You will have an individual session at this time to get feedback from that evaluation.

Your Stage of Change

Now, rate yourself as to what stage you are in as to making changes in your AOD use patterns and in your CC thinking and conduct.

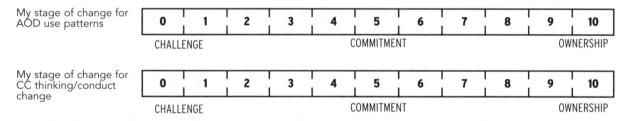

CONGRATULATIONS! YOU HAVE SUCCESSFULLY COMPLETED PHASE I, THE CHALLENGE TO CHANGE. YOUR DECISION? WILL YOU COMMIT YOURSELF TO PHASE II - THE COMMITMENT PHASE OF TREATMENT?

PHASE II

commitment to change

SSC is about getting positive outcomes from yourself, others and your community.

Strengthening Skills for Self-Improvement, Change and Responsible Living

Phase I challenged you to make a commitment or promise to change. You met this challenge by finishing *Phase I.* You worked hard and gave time and energy to preventing relapse and recidivism. Your decision to continue in *SSC* means you are putting this commitment into action.

But there is more to *SSC* than responsible living. It is also about positive action and positive outcomes. It is about learning to live a happy, meaningful and fulfilling life. *Phase II* is about learning to enjoy life as you continue your journey of self-improvement, change and responsible living.

A *Phase II Orientation Session* will be done in a small group or in an individual session with your counselor. *Phase II* is made up of special programs that build and strengthen the skills to have a healthy relationship with yourself, with others and your community. *Phase II* session content is short and to the point. Most of the sessions will be spent in practicing and relating session skills and ideas to everyday living.

There are three modules in *Phase II.*

Module 8:   Mental Self-Control: Managing Thoughts and Emotions

Module 9:   Social and Relationship Skills Building

Module 10: Skills for Social and Community Responsibility

"It is caring about others and living in harmony with our community that makes us human."
--UNKNOWN

PREPARATION SESSION FOR PHASE II

Looking Back at Phase I

Phase I was about telling your story and sharing your thoughts, beliefs, emotions and behaviors. You began to sort out these thoughts, beliefs, feelings and behaviors and identified those that lead to bad outcomes. Here is a summary of the knowledge you gained and skills you learned and practiced.

▶ Built trust and harmony in your treatment provider and your group.

▶ Learned the tools, rules and targets for change.

▶ Saw how thoughts lead to behaviors and how both are strengthened.

▶ Learned and practiced cognitive and behavioral change skills.

▶ Developed and practiced the skills of active sharing and active listening.

▶ Identified and corrected thinking errors.

▶ Learned about alcohol and drug use and abuse patterns and pinpointing your own substance use problems.

▶ Saw how criminal conduct and its cycles fit you and evaluated your own criminal conduct pattern.

▶ Learned about and how to control cravings and urges and learned and practiced refusal skills.

▶ Saw the pathways to relapse and recidivism and R&R prevention.

▶ Developed a specific R&R prevention plan.

▶ Saw the stages and process of how people change and saw what stage you are in.

▶ Did an in-depth self-assessment to spot targets for change.

▶ Developed a plan for change and updated that plan as you prepare for *Phase II*.

Looking Forward to Phase II

Phase II involves following through with your **commitment to change your thinking** that leads to drug abuse and to criminal conduct. It involves building and learning skills to continue on the path of self-correction, change and responsible living. This phase includes 22 skill development and practice sessions that focus on:

▶ Cognitive or mental self-control;

▶ Social and relationship building;

▶ Community responsibility.

Sessions dealing with each of these areas are grouped together. For example, all of the **mental self-control** sessions are together. If you are in an open group setup, then you might enter *Phase II* when your group is working on the **community responsibility** sessions. After your group finishes this group of sessions, it will go to sessions dealing with **cognitive or mental self-control,** then on to **social and relationship** building skills.

However, these three areas are linked together. Successful mental self-control is a key to success in building healthy relationships. These two areas are important keys to being prosocial and responsible in your community and society.

Skill Building is About Positive Actions and Outcomes

A big part of *Phase I* was learning and practicing the cognitive-behavioral (CB) map for learning and change: **Events and situations lead to thoughts, which result in emotional and behavior outcomes.** The outcomes can be good or resolve problems. Or, the outcomes can be negative or lead to more problems. At the beginning of each *Phase I* session we did the *CB Map Exercise.* Group members took an event, identified thoughts coming from the event, and then looked at their emotional and behavioral outcomes - good or bad.

In *Phase II* we center our work on these same aspects of CB learning and change. However, in *Phase II*, we also use the *CB STEP* method that focuses on the positive change process of the *CB Map:* **SITUATIONS - THINKING CHANGE - EMOTIONS - POSITIVE ACTION.** Here is how we relate it to the CB Map.

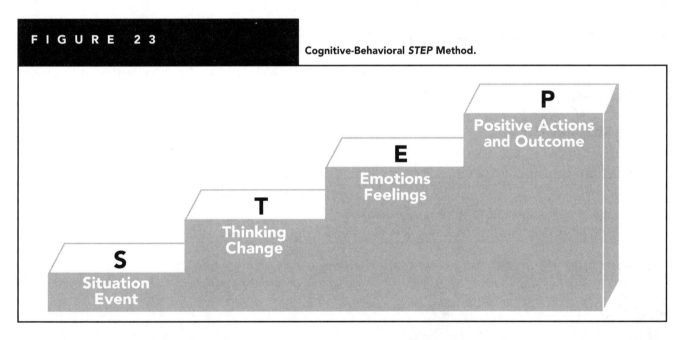

FIGURE 23

Cognitive-Behavioral *STEP* Method.

P Positive Actions and Outcome

E Emotions Feelings

T Thinking Change

S Situation Event

We use *STEP* when working on changes to bring about positive actions and outcomes. For example, we may focus on **situations** (S) that lead to negative **thinking** (T). How can we change our T to **thoughts** and **beliefs** that lead to positive **emotions** (E) and **positive** actions or behaviors (P)? In the *CB MAP* (Figure 2, page 14), actions or behavior could be adaptive (good) or maladaptive (bad). Now, we want the outcome to be POSITIVE. We want our skill use to result in positive behaviors that lead to positive outcomes such as prosocial behavior, drug-free living, positive relationships with others and our community.

A Review to Prepare for Phase II

To prepare for *Phase II*, we review the **work** we did in *Phase I*.

▶ Review the goals and objectives of *SSC - Figure 1,* page 11 and program agreements and guidelines, page 12.

▶ Look over what you wanted to get out of *SSC,* page 17.

▶ Review the process of learning and change, how thoughts and behaviors are strengthened, the *CB Map - Figure 2*, page 14, and *Sessions 3* and *4.*

▶ Review your AOD use patterns, page 63, your AOD use and problem profile, page 80 and your AOD classification, page 82.

▶ Review the pathways and skills to preventing relapse and recidivism (page 130) and your recidivism prevention goal (page 126) and relapse prevention goal (page 127).

▶ What were the basic mental and behavioral change skills you learned?

▶ Look over your *TAP Charting.* You continue this in *Phase II.*

▶ Look at the *SSC Scales* that you did at the end of each session, and **re-rate yourself on each scale.** Your counselor will walk you through these, giving you the page numbers.

▶ Be sure that your *Master Assessment Plan (MAP)* is up to date.

▶ Discuss the strengths you take into *Phase II.*

▶ Finally, review *Program Guide 1,* page 291, your *Master Skills List (MSL).* You worked on some of these skills in *Phase I.* The main focus of *Phase II* is these skills.

Session Structure

We will continue using the *CB Map Exercise,* share your weekly *TAP Charting* and review the last session. We will use *STEP* to learn how to bring about positive outcomes. Group members share and discuss session material and exercises. We focus on the session's topic and skills as they relate to our past and present problems. HAVE A GREAT PHASE II JOURNEY.

MODULE 8

Self-control comes through controlling our thoughts, attitudes and beliefs and leads to positive outcomes. This module works on strengthening the mental self-control and change skills to help you develop a healthy mental world. The objectives are to apply mental self-control skills to:

Mental Self-Control: Managing Thoughts and Emotions

▶ Recognize and manage negative thoughts and negative thinking;

▶ Recognize and manage errors in thinking;

▶ Recognize and manage stress and the emotions of anger, guilt, and depression.

These cognitive skills are also the basis of developing a healthy relationship with others and our community.

Self-control leads to positive outcomes

Module 8 has eight sessions.

Session 21: Practicing Mental Self-control and Change Skills

Session 22: Recognizing and Being Aware of Negative Thinking

Session 23: Managing and Changing Negative Thinking and Beliefs

Session 24: Recognizing and Changing Errors in Thinking

Session 25: Understanding Stress, its Causes and Roots

Session 26: Managing Stress and Emotions

Session 27: Managing and Regulating Anger

Session 28: Managing Guilt and Depression and Increasing Positive Emotions

SESSION INTRODUCTION AND OBJECTIVES

In this session, we work on how to map our thoughts, and search for and identify our beliefs. We also review and practice the skills we learned in *Session 19* to get positive outcomes.

OBJECTIVES OF SESSION AND KEY TERMS

➠ Reviewing the process for changing thinking and behavior.

➠ Practice using the skills of mental self-control.

➠ Key terms: core beliefs, thought mapping, thought chain, belief searching.

SESSION CONTENT AND FOCUS

REVIEW HOW THOUGHTS AND BELIEFS ARE HOOKED TOGETHER

The first step in change is to change our thoughts. Changing thoughts works in the short-run; but for long-term good outcomes, we need to change our core beliefs.

Exercise: See how you hooked thoughts with beliefs in *Worksheet 49,* page 149. Look at your core belief list in *Worksheet 50,* page 149, that support your substance abuse and criminal conduct. Do you need to add to that list?

THOUGHT MAPPING AND BELIEF EXPLORING

Identifying and changing beliefs is the key to long-term positive outcomes. We can explore and identify our beliefs by mapping the thought chain that leads "down to" or "up from" those beliefs. We understand core beliefs if we see the thought chain they support. *Figure 24* shows how this works. It also helps tell the difference between thoughts and beliefs.

Exercise: Use *Worksheet 51,* page 161, to do thought mapping and belief searching. Put an event and work down filling in thoughts in the four "thought chain" spaces. Then discover the core belief that underlies those thoughts. Write in the outcomes that will come from the core belief and the thought chain. Give both emotional and action outcomes.

Leatn to map your thoughts and beliefs.

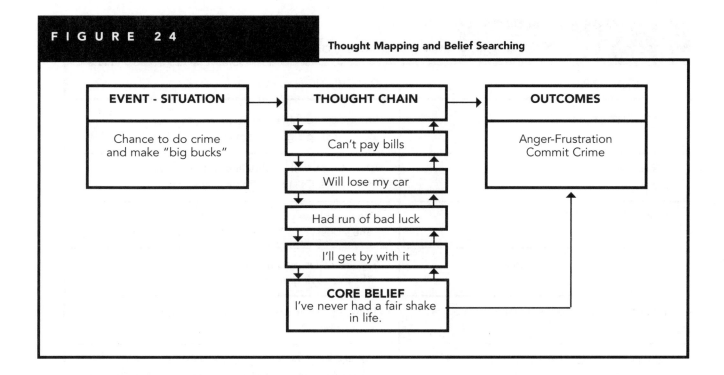

FIGURE 24

Thought Mapping and Belief Searching

EVENT - SITUATION	THOUGHT CHAIN	OUTCOMES
Chance to do crime and make "big bucks"	Can't pay bills Will lose my car Had run of bad luck I'll get by with it **CORE BELIEF** I've never had a fair shake in life.	Anger-Frustration Commit Crime

MENTAL SKILLS FOR SELF-CONTROL AND GOOD OUTCOMES

Table 6, on the following page, summarizes the self-control and mental change skills we have learned. We have added one new skill: **Acceptance.** This is accepting the thoughts and moving on. **Example:** "She doesn't understand me." Self-talk: "That's OK, I accept this. It's OK that I think at times that she doesn't understand me."

We practice these skills in four ways, all leading to use in our daily living, as shown in *Figure 25.* **1) See -** Visualize the skill, such as a stop sign; **2) Hear -** listen to ourselves say the skill out loud; **3) Act -** Role play the skill by telling someone thoughts and the other person says out loud a skill that can change those thoughts; **4) Write or journal** the skill.

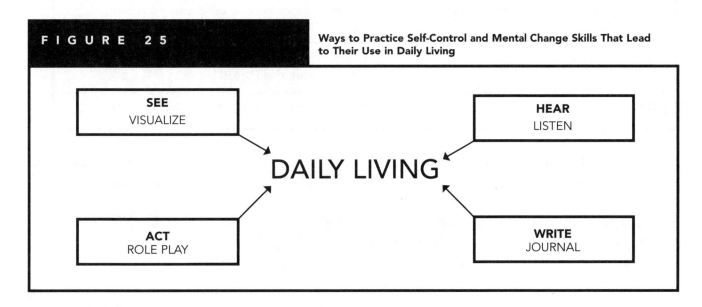

FIGURE 25

Ways to Practice Self-Control and Mental Change Skills That Lead to Their Use in Daily Living

SEE VISUALIZE		HEAR LISTEN
	DAILY LIVING	
ACT ROLE PLAY		WRITE JOURNAL

NAME OF SKILL	DESCRIPTION OF SKILL
THOUGHT STOPPING	Stopping thoughts by shouting "stop" or visualizing a stop sign or slamming on brakes
ACCEPTANCE	Accepting the thoughts and not changing them. "It's OK to think this way sometimes."
SHIFTING THE VIEW	Changing how you think about someone: "She's bossy" to "she's just trying to help me"
THINKING "THEIR POSITION"	Say the other person's view to yourself: "They're saying......"
THINKING "TAKING RESPONSIBILITY"	Thinking "what part of this is my fault, my responsibility"
PLANTING A POSITIVE THOUGHT	Replace negative with positive thought: "It's not working" to "it will work out just fine"
THOUGHT REWARD	Reward thinking that leads to good outcomes: "I'm proud I did that - good thinking"
EXAGGERATE OR OVERSTATE THE THOUGHT	Your thoughts of worrying about the job: "I'm going to worry myself sick for 50 hours"
CONDITIONING: MAKE THOUGHTS WEAKER	Thinking about doing a crime: Imagine being put in jail cell and "hear" the door slamming
CONDITIONING: MAKING THOUGHTS STRONGER	Thinking about positive outcomes when deciding not to use drugs
GOING TO COURT WITH YOUR THOUGHTS	Thought: "I want to steal" - get evidence that it doesn't make sense, then make a verdict
COPING STATEMENTS THAT AFFIRM "I CAN HANDLE IT"	Statements that increase self-mastery and confidence: "I've solved bigger problems"
RELAXATION SKILLS	Muscle relaxation; imagine calm scenes; mental-physical focus; deep breathing
THOUGHT REPLACEMENT	Replace angry thoughts with positive thoughts

Exercise: Use the *Table 6* skills to change the thoughts and beliefs in *Worksheets 48, 49 and 50*, pages 148 and 149. Use the "see," "hear," "act," and "write" methods of practicing these skills.

Exercise: Use the above skills to change John's thinking in the example on page 32. What skill would you use to change his expectation "If I stop off and have a few, I'll feel better?"

Exercise: Role play events that lead to thoughts about using drugs or doing a crime. One group member shares a thought about using drugs or doing a crime to another. Another group member uses the thought change skills and applies the *STEP* method to get a positive outcome.

S	→	T	→	E	→	P
(Situation)		(Thinking Change)		(Emotions)		(Positive Action)

SESSION ACTIVITIES AND CLOSURE GROUP

1. Do *Worksheet 51.* Update your *Master Skills List,* page 291. Do this week's TAP charting.

2. *SSC Scale:* Rate yourself as to your being able to use the mental self-control skills in *Table 6.*

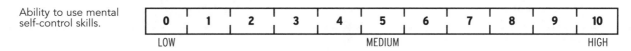

Ability to use mental self-control skills.

0	1	2	3	4	5	6	7	8	9	10
LOW					MEDIUM					HIGH

3. Discuss how the mental self-control skills are working for you.

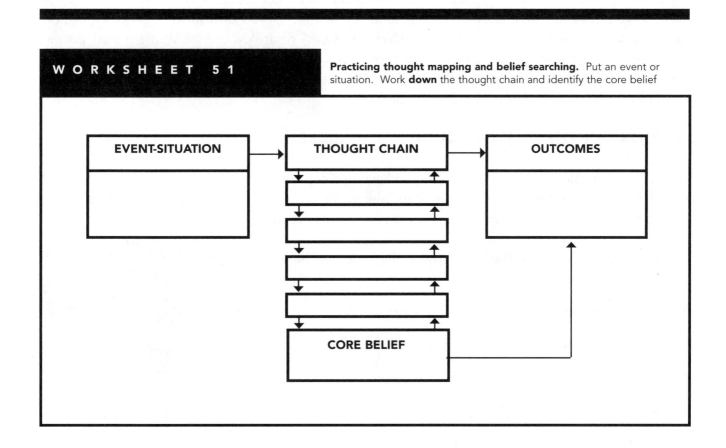

WORKSHEET 51

Practicing thought mapping and belief searching. Put an event or situation. Work **down** the thought chain and identify the core belief

EVENT-SITUATION → THOUGHT CHAIN → OUTCOMES

CORE BELIEF

SESSION INTRODUCTION AND OBJECTIVES

This is the first of two sessions that focus on negative thinking. In this session we look at how negative thoughts and attitudes influence our lives. Then we learn to identify negative thinking

> ### OBJECTIVES OF SESSION AND KEY TERMS
>
> ➠ See how negative thinking leads to problem outcomes.
>
> ➠ Learn to recognize negative thoughts and beliefs.
>
> ➠ Key terms: negative thinking, errors in thinking, negative thought mapping and negative belief searching.

SESSION CONTENT AND FOCUS

HOW NEGATIVE THOUGHTS AND BELIEFS LEAD TO PROBLEM OUTCOMES

Negative thinking can become a way of life. It leads to negative and angry behavior. Negative thinking is often irrational. It leads to negative emotions and to tension. The escape may be to commit a crime. We can get a strong negative feeling about the world. "The world sucks!" When we believe that long enough, it makes it easier to "do what you want," regardless of how it might hurt people. Negative thinking leads to negative feelings about oneself including lack of self respect, anger and depression. **Negative thinking works against positive outcomes.** It works against what you want to accomplish. It throws a damper on feeling good.

RECOGNIZING NEGATIVE THOUGHTS AND BELIEFS

Before you can change negative thoughts, you have to recognize them. This means being **mindful of** negative thoughts. Often they are errors in thinking. In *Session 10,* we saw that thinking errors can lead to criminal conduct. Here are some examples of negative thinking.

▶ **Expecting the worst:** The worst always happens. "I know it won't work out."

▶ **Self put-downs:** "I'm no good." "I deserve it."

▶ **Jumping to conclusions:** "I'm going to get fired."

▶ **Castastrophizing:** "Something terrible is going to happen."

▶ **Self-blame:** "I deserve it."

▶ **Magnifying:** "It couldn't be worse. I'll lose everything."

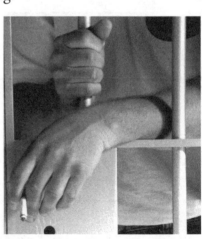

Negative thinking can lead to bad outcomes.

Exercise: First, as a group, read the thinking errors in *Worksheet 25*, page 92. Then, take turns sharing a negative thought. Group members will see if the negative thought fits one of the above thinking errors on the previous page or one in *Worksheet 25*, page 92.

Exercise: As a group, do a thinking report around negative thoughts that lead to using substances and getting high. Remember the five parts of the thinking report: 1) SITUATION 2) THOUGHTS 3) ATTITUDES AND BELIEFS 4) EMOTIONS 5) OUTCOME.

NEGATIVE THINKING CAN LEAD TO RELAPSE AND RECIDIVISM

Think about the times that you went out and used drugs or committed a crime. Did you have some angry or negative thoughts? Were you angry at someone close to you? Did you think, "screw them, I don't care?"

Exercise: Use *Work Sheet 52,* page 164 and list negative thoughts you had before you used drugs or committed a crime.

NEGATIVE THOUGHT MAPPING IN SEARCH OF NEGATIVE BELIEFS

Underlying our negative thinking are core negative beliefs. Use *Worksheet 53,* page 164 and give a situation that leads to a negative thought chain. These could be errors in thinking. List four negative thoughts. Then, figure out what is your core negative belief. What is the outcome for this negative thought and belief chain.

SESSION ACTIVITIES AND PROCESS GROUP

---

1. Do *Worksheets 52 and 53.* Update your *Master Skills List,* page 291. Update your *MAP,* page 295. Do this week's *TAP Charting,* page 300.

2. Rate yourself as to your being able to clearly see your negative thinking and beliefs.

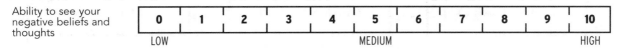

Ability to see your negative beliefs and thoughts

0	1	2	3	4	5	6	7	8	9	10
LOW					MEDIUM					HIGH

3. Use the process group to talk about how negative thinking has affected your life. The group can also be used to deal with issues and problems you have been facing. How are the skills of *SSC* helping you deal with these problems?

List negative thoughts you had before using drugs or before committing a crime

NEGATIVE THOUGHTS THAT YOU HAD BEFORE USING DRUGS	NEGATIVE THOUGHTS THAT YOU HAD BEFORE COMMITTING A CRIME

Practicing negative thought mapping and negative belief searching. Put an event or situation. Work down the thought chain and identify the core belief.

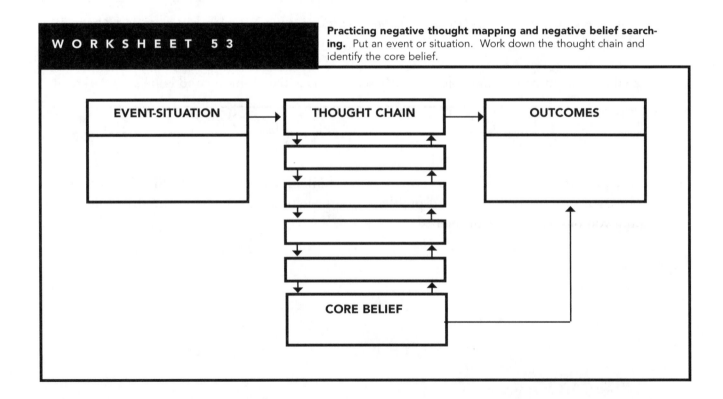

SESSION INTRODUCTION AND OBJECTIVES

You are in control of what you think or say to yourself. This allows you to choose your actions. The actions can lead to bad or good outcomes. You might say, "I had no choice, they made me do it." You always have a choice of what you think.

> ## OBJECTIVES OF SESSION AND KEY TERMS
>
> ⮕ Review how we recognize our negative thoughts and beliefs.
>
> ⮕ Apply mental skills to change negative thinking and beliefs.
>
> ⮕ Key terms: realistic positive thinking, *CB STEP* method, positive thought arming.

SESSION CONTENT AND FOCUS

We use self-talk to replace negative thoughts or beliefs. But self-talk can be negative and irrational. Our goal is to replace negative self-talk with positive self-talk.

THERE IS POWER IN REALISTIC POSITIVE THINKING

We have heard about the "power of positive thinking." But healthy positive thinking has two parts.

▶ Realistic thinking based on sensible goals; and

▶ Using skills to change negative thinking and outcomes.

Example: "I'll never get this job done" is **negative thinking.** But, "I'll finish it in two weeks" is realistic thinking based on changing thoughts for better outcomes. The power is in being sensible and more self-skilled. This gives us **self-mastery** or what we call **self-efficacy.**

USE THE *STEP METHOD* IN CHANGING NEGATIVE THINKING

Remember: negative thoughts and beliefs are often errors in thinking and are irrational (crazy, unsound, silly). We can change these thoughts to make them sensible and rational. The *CB STEP* method can be used to change irrational negative thinking to rational and positive thinking and positive action.

The *STEP* method is the part of the *CB Map* that leads to positive action and outcomes. We review the parts to *STEP.*

S	→	T	→	E	→	P

SITUATION   **THINKING CHANGE**   **EMOTIONS**   **POSITIVE ACTION OUTCOMES**
(EVENT)   (THOUGHTS/BELIEFS)   (FEELINGS)   (POSITIVE BEHAVIORS)

S **SITUATION:** Know the Ss that lead to negative and irrational thinking and beliefs.

T **THINKING CHANGE:** Identify - be **mindful** and aware of the specific negative thoughts and the underlying beliefs that are part of the thinking. Then apply skills to change **thoughts** and **beliefs.**

When we change our negative thoughts we experience power.

- **Thought stopping:** Tell yourself to STOP the thought. Imagine a stop sign. Slam on the "thought brakes."

- **Argue against** or dispute the negative thinking. Tell yourself that your negative thoughts are irrational, foolish.

- **Positive thought planting:** Put a positive thought in its place. Every time you have that thought, replace it with a positive thought: NEGATIVE THOUGHT? REPLACE WITH A POSITIVE THOUGHT.

E **EMOTIONS:** What feelings do you have now? Do positive thoughts and beliefs lead to positive emotions? Say those feelings to yourself. "I feel good. I feel confident. I feel relaxed."

P **POSITIVE ACTION AND OUTCOMES:** What was your positive action? Did you handle the situation better?

POSITIVE THOUGHT ARMING

Arm yourself with positive thoughts that are there ready to use. Use *Worksheet 54* to make a list. Here are some examples.

- REMEMBER THE GOOD THINGS: What you achieved, people who care about you, fun you have had.

- STATEMENTS OF HOPE: Positive self-statements, "I can manage this situation;" "This is hard, but I can do it."

- SELF-REWARDS: After doing something well, reward yourself with positive self-talk. "I came close to using, but I did a good job controlling myself." Self-reward is a key to strengthening change.

Exercise: Each group member is asked to share a past event that led to a negative outcome. Use *STEP* and the positive thoughts you put in *Worksheet 54* so that the event leads to a positive outcome.

SESSION ACTIVITIES AND PROCESS GROUP

1. Do *Worksheet 54*. Update your *Master Skills List*, page 291. Update your *MAP*, page 295. Do this week's *TAP Charting*.

2. Use the *SSC Scale* to rate yourself as to your being able to change your negative thinking and beliefs.

Ability to change negative thoughts and beliefs

0	1	2	3	4	5	6	7	8	9	10
LOW					MEDIUM					HIGH

3. Use the process group to talk about how negative thinking has affected your life. Share with the group issues and problems you have been facing. How are the skills of *SSC* helping you deal with these problems?

WORKSHEET 54

Positive thought arming: Make a list of six (6) positive thoughts that you can arm yourself with. Use self-talk to practice these positive thoughts. Each time this week you have a negative thought, use one of these positive thoughts.

MAKE A LIST OF SIX POSITIVE THOUGHTS TO ARM YOURSELF WITH - READY TO USE
1.
2.
3.
4.
5.
6.

SESSION INTRODUCTION AND OBJECTIVES

Thinking errors are distorted or illogical thoughts, attitudes and beliefs about ourself, others and the world. They are so automatic that we accept them without facts to support them. These errors can get us into trouble with relationships and the law.

OBJECTIVES OF SESSION AND KEY TERMS

→ Recognize distorted thinking patterns (thought-habits) and see how they can lead to bad or undesirable outcomes.

→ Apply the mental skills to change errors in thinking.

→ Key terms: thinking errors, entitlement trap.

SESSION CONTENT AND FOCUS

REVIEW YOUR WORK ON THINKING ERRORS

Negative thinking can often be based on facts. But, errors in thinking have little or no facts to support them. Errors in thinking are just that - errors.

Exercise: Again, rate yourself on the list of thinking errors in *Worksheet 5,* page 35. Have you changed your ratings? Do you see how more of the errors are part of your CC (criminal conduct)?

Exercise: Look at *Worksheet 25*, page 92. See if you want to add more prosocial thoughts to the antisocial thinking errors.

COMMON THINKING ERRORS

Thinking errors are often automatic thoughts: **expectations, appraisals, attributions and decisions.** Most thinking errors are **appraisals** - your judgment or evaluation of yourself or others or the meaning of an event. Here are four of the most common thinking errors that are roadblocks to change.

▶ **"I had no choice:"** We always have choices on what to think.

▶ **"Everyone does it."** "Everyone breaks the law." Not true. Most people do not break the law. "Everyone drinks." But 30% of Americans do not drink alcohol.

▶ **"I'm right and my thoughts don't need changing."** Stubborn refusal to think differently gets you into trouble. There is always more than one way to think about an issue.

▶ **"I have something coming."** I deserve better than this." This is the entitlement trap. We look again at this below.

CORRECTING THINKING ERRORS USING THE *CB STEP* METHOD

S **SITUATION:** Know the Ss that lead to thinking errors.

T **THINKING CHANGE:**

▶ First, see the error. Listen when people say you're wrong. What thinking errors do you use most? What core beliefs support them? Use *Worksheet 5,* page 35, and *Worksheet 25,* page 92, to help you see the thinking errors you use most.

▶ Second, use mental skills to change the errors. When you think, "I'm right," **question it.** What might make me wrong? **Test it.** "Do I have friends who don't use drugs?" Use "their **position skill**" for a test. What skills in *Table 6,* page 160, will help change thinking errors?

E **EMOTIONS.** Are you less tense thinking you don't have to be right? Are you relieved you don't have to fight to "be right"?

P **POSITIVE ACTION AND OUTCOMES:** What are your positive behavior outcomes? Are you doing more listening and less defending your thinking errors?

PRACTICE CHANGING THINKING ERRORS

Exercise: For the thinking errors in *Worksheet 5,* page 35 and *Worksheet 25,* page 92, use the change skills in *Table 6,* page 160, to correct them. Take turns doing this.

Exercise: Use the skill "Shifting the view." For the thought "I'm always getting screwed," shift the view. Try this one: "There are people who have helped me and not 'screwed' me." Now use "shifting the view" on the four common thinking errors given on the previous page.

THE ENTITLEMENT TRAP

Because of past problems and hurts, some people think they have been a victim (which is often true). They see themselves being punished, badly treated. But their error in thinking is: "I have something coming" - "entitled." They take this attitude into relationships. This prevents them from being responsible to others and their community. They use this as an excuse for criminal conduct. Listen to this story told by a judicial client.

I went through a tough divorce. My kids are out of state - can't see them. My dad abused me. Mom died when I was nine. Sure, I use drugs and even sell them. Got busted once. Do some stealing. But I take my chances. I got this much coming.

Exercise: What thinking errors is this person into? Role play this person with another person helping them use skills to change the error "I'm entitled to sell drugs and steal."

Exercise: Using *Work Sheet 55,* do a Thinking and Re-thinking Report on the "entitlement trap," a situation where you thought you had something coming. Then do a Re-thinking Report on that event.

SESSION ACTIVITIES AND PROCESS GROUP

1. Do *Worksheet 55.* Update your *Master Skills List,* page 291 and *MAP,* page 295. Do this week's *TAP Charting,* page 300.

2. SSC Scale: rate yourself as to your being able to change your thinking errors.

Ability to change thinking errors

0	1	2	3	4	5	6	7	8	9	10
LOW					MEDIUM					HIGH

3. Use the process group to share the thinking errors you use that are most apt to lead you back to criminal conduct - recidivism.

WORKSHEET 55	**Thinking and Re-thinking Report:** Use an event or situation where you thought you had something coming - the "entitlement trap." Then, re-think the event, thoughts, beliefs, feelings, outcome.

THINKING REPORT ON ENTITLEMENT TRAP	RE-THINKING REPORT ON ENTITLEMENT TRAP
EVENT	EVENT
THOUGHTS	THOUGHTS
BELIEFS	BELIEFS
FEELINGS	FEELINGS
OUTCOME	OUTCOME

SESSION INTRODUCTION AND OBJECTIVES

For the AOD user, stress is a two-edged sword. One edge is that we can become dependent on drugs to reduce stress. The other edge is that stress can come from the problems resulting from AOD use. Also important, stressful events are triggers for relapse and recidivism. The purpose of this session is to understand stress and to see how stress relates to your life. In the next session we learn skills to cope with stress. In other sessions, we look at how to manage the emotions related to stress: guilt, anger and depression.

OBJECTIVES OF SESSION AND KEY TERMS

➡ Understand stress, its sources and roots, and what it does to us and how it is related to R&R.

➡ Look at what has caused stress in your life.

➡ Key terms: roots of stress, unable to cope, coping.

REVIEWING YOUR MP AND MAP

If you rated yourself high on AOD use to deal with emotional discomfort and psychological problems on your *MP,* you may be dependent on AOD use to manage stress. Update your *MP* and *MAP.*

SESSION CONTENT AND FOCUS

The CB approach tells us that it is not the outside or inside events that make us stressful, but our thoughts about and our reactions to those events.

UNDERSTANDING STRESS

Stress is our response to thinking or judging that the demand of an event or situation goes beyond our being able to cope with the situation. **Coping** is the key word. Stress is based on our automatic thoughts about inside or outside events.

▸ **Expectations:** You **expect** (worry about) something bad will happen to you because of the outside events.

▸ **Appraisals:** You judge that the demands of the event go beyond your ability or resources to meet those demands.

▸ **Attribution:** You blame the causes of your stress to outside events or to upsetting memories of past events.

▶ **Decision:** You **decide** you cannot handle the demands of the outside world.

Exercise: Use the *CB Map Exercise (Figure 2,* page 14) to understand how stress works. What were the stress-thoughts? What were the emotional and action outcomes?

THE ROOTS AND SOURCES OF STRESS

Stress comes out of the mixing (interaction) of your inside world with events or situations in your outside world. It has two roots.

Your inside world. We call these "internal stressors:" the memory of past major negative or difficult experiences such as divorce, loss of loved one, childhood traumas. These are now "internal" but are set off by on-going life experiences.

▶ The stressor event may be inside you if you cannot tie the mental, physical or emotional responses to something outside.

▶ Such "internal events" could be a memory of a past trauma or loss, high need to be successful, having failed in a job.

▶ Internal stressors will be based on outside events that have happened sometime in the past.

Your outside world. There are three major outside roots of stress.

▶ Major negative life events such as death of loved one, divorce, loss of job or major illness.

▶ Daily negative or difficult life events such as demands of family and work. These are "external."

▶ Major and minor positive happenings such as a new job, getting married, having a baby or a salary raise.

Exercise: Do *Worksheet 56,* page 175. List some stressful events that have happened to you this past year. They may be "outside " or "inside." Give your responses. **Example: Event:** short of money, can't pay the bills. **Thoughts:** I always have to bring in the money. **Beliefs:** I never get help from anyone. **Emotions:** anger because partner doesn't earn money. **Behavior:** blame partner, get into fight.

STAGES AND EFFECTS OF STRESS ON THE BODY

Long periods of exposure to stress can hurt the body. It can cause us to become physically ill. Research has shown that we go through three steps when faced with stress:

▶ **Alarm:** the body steps up its inside resources to fight the stressor or cause of stress.

▶ **Revolt:** The body resists and fights the stressors. Body chemicals are released to help us cope. For awhile, these chemicals help keep the body in balance.

▶ **Exhaustion:** The body gets tired. We might collapse. We are more likely to get sick or emotionally upset. Now, because of ongoing stress, the chemicals that once helped us now makes us weaker.

The answer: avoid ongoing stress and use ways to cope and manage stress, our topic for next session.

SIGNS OF STRESS AND EFFORTS TO COPE

Stress can throw us out of balance. We call this balance *homeostasis.* The body and mind work at keeping balance through coping responses. These are the efforts to control or cope with the stress reactions inside of you. But they also are signs of stress.

▶ **Mental:** Mental **worry** is a major cause of stress. Worries are thoughts and views of what might happen. Your thoughts are the key. When we manage stress this comes first. If our thoughts fail to give us self-control we lose control over body, emotions and behaviors.

▶ **Physical:** Our body becomes upset. Our heart beats fast, we get sweaty, feel weak. We breathe hard and lose control of breathing. We hunger for air or oxygen. Being in control of breathing helps us to be in control of our stress response.

▶ **Emotional:** These are your efforts to cope with stress. They are signs of stress.

  • **Anxiety:** We feel uneasy, anxious. We can't pin down why.

  • **Panic:** a sudden intense fear or anxiety with body symptoms - hard to breathe, tight chest, heart beats fast.

  • **Emotional stress syndromes:** guilty, angry or depressed. We look at the guilt-anger cycle below, in *Session 34.* We take a close look at anger in another session. Managing anger, guilt and depression helps us to manage our stress.

▶ **Behavioral:** You may drink, go running, go to a movie, gamble, smoke a cigarette, talk with a friend. Sometimes they are positive and help us cope.

HOW PROBLEMS COME FROM THE REACTION TO STRESS

Your coping effort fails to give you the self-control to solve what you think are the demands of outside events or your inside world. Those very efforts to cope cause you problems. Some examples.

▶ Your physical effort to cope with worry causes an **ulcer.**

▶ Getting angry as a way to cope leads to getting **violent.**

▶ Your use of alcohol to cope with emotional responses of stress now causes problems or you develop an **alcohol problem.**

<u>Exercise:</u> Group members are asked to share actions they have used to cope with the stress that have ended up causing more stress and problems.

HOW STRESS TRIGGERS RELAPSE AND RECIDIVISM (R&R) CYCLE

Look at *Figure 8,* page 71, the MB-ICC. **Exercise:** Discuss how this cycle explains how stress can trigger R&R. *Figure 26* below shows what happens to many who abuse drugs and commit crimes.

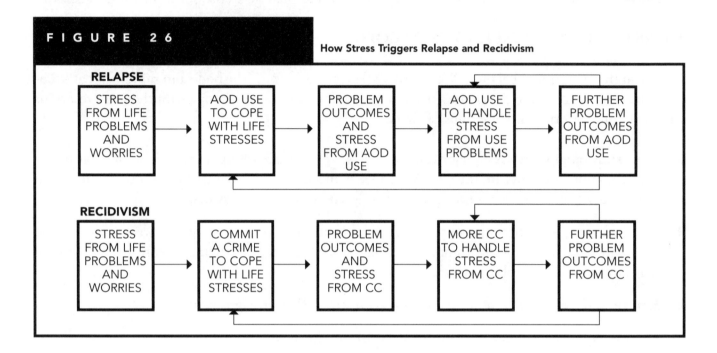

FIGURE 26

How Stress Triggers Relapse and Recidivism

RELAPSE

STRESS FROM LIFE PROBLEMS AND WORRIES → AOD USE TO COPE WITH LIFE STRESSES → PROBLEM OUTCOMES AND STRESS FROM AOD USE → AOD USE TO HANDLE STRESS FROM USE PROBLEMS → FURTHER PROBLEM OUTCOMES FROM AOD USE

RECIDIVISM

STRESS FROM LIFE PROBLEMS AND WORRIES → COMMIT A CRIME TO COPE WITH LIFE STRESSES → PROBLEM OUTCOMES AND STRESS FROM CC → MORE CC TO HANDLE STRESS FROM CC → FURTHER PROBLEM OUTCOMES FROM CC

LOOKING AT YOUR STRESS

Exercise: Let's look at what might be the roots or sources of your stress. Put a check if you have had any of these happen to you.

- ☐ Serious childhood illness and distress.
- ☐ Loss of someone close or loved one in childhood.
- ☐ Loss of close family member.
- ☐ Loss of spouse or intimate partner.
- ☐ Divorce or separation from intimate partner.
- ☐ Loss of important job or work position.
- ☐ Making a difficult geographic move.
- ☐ Negative outcomes from AOD use.
- ☐ Legal problems.

Stress comes from thoughts about what is happening to us.

If you checked several of these, you may have had more than the average amount of stress in your life.

Exercise: Do *Worksheet 57,* page 176. Answer each question based on the past year. Then check whether you think each of these were related to your use of alcohol (or other drugs). If your score was **5 to 9,** you have been experiencing some stress in your life. A score of **10 to 15** means you probably have had at least moderate stress. A score of **16 or above** indicates that you may have had a high amount of stress in the past year. In the last column, write down **how** your AOD use or criminal conduct (CC) may have been a part of or a response to each situation.

SESSION ACTIVITIES AND PROCESS GROUP

1. Do *Worksheets 56* and *57*. Update your *Master Skills List,* page 291 and MAP, page 295. Do this week's *TAP charting.*

2. Using the *SSC Scale*, rate yourself as to your being able to understand your own stress and the causes of your stress.

Level of understanding
my stress

0	1	2	3	4	5	6	7	8	9	10
LOW					MEDIUM					HIGH

3. Use the process group to share the areas of stress in your life. If you do not see yourself as having stress, why don't you?

WORKSHEET 56	**Negative stressful events that have happened in the past year:** Your mental, emotional and behavior responses to those events.		
STRESSFUL EVENTS	MENTAL RESPONSES	EMOTIONAL RESPONSES	BEHAVIOR RESPONSES

Events or situations that cause stress: Answer these questions as to whether these have been sources of stress for you over the past year. Check the column that best fits your answer. For each "sometimes" check, give yourself one point; for each "a lot" check, give yourself two points. In the last column, write down how your AOD use or CC may have been a part of these events.

HAVE THESE SITUATIONS IN YOUR LIFE CAUSED YOU STRESS IN THE PAST YEAR?	0 NO	1 SOME	2 A LOT	AOD USE OR CC WAS A RESPONSE TO THESE
1. Too many job demands				
2. Demands of family life				
3. Conflict with spouse/partner				
4. Not having a job or work				
5. Keeping up my home/house				
6. Not enough money to pay bills				
7. Demands from relationships				
8. Legal problems				
9. Use of alcohol or other drugs				
10. Medical problems or illness				
11. Divorce or separation				
12. Death of loved one				
TOTAL SCORE: USE SCORING GUIDE DESCRIBED ABOVE				

SESSION INTRODUCTION AND OBJECTIVES

In *Session 25,* we looked at stress, its roots and causes, how it is related to R&R and the areas of stress in your life. Now we look at specific stress reactions and how to manage these reactions.

OBJECTIVES OF SESSION AND KEY TERMS

➡ Understand stress and your specific stress responses.

➡ Learn the skills and steps to manage stress and worry.

➡ Use the Stress Scale and Stress Ladder to understand your levels of stress.

➡ Key terms: worry, anxiety, panic, stress scale, stress ladder.

SESSION CONTENT AND FOCUS

THE STATES OF STRESS

Stress shows itself in three ways.

- **Worry:** Fear or uneasiness about something you **can pin down.** You worry you will get sick. Worriers blow up the possible bad outcomes and ignore information. They play down their ability to handle problems. They want things to be perfect. Most worries are based on errors in thinking.

- **Anxiety:** Fear or uneasiness that **cannot be pinned down** to a cause. Or, if is related to a specific event, the possible outcomes can't be pinned down.

- **Panic:** A sudden attack of fear and anxiety. Its symptoms: fast heartbeat, hard time breathing, pain in chest, getting sweaty.

IDENTIFYING YOUR STRESS RESPONSES

What are your specific responses to stress? **Exercise:** Complete *Worksheet 58,* page 181, *Stress Response Questionnaire.* The higher your score, the stronger your stress responses. A score above 20 suggests strong and even unhealthy stress responses. A score above 30 suggests even stronger and very unhealthy stress responses. A score less than five suggests a strong defense against admitting to stress.

STEPS IN MANAGING STRESS: WORRY, ANXIETY, PANIC

Basic rule: Manage the stress reaction before managing the stress event. You may not follow these steps in exact order. But, in managing stress, you will use most of these steps.

Step 1:   **Ask: What's happening to me?**   What are my stress reactions or symptoms? Knowing your stress reactions will help prepare you for managing stressful events. *Worksheet 58, page 181,* will help you identify those symptoms or reactions.

Step 2:   **How stressed or worried am I?** **Exercise:** Write below a stressful event or time in your life. Using the scale on the right, rate the level of this stress from zero to 10.

A STRESSFUL EVENT OR TIME IN YOUR LIFE

STRESS SCALE

10	HIGH STRESS
9	
8	
7	
6	
5	MODERATE STRESS
4	
3	
2	
1	LOW
0	STRESS

A STRESSFUL EVENT OR TIME IN YOUR LIFE

_____

_____

Step 3:   **Ask: What's bothering me?**   What am I stressed or worried about? What are my thoughts about the stress event? Prepare for stress by knowing your stress areas. *Worksheets 56* and *57* in *Session 25,* pages 175 and 176, will help you with this.

Step 4:   **Manage your stress or worry with these skills.**

▶ **Use the self-control skill**s in *Table 6,* page 160 and the relaxation skills in *Table 7,* page 180. Talk with your counselor if you think the relaxation skills don't work for you.

▶ **Test the worry and use the time test.** How big of a problem is this? What's the worst that can happen? Does my worry make sense? Will it make a difference in a month, a year, five years, 10 years? **Use the stress scale - zero to 10.**

▶ **Ask: What is the problem?** Most stress events are caused by some unsolved problem. We look at problem solving in *Module 9.* After you manage the stress reaction, work on solving the problem.

▶ **Ask: Is this a good (useful) worry or bad (useless) worry?** Useful worries are about something that can happen and you can do something. If you can't do anything about it, it may be a useless worry. Good stress can motivate you to positive action.

Exercise: The *Stress Scale* above shows a stressful event or time in your life. Now, using the *Stress Scale* to the right, put a check by the number that shows how much overall stress you are having at this time. When you are having stress, rate that stress using the Stress Scale. Ask, "Where am I?" A 10? A one? When your stress is high, put extra effort into using the above skills.

Step 5:   **Look back at the stress episode.** Was it silly to worry? Have you done this before? Did you problem solve? Did the stress and worry help you get a positive outcome? How am I doing?

Exercise: For each stress response in *Worksheet 58,* page 181, that you did not check "never," write down one skill you would use to handle it.

THE STRESS LADDER

Choose another action: take a ride, go for a walk, go to a movie.

Exercise: Using *Worksheet 59,* page 182, list five areas of stress or worry in your life at this time. Make FIVE the most stressful and ONE the least. Using the Stress Scale under Five at the bottom of *Worksheet 59,* rate that area of stress. How does it compare with your rating of a stressful event or time in your life that you wrote down on page 178? Rate the other four areas in *Worksheet 59,* page 182, using the *Stress Scales* at the bottom of the worksheet.

You are asked to talk about only those areas you are comfortable sharing with your group. Ask for a session with your counselor if you would like additional help in dealing with a past or present stressful event.

Exercise: Use the *STEP Method* to bring number FIVE in *Worksheet 59* to a positive outcome. Role play the event and positive outcome. (The *STEP Method* is different from the steps we use to manage stress.)

S SITUATION—> **T** THINKING CHANGE—> **E** EMOTIONS— **P** POSITIVE ACTION

POSITIVE FACES OF WORRY AND ANXIETY

Anxiety and worry can spur us to action and alert us to bad outcomes. They tell us something is wrong. They are alarms that tell us we might be doing too much. Healthy anxiety keeps us from relapse and recidivism. Many adult judicial clients do not worry enough to prevent seeing the bad outcomes of AOD abuse and criminal conduct.

SESSION ACTIVITIES AND PROCESS GROUP

---

1. Do *Worksheets 58* and *59.* Update your *Master Skills List,* page 291 and MAP, page 295. Do this week's *TAP charting.*

2. Use the *SSC Scale* to rate yourself on being able to manage stress.

My ability to use skills to manage stress	0	1	2	3	4	5	6	7	8	9	10
	LOW					MEDIUM					HIGH

3. Use the process group to share the stress in your life. If you do not see yourself as having stress, why don't you?

TABLE 7	**Summary of Relaxation and Stress Management Skills:** Practice these skills if they work for you by sitting in a comfortable chair. But you can use them at any time or any place. For some exercises, it might be helpful to close your eyes.

SKILL NAME	DESCRIPTION AND APPROACH
CALM SCENE RELAXATION	Imagine walking on the beach, watching the sunset, laying by a stream in the mountains
BODY RELAXATION	Focus on parts of your body and tell them to relax: my arms are heavy, my hands are warm, I am relaxed. Go through all your body parts. Practice relaxing thoughts: "I feel relaxed, I am calm, I am feeling soothed. I feel quiet."
CALM BREATHING	Focus on your breathing. Breathe slow and steady, in and out for five minutes. Breathe into your stomach, making your stomach rise and fall. Let the air out completely. As you breathe, imagine your heart breathing in and out, taking in oxygen and breathing out stress. As you let out the air, feel yourself sink into the chair.
DEEP BREATHING	From normal breathing, make each breath deeper until you breathe deep five times. Breathe in through your nose and out through your mouth, puckering your lips and blowing out slowly. After five deep breaths, go back to normal breathing. **Do no more than five deep breaths at a time.**
MUSCLE RELAXATION	Put your hands on the chair arms and breathe normal and steady. Take about ten minutes for this exercise. Tighten each muscle group for a few seconds and then gradually let the muscles relax slowly. Do each two times. First, squeeze your eyes closed and then relax the eye muscles. Then, squeeze your hands on the chair arms and gradually let the muscles relax. Squeeze your arm muscles and let them go gradually. Don't squeeze real hard, but tighten them up and then relax them. Go through all of your muscles, your shoulders, your stomach, your thighs, legs and toes. Squeeze gently but tightly. At the end of this exercise, think of a calm scene. Take your time.
STRETCHING RELAXATION	Stretching lets the tension go out of the muscles and hooks the parts of our body together. **If you have a medical condition, check with your doctor first before doing stretching exercises.** Lay on your back and pull one knee to your chest, stretch the leg back and do the same with the other knee. Pull both knees to your chest. Do these several times. Do several situps, but do them easy and slow. Feel the muscles stretch. Lay on your stomach and push your upper body up by your hands and arms. Do it gently. Lay on your side, pull your leg to your chest, then straighten it out and swing it slowly back. Feel the back muscles stretch. Always be gentle and slow. Do this on the other side. Now, come up with other stretching exercises. Get a book on stretching.
ACTIVE RELAXATION	Walk 15 minutes a day. Swing your arms for awhile. Put your hands behind your back and walk for awhile reflecting on how good you feel. Do as much lifestyle walking each day as you can. Use a hand-sized, soft ball and do hand exercises each day. Work out a couple times a week by playing a sport like tennis, going to the gym.

SKILL NAME	DESCRIPTION AND APPROACH
GROUNDING	Grounding focuses on the outside world and on the now, not the past or future. Describe what is around you: sights, sounds, colors, temperature, objects. Say or read out loud a saying, such as the *Serenity Prayer*. Think of somthing funny. Examples: the chair is wood, the wall is green, there is one window, the sky is blue, the breeze is cool. This will help you focus away from your stress.

W O R K S H E E T   5 8

Stress Response Questionnaire: Check those that you have had in the past year. Then, in the right margin, for each reaction that you check "sometimes," "a lot," or "all the time," put one skill you would use to handle that stress reaction.

YOUR REACTIONS TO STRESSFUL SITUATIONS	0 NEVER	1 SOMETIMES	2 A LOT	4 ALL THE TIME
1. Feel jumpy or nervous				
2. Restless and on edge				
3. Get tired and worn out				
4. Get irritated, angry, blow up				
5. Jump to conclusions				
6. Get all worried and tense				
7. Get a tension headache				
8. Muscles get tight/tense, back pain				
9. Lot of negative thoughts				
10. Can't sleep/restless sleep				
11. Can't think/mind goes blank				
12. Blow things up in your mind				
13. Worry something bad will happen				
14. Get into arguments				
15. Fear going out of home in public				
16. Get sweaty, hot when anxious				
17. Shortness of breath when anxious				
18. Heart beats fast when anxious				
TOTAL SCORE				

The Stress Ladder: List your five areas of stress. For FIVE, list the most stressful area. For ONE, list one of your least stressful areas. Then, go up the ladder from TWO to FOUR and list your increasing stress areas. In column 2, list skills to handle those stresses. Then rate each area using the Stress Scale.

LIST YOUR AREAS OR SITUATIONS OF STRESS IN YOUR LIFE NOW	LIST SKILLS TO MANAGE THE STRESS AREA
FIVE: GREATEST WORRY OR STRESS AREA	
FOUR:	
THREE:	
TWO:	
ONE: LEAST WORRY OR STRESS AREA	

RATE EACH AREA USING THE STRESS SCALE

Stress Area Five

STRESS SCALE

10	HIGH STRESS
9	
8	
7	
6	MODERATE STRESS
5	
4	
3	
2	
1	LOW STRESS
0	

Stress Area Four

STRESS SCALE

10	HIGH STRESS
9	
8	
7	
6	MODERATE STRESS
5	
4	
3	
2	
1	LOW STRESS
0	

Stress Area Three

STRESS SCALE

10	HIGH STRESS
9	
8	
7	
6	MODERATE STRESS
5	
4	
3	
2	
1	LOW STRESS
0	

Stress Area Two

STRESS SCALE

10	HIGH STRESS
9	
8	
7	
6	MODERATE STRESS
5	
4	
3	
2	
1	LOW STRESS
0	

Stress Area One

STRESS SCALE

10	HIGH STRESS
9	
8	
7	
6	MODERATE STRESS
5	
4	
3	
2	
1	LOW STRESS
0	

SESSION INTRODUCTION AND OBJECTIVES

There are three big emotions that are related to stress: anger, guilt and depression. In this session, we focus on **managing and regulating** anger to get trouble-free outcomes. When anger turns to aggression and violence, it leads to bad outcomes for others and society. We look at aggression and violence in *Module 10*.

OBJECTIVES OF SESSION AND KEY WORDS

➠ Understand and recognize angry thoughts and feelings.

➠ Become aware of the events that trigger anger for you.

➠ Learn the clues and signs of getting angry.

➠ Learn and practice the skills of handling anger.

➠ Key terms: angry thoughts/feelings, constructive and destructive anger, triggers, high charged events, *Anger Scale*.

SESSION CONTENT AND FOCUS

UNDERSTANDING ANGER

When growing up, we were often not allowed to show angry feelings. We may not have had a chance to understand anger and learn skills to express and handle anger. Here are important ideas about anger.

▶ **Events do not cause anger.** It is our thoughts about these events that lead to angry feelings and actions. We control our anger by controlling these thoughts.

▶ **It is the actions or behaviors coming from anger that are good or bad,** not the emotion or feeling of anger itself.

▶ **Anger is a big part of substance abuse and criminal conduct.** Hurting others is an angry act. Criminal conduct hurts others. It is an angry act. Getting high or drunk are angry acts if they hurt others. What are your thoughts about this?

▶ **Anger is usually caused by some problem.** A part of handling anger is problem solving. We look at this in *Module 9*.

▶ **It's not true that you have to get angry to keep it from building.** "Getting it off your chest" may make you feel better, but it doesn't solve the problem behind the anger. Talking about it, not "blowing up," keeps it from building.

- **Hostility, resentment, anger, aggression and violence are negative emotions and actions.** In *Module 9,* we look at how anger and aggression can be harmful to relationships. In *Module 10,* we look at physical aggression and violence.

- **Constructive anger** expresses the emotions in such a way that you feel better afterwards. It builds communication. It can help you to be assertive. It can trigger problem-solving.

- **Destructive anger** leads to bad decisions. It makes people angry and aggressive. It blocks communication. It leaves us feeling helpless. It knocks down our self-worth. **It can cause you to lose your freedoms.**

- **Rating you anger:** Everyone will experience angry feelings. How angry we feel depends on what is going on in our lives. Think about situations during the past year when you have been angry. Using the scale on the right, rate the level of your anger from zero to ten in those situations.

- **Stuffed anger comes out when people are tired or on drugs.** We blow up, hurt others. This reaction is followed by guilt which prevents dealing with the anger. We look at guilt in *Session 28.*

<u>Exercise:</u> Think of a situation or event that happened in the **past couple of weeks** that triggered anger. Use the second *Anger Scale* to the right and put and X to show your level of anger for that event.

CLUES AND SIGNS OF ANGER

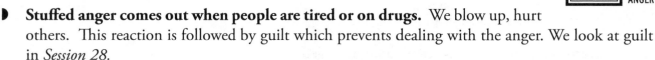

- **Physical:** tense muscles; shakiness; red in the face; sweating; rapid breathing; fast heart beat; sweating; clenching fists. Anger increases blood flow to the brain and pumps our adrenalin.

- **Mental:** agitated; irritable; feelings are hurt; humiliated and insulted; tense, on edge; impatient; feeling out of control.

- **Actions:** fly off the handle; restless; quick body motions; lose temper, get physically violent.

- **Angry self-talk:** thoughts of being "short changed;" not treated fairly; feeling like a victim; "they deserve it;" thinking your personal space is violated, feel being pushed.

HIGH-CHARGED EVENTS THAT LEAD TO ANGRY THINKING

- **Relationship conflicts and problems:** not being understood, feeling powerless, not feeling approved of, having needs blocked and not getting what you want from another person.

- **Non-interpersonal** problem such as being stuck in traffic, losing your billfold.

SELF-CONTROL SKILLS FOR REGULATING ANGER

Skill 1: **Know what triggers your anger:** Being attacked, unable to reach your goals, being blamed.

Exercise: Using *Worksheet 60,* page 186, list five triggers to anger in column one. Use the *Anger Scales* at the bottom of *Worksheet 60,* to rate the level of anger you could feel from each trigger.

Skill 2: **Be mindful or aware of your angry feelings and thoughts.** Look at the clues listed above. **Exercise:** In column two, *Worksheet 60,* for each trigger, list one angry thought.

Skill 3: **Use the mental self-control tools** in *Table 6,* page 160 and the **relaxation skills** in *Table 7,* page 180, when your anger is aroused or is building. Without self-control, your anger is destructive. You just get angry. Use self-talk: "CALM DOWN AND STAY COOL." Hear your own voice calm yourself. **Exercise:** On *Worksheet 60,* column three, put skills to manage angry triggers and thoughts.

When your anger builds, use self-talk to "calm down and stay cool."

Skill 4: **Communicate or express your angry thoughts, not just your feelings.** Use "I" message. "I'm angry about this." If you use the "you message," or blame, you act out your anger, yell, or get physical. You express anger not just to get it off your chest, but to communicate the angry thoughts. Take responsibility for your anger. Think: "It's my anger. I own it. It's not someone else's fault." If you yell, **they can't hear what you think.**

Skill 5: **Problem solve** when the anger starts to build. Anger is usually about some problem - conflict with another person, losing something. What is the problem? Choose an action that replaces the angry thoughts. We study problem solving in *Module 9.*

Skill 6: **Reward yourself** after you succeed in handling the anger in a positive way. Share your positive actions with someone close.

PRACTICE IN SELF-CONTROL

The **key:** use self-control skills. The **goal:** prevent relapse and recidivism. The **skill:** learn to express and communicate your angry thoughts, not just your feelings.

Exercise: Role play being angry at someone and use the above skills.

Exercise: With the help of your counselor, pick a scene that arouses anger. Use the *STEP method* to change your thoughts to get a good outcome. Use the skills in *Table 6,* page 160, and *Table 7,* page 180, that work for you. You may be asked to role play the STEP process.

Exercise: With the help of your counselor, pick another situation that makes you angry. Your counselor will then lead you through the self-control skills in Table 6 and the relaxation skills in *Table 7* that help you manage your anger.

SESSION ACTIVITIES AND PROCESS GROUP

1. Do *Worksheet 60.* Update your *Master Skills List, Master Assessment Plan,* and do your *TAP charting.* For homework, do a *Thinking Report* on an event that happens this week in which you become angry and a *Re-thinking Report* on that event.

2. Rate yourself on this *SSC Scale* as to your ability to manage anger.

My ability to use skills to manage anger	0	1	2	3	4	5	6	7	8	9	10
	LOW					MEDIUM					HIGH

3. Use the process group to share your anger triggers.

List five triggers or situations that can set off angry thoughts and feelings:
Then write down angry thoughts or beliefs that come from those triggers. List self-control and relaxation skills you can use to manage angry thinking. Rate the level of anger you might feel from these triggers using the anger scales below.

WORKSHEET 60

YOUR ANGER TRIGGERS	ANGRY THOUGHTS/BELIEFS	SELF-CONTROL SKILLS
1		
2		
3		
4		
5		

RATE EACH TRIGGER USING THE ANGER SCALE

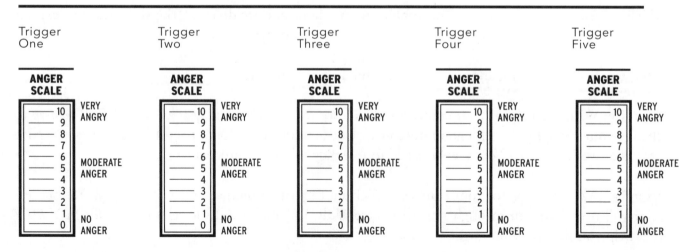

Trigger One	Trigger Two	Trigger Three	Trigger Four	Trigger Five
ANGER SCALE	ANGER SCALE	ANGER SCALE	ANGER SCALE	ANGER SCALE

SESSION 28: Managing Guilt and Depression and Increasing Positive Emotions

SESSION INTRODUCTION AND OBJECTIVES

The negative emotions of guilt, depression and sadness can also lead to relapse and recidivism. Just as with anger, we may not have learned skills to express and manage guilt and depression. This session looks at how to be mindful of and manage guilt and depression to get more positive outcomes. It also looks at increasing positive emotions in your life. WE START THIS SESSION by sharing your *Thinking and Re-thinking Report* homework.

OBJECTIVES OF SESSION AND KEY TERMS

➡ Understand and become aware of guilt and depression.

➡ Learn skills to regulate and manage depression and guilt.

➡ Learn to identify and increase positive emotions.

➡ Key terms: Being mindful, balancing emotions, managing guilt and depression, *Guilt Scale, Depression Scale,* increasing positive feelings.

SESSION CONTENT AND FOCUS

BEING MINDFUL: PUTTING A NAME TAG ON OUR EMOTIONS

Putting name tags on our negative and positive emotions is hard. It requires being **mindful and accepting.** Here are some skills to help you be more aware of how thoughts and feelings are related.

Skill 1: **Notice your body states.** A flushed face may be anger. A sinking of the stomach may be sadness. Being tired may be depression. A surge of energy may be joy.

Skill 2: **Know what sparked or aroused the emotion.** This tells you what the emotion is. If you think you were treated badly, it is probably anger. If you were disappointed, it may be depression. If you let someone down, it might be guilt. If you received a compliment, it might be pride.

Skill 3: **Understand your action urges.** Wanting to strike out means anger. Wanting to run means hurt and sadness. Wanting to undo the situation may be guilt. Wanting to hug might be love.

Skill 4: **Join or take part in the emotion with self-control.** Always let your "head rule your emotions." This applies to both positive and negative emotions.

Skill 5: **Look at the outcome.** What is your reaction? The reaction of others? Are you tired? Are others angry with you? Do you feel pleasure?

UNDERSTANDING AND MANAGING GUILT

Anger can lead to guilt; guilt can prevent us from managing anger. We look at the *guilt-anger cycle* in *Module 9,* since it gets in the way of good relationship outcomes.

▶ **Guilt or lack of guilt may play a part in AOD misuse and can lead to criminal conduct.**

▶ **Appropriate guilt is good.** It should follow actions harmful to others. It guides us in what is right or wrong. It is necessary for responsible and prosocial actions. It is part of our conscience.

▶ **Inappropriate and excessive guilt** keeps us from expressing our thoughts and feelings in a wholesome, open and honest way. Storing up angry thoughts because of excessive feelings of guilt may lead to uncontrolled anger.

▶ **Know if your guilt is based on reality.** We can manage realistic guilt. Share it openly, by saying, "I feel bad. I'm sorry that happened."

▶ **Some "shoulds" and "oughts" are healthy.** They help us to be morally responsible to others and the community.

▶ **Rating your guilt: everyone has feelings of guilt.** Your level of guilt depends on what is going on in your life. Think of a time or situation when you felt guilty. Use the Guilt Scale on the right to rate that situation from zero to ten.

▶ **Exercise:** Think of the last time you felt guilty. Was it good or negative guilt? Rate that guilt on the second Guilt Scale to the right. Use the *STEP Method* to bring your guilty thoughts in that situation to a positive action and outcome.

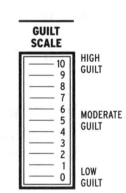

S SITUATION - leading to guilty feelings.

T THINKING CHANGE - change guilty thoughts to ones that are more appropriate to the situation.

E EMOTION - have those thoughts lead to a positive emotion or a feeling of guilt that is more appropriate.

P POSITIVE Action and Outcome.

UNDERSTANDING AND MANAGING DEPRESSION

When we are depressed, we feel gloom, despair, dejected and deflated. We don't care. It may start out as a feeling. It may end up as a state or condition. We may not only feel depressed. We may be depressed. Everyone gets depressed from time to time. Some depression is normal.

Being mindful of your depression

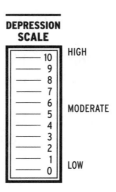

DEPRESSION
SCALE

The first step in changing depressed thoughts is to be aware of those thoughts and the feelings coming from those thoughts. **Exercise:** Write in the space below a time you were depressed. Use the *Depression Scale* on the right to rate that depression from zero to 10.

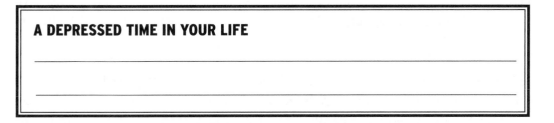

A DEPRESSED TIME IN YOUR LIFE

_____

_____

Exercise: Using the second *Depression Scale* on the right, put an X at your level of depression over the last two weeks.

Some causes of depression

▶ Not dealing with our anger and pushing it down deep inside.

▶ Being in a hopeless situation.

▶ Using depression to cope with stress, anger and guilt.

▶ Being in a helpless situation. Not able to do anything about your problems.

▶ Know the difference between depression, grief and sadness. It is normal to feel sad and have grief over real losses in your life. Sadness and grief have normal stages.

Triggers for relapse and recidivism

▶ Alcohol or other drugs are used to cope with depression. But, AOD use can make us more depressed. This puts you into the mental-behavioral impaired control cycle.

▶ Depression can trigger recidivism. If you are depressed and find yourself in a high risk recidivism situation, you might say, "I don't care. Just as well do it."

Measuring your depression

Exercise: Complete *Worksheet 61, page 191, The Depression Questionnaire (DQ).* The higher the score, the more depression you are disclosing. A score in the range of 30 or above suggests a high range of depression and you may want to seek some help. A score of 20 to 30 suggests enough depression to get an opinion from a counselor or specialist. A score of 10 to 20 suggests some depression, but may be in the low range. A score of zero suggests you may be defending against feeling depressed. Talk with your counselor about your score.

Skills and Strategies in Managing and Coping with Depression

Skill 1: **Know the triggers** - past and present events - to your depressed thinking. **Exercise:** Complete the first column of *Worksheet 62,* page 192.

Skill 2: **Be aware and mindful of depressed thoughts and beliefs.** "I don't care," "I'm worthless," "What's the use." The DQ will help tell how much depression you might have. Negative thinking is part of depression. **Exercise:** Do the middle column of *Worksheet 62,* and list depressed thoughts and beliefs.

Skill 3: **Change depressed thoughts and beliefs.** Use the skills in *Session 19,* page 146, and *Table 6,* page 160, to change your negative and depressed thinking. Use the positive thoughts you armed yourself with. **Exercise:** On *Worksheet 62,* page 192, list skills you can use to change your depressed thoughts and beliefs.

Skill 4: **Take action.** Helpless and hopeless thinking can lead to depression. Do relaxation skills. Act. Take charge of your life. Be in control. Seek some help if necessary.

POSITIVE FACES OF OUR MOODS

Anxiety, stress and anger can spur us to action. Depression can help control stress. Sometimes, it is healthy to say: "I don't care what happens. I've done all I can." To let go, and not have to be in control, to get distance from what overwhelms us. Healthy guilt helps us to be concerned about how our actions affect others and to care.

OVERCOMING NEGATIVE EMOTIONS BY INCREASING POSITIVE FEELINGS

We have been working on managing negative emotions to get trouble-free outcomes. **Self-control also involves making positive outcomes by increasing positive feelings of joy, love, pride.** Increasing positive feelings balances out the negative ones. Here are several ways to increase our positive emotions.

> **Being mindful** or aware of your positive emotions. **Exercise:** Use *Worksheet 63,* page 192, and rate yourself on the positive emotions. What emotions are you high on? Low on? Want to increase?

> **Develop a list of thoughts** that lead to positive feelings. **Exercise:** To the right of each positive emotion on *Worksheet 63,* write a thought that will lead to that feeling or emotion.

> **Develop a list of activities** that lead to positive emotions and outcomes.

> **Delaying rewards** will help you get positive feelings. "I'll work hard this week and have fun this weekend."

> **Give yourself credit** for positive emotions.

> **Find pleasure in everyday, simple things** - morning cup of coffee, taking a walk.

SESSION ACTIVITIES AND PROCESS GROUP

1. Do *Worksheets 61 through 63.* Update your *Master Skills List* and do your *TAP charting.* For homework, do a *Thinking Report* on an event that happens that caused you some depression.

2. Use the *SSC Scale* to rate yourself on your ability to manage guilt and depression.

My ability to use skills to manage guilt

0	1	2	3	4	5	6	7	8	9	10
LOW					MEDIUM					HIGH

My ability to use skills to manage depression

0	1	2	3	4	5	6	7	8	9	10
LOW					MEDIUM					HIGH

WORKSHEET 61

Depression Questionnaire (DQ): Answer the questions as to how they apply to you at this time in your life. For each "sometimes" answer, score "1," for each "often" answer, score a "2."

APPLY AT THIS TIME IN YOUR LIFE	0 NEVER	1 SOMETIMES	2 OFTEN
1. Get tired easily			
2. Sit around and do nothing			
3. Lower sexual drive than usual			
4. Jumpy and quick to react			
5. Hard time doing my work			
6. Loss of appetite and weight			
7. Not sleeping well			
8. Gained lot of weight			
9. Sleeping way too much			
10. Feel like a failure			
11. Have a lot of negative thoughts			
12. Lost interest in things			
13. Feeling sad and not happy			
14. Feel disappointed in myself			
15. Hopeless about the future			
16. Cry a lot			
17. Feel like not wanting to live			
18. Can't think clearly			
19. Feel overwhelmed			
20. Feel guilty			
TOTAL SCORE			

List the triggers that can set off depression for you. Write down depressed thoughts and beliefs. Put skills you can use to change your depressed thoughts.

DEPRESSION TRIGGERS	DEPRESSED THOUGHTS/BELIEFS	CONTROL SKILLS

Rate yourself on these positive emotions. Put a check on the rating that fits you. Then, to the right of each scale, write a thought that will bring you those emotions.

FEELINGS	LOW MEDIUM HIGH	A THOUGHT THAT BRINGS ON THIS FEELING
Happiness	1 2 3 4 5 6 7 8 9 10	
Pride	1 2 3 4 5 6 7 8 9 10	
Joy	1 2 3 4 5 6 7 8 9 10	
Hopeful	1 2 3 4 5 6 7 8 9 10	
Calm	1 2 3 4 5 6 7 8 9 10	
Confident	1 2 3 4 5 6 7 8 9 10	
Relaxed	1 2 3 4 5 6 7 8 9 10	
Love	1 2 3 4 5 6 7 8 9 10	
Faith	1 2 3 4 5 6 7 8 9 10	

MODULE 9

An important trigger for backsliding into substance abuse and criminal conduct is relationship problems. The mental self-control skills you learn in *Phase I* and in *Module 8* give the foundation for positive relationships with others and the community. This module works on building and strengthening social and relationship skills. Handling conflicts and building positive relationships will help you in two important ways:

Social and Relationship Skills Building

Communication skills lead to positive relationships.

- to prevent relapse and recidivism;

- to give you support in your journey of change.

We use the STEP method that focuses on the positive change process of the *CB Map:* **S** SITUATION → **T** THINKING CHANGE → **E** EMOTIONS → **P** POSITIVE ACTION AND OUTCOMES. Your counselor will review *STEP* with you. Here are the learning and therapy objectives of this module.

- Strengthen communication skills to increase positive outcomes in relationships.

- Learn and practice the skills of problem solving and being assertive.

- Learn to manage and regulate anger in relationships.

- Learn skills to develop close family and intimate relationships.

Module 9 has seven sessions.

Session 29: Strengthening Communication Skills
Session 30: Starting a Difficult Conversation and Keeping it Going
Session 31: Giving and Receiving Praise and Positive Reinforcement
Session 32: Skills in Problem Solving
Session 33: It's Your Right: Developing Assertiveness Skills
Session 34: Managing Anger in Relationships: The Guilt-Anger Cycle
Session 35: Developing and Keeping Close and Intimate Relationships

SESSION INTRODUCTION AND OBJECTIVES

Communication skills are the foundation for positive and healthy relationships. Positive relationships give you support in your efforts to change and in managing high-risk exposures that lead to R&R. In *Module 5,* we learned about nonverbal communication and the communication skills of active listening and active sharing. In this session, we review and practice these skills in greater depth. WE START THIS SESSION by sharing your *Thinking Report* homework on an event that caused you some depression and then do a *Re-thinking Report* on that event. We then do the *CB Map Exercise* using an event of poor or bad communication.

OBJECTIVES OF SESSION AND KEY TERMS

➡ Review the skills of active sharing and active listening and the *Johari Window.*

➡ Learn and practice the specific skills of active sharing and active listening.

➡ Key terms: accurate thought, feeling and action sharing; open receiver; open responder; defensive listening; invitation to share; restating; reflecting.

SESSION CONTENT AND FOCUS

The *Johari Window,* page 99, gives us a view of how active sharing and listening take place. Your counselor will review this.

SKILLS OF ACTIVE SHARING

Active sharing or self-oriented communication is done through the skills of 1) self-disclosure and 2) receiving feedback. The goal is to make your disclosure and sharing clear, correct and **accurate.** The challenge is getting the other person to listen to and understand what we have to say. It also means we listen to and receive feedback from the other person about what we have shared.

The skills of sharing

▶ Use "I" and "me" messages and not "you" messages. Remember the four parts to this communication.

  • I think • I feel • I need • I do or act

▶ Talk about yourself, not the other person.

▶ Have ready-to-go opening statements you can use to start your active sharing. "I need to talk with you"; "This is what happened to me."

- Use the four kinds of active sharing statements: **Thought sharing:** "It's cold out." **Feeling sharing:** "I'm angry and upset." **Need sharing:** "I need your help doing the dishes." **Action sharing:** "I got drunk."

- Get closure and then give the other person a chance to talk.

The skills of receiving feedback

- Be an **open receiver.** Imagine talking on a phone with no receiver, no "over." That happens when you don't have an open receiver. You don't hear the other person respond.

- Be an **open responder.** Don't push the feedback away. Don't be a **defensive listener.**

Exercise: As a group, develop a set of opening statements for active sharing. Your counselor will put them on a flipchart. In the first part of *Worksheet 64*, page 197, write down four opening statements for active sharing that work for you.

Exercise: Share something you did last weekend, using all of the sharing skills: **I think, I feel, I need, I do.**

ACTIVE LISTENING

Active listening involves three skills: **attending, inviting others to share and giving feedback.** The challenge is **accurate listening** and giving **accurate feedback** the other person accepts.

Look at the person and pay attention to what is being said.

The skills of attending

- Look at the person and have comfortable eye contact.

- Listen to the person's body language or nonverbal "talk:" posture, facial expression, voice tone, asking for personal space, body gestures.

- If you don't understand, ask an open question.

- Use body language to "say" you are listening: nod your head; hold your hands open to receive the message.

- Do some active sharing of your own.

The skills of inviting

- Open questions: "What are some things you are going to do today?" Avoid closed questions: "Did your day go well?" "Are you happy?"

- Open statement: "Tell me some of your feelings." This is more powerful.

The skills of giving feedback or reflecting

▶ **Restating** or mirroring what the person is saying.

▶ **Reflecting: thoughts** - "You're thinking about quitting;" **feelings** - "You seem upset;" **action** - "You went to the bar."

▶ **Confirming:** "I understand you're angry that I didn't call."

Exercise: First, each group member uses a **closed question** in inviting another member to share. What happens? Then, practice both **open questions and open statements.**

Exercise: As a group, develop a set of invitation skills. Your counselor will put them on a flipchart. Use the second part of *Worksheet 64* to write down four invitation skills to use in active listening.

Exercise: As a group, develop a set of feedback or reflection skills. Your counselor will put them on a flipchart. Use *Worksheet 64* to write down four feedback statements that work for you.

Exercise: Break into groups of three. One person practices **active sharing** by talking about a problem he/she has. Another practices **active listening.** The third person gives **feedback** on how the other two are doing with the communication skills.

SESSION ACTIVITIES AND PROCESS GROUP

1. Do *Worksheet 64.* Update your *Master Skills List* and your *MAP.* Do this week's *TAP charting.*

2. *Homework exercise:* Practice the skills of active sharing and active listening. Do a *Thinking Report* on one episode where active listening worked.

3. Use the *SSC Scale* to rate yourself as to how skilled you are in using active sharing and active listening. Compare your ratings with the ones you made on pages 100 and 104.

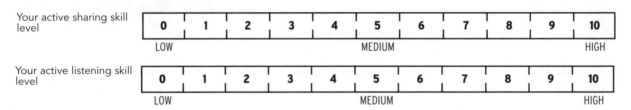

4. Use the process group to talk about whether you think the skills of active listening will help you have more positive relationships. Be honest! If you don't think they will work for you, say so!

Make a list of statements to use in active sharing and active listening communication following the examples.

MAKE A LIST OF READY-TO-GO OPENING STATEMENTS FOR ACTIVE SHARING

Example: I want to tell you what is happening today.

1.

2.

3.

4.

MAKE A LIST OF OPEN QUESTIONS AND OPEN STATEMENTS FOR ACTIVE LISTENING

Example: Tell me some things you did today.

1.

2.

3.

4.

MAKE A LIST OF FEEDBACK AND REFLECTION STATEMENTS FOR ACTIVE LISTENING

Example: Sounds like you had a good day.

1.

2.

3.

4.

SESSION 30: Starting a Difficult Conversation and Keeping It Going

SESSION INTRODUCTION AND OBJECTIVES

For some people, starting a conversation and keeping it going is difficult. Yet, these skills open doors to meeting new people, buying a car or getting a job. Sometimes people are lonely and isolated because they do not feel confident relating to others. Often, this is due to shyness or a reluctance to start talking with someone. People use drugs to loosen up.

Most people can chit-chat, "shoot the breeze." But starting a difficult conversation and keeping it going may be hard. We avoid conflict and touchy issues. A few drinks may help in approaching a sensitive issue. You can easily talk to your spouse about going to the store, but not about his getting home late. It is easy to talk with your neighbor about the weather, but not about his barking dog. This session is about starting a conversation **and** about starting a difficult conversation.

WE START by going over your homework and *Thinking Report* on active listening, sharing your *TAP Charting* and doing the *CB Map Exercise*.

OBJECTIVES OF SESSION AND KEY TERMS

➡ Review the skills of active sharing and active listening.

➡ Learn and practice the skill of starting a conversation with the goal of learning to start a difficult conversation.

➡ Key words: active listening, active sharing, set the stage, keep to the point, keep focus on you, Use "I" messages, end on positive note.

SESSION CONTENT AND FOCUS

GUIDELINES AND SKILLS FOR STARTING A CONVERSATION

▶ **Small talk is OK.** You don't have to have an "important" topic.

▶ **Talk about yourself.** Use "I" messages. When you are finished, does the other person know something about you?

▶ **Listen and observe.** Is the person open to talking?

▶ **What is of interest to the other person?** Tune into that.

▶ **Speak clearly and slowly.** Some people have a hard time hearing.

▶ **Use active listening.** You don't have to do all the talking. Encourage the other person to talk.

State what you hear the person saying. Ask: "What do I know about this person?"

- **Learn to story-tell.** It's simple. Just tell someone what happened to you on the way to work.

- **END ON A POSITIVE NOTE.** Be graceful if you end the conversation. "I have to go now, but nice talking with you."

SKILLS AND STEPS IN HANDLING A DIFFICULT CONVERSATION

This requires skillful use of active sharing and active listening. Here are the skills and steps.

Step 1: **Set the stage.** Make time for it. Don't sandwich it in between T.V. programs. Tell the person: "I need to talk with you and need some of your time."

Step 2: **Negotiate (work out) the setting and terms.** Is this just sharing or do you want to solve a problem? After you state your need, give the other person opportunity to be part of the decision of when and how. Set the terms early on. If you want to problem solve or make decisions, make that clear to begin with.

Step 3: **Keep to the point and keep the focus on you.** Share with the person what you have to say. Make the agenda yours. Use "I" messages. Avoid "you" statements. If you blame, it will only make the person defensive. If you want the person to listen, don't talk about them. Talk about yourself. Get closure on your statement. Don't go on and on.

Step 4: **Give the other person a chance to state their position and respond.** Then, state their position back to them. Use active listening skills. Converse back and forth.

Step 5: **Decide between the two of you if you want to move to problem solving.** It is probably best to keep this for another time if you did not negotiate this to begin with.

Step 6: **End on a positive note.** Be content with having made your statement and conversing about it with the other person.

<u>Exercise:</u> One or two group members will be asked to role play having a sensitive or touchy conversation with someone important in their life. Give feedback. Did they stick with the above steps?

<u>Exercise:</u> One or two group members are asked to role play talking about a sensitive issue with someone, but not use the word "you" at any time. Use only "I." This keeps you on your agenda.

<u>Exercise:</u> Break into pairs and practice starting a conversation, using the above skills.

<u>Exercise:</u> Using *Worksheet 65,* page 200, describe a conversation you started around a sensitive and difficult topic that did not turn out well. Do the right column to describe how you would do it differently to get a better outcome.

SESSION ACTIVITIES AND PROCESS GROUP

1. Do *Worksheet 65.* Update your *Master Skills List* and your *MAP.* Do this week's *TAP charting.*

2. Rate yourself as to how skilled you are in managing a conversation around a sensitive or touchy topic.

Your skill in managing a difficult conversation

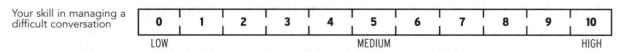

| 0 | 1 | 2 | 3 | 4 | 5 | 6 | 7 | 8 | 9 | 10 |
| LOW | | | | | MEDIUM | | | | | HIGH |

3. Use the process group to talk about relationship problems that might have come up in your mind during this session.

Difficult conversation: In the first column, describe a difficult conversation you started that did not turn out well or led to a conflict. In the second column, using the skills we have learned, write down how you would now start the conversation. What would you now say? Write down what you think the other person's response would now be and expected outcome.

WORKSHEET 65

DESCRIBE A DIFFICULT TOPIC CONVERSATION YOU STARTED THAT HAD A BAD OUTCOME	HOW WOULD YOU DO IT DIFFERENTLY, USING THE SKILLS YOU HAVE LEARNED
Describe situation and who with.	Describe situation and who with.
What did you say to start the conversation?	How would you start the conversation now and keep it going?
What was the other person's response?	Given your different approach, how do you think the other person would now respond?
What was the outcome?	What would the outcome now be?

SESSION INTRODUCTION AND OBJECTIVES

Healthy and successful relationships involve giving and receiving positive reinforcements and compliments and the sharing of positive experiences. Our chances of receiving in a relationship increase when we give. Our chances of giving increase when we receive from that relationship.

We may not share the good things we think about our friends and family members because we assume they just know we like them or care about them. Yet, we find it easier to tell other people how much we appreciate them, but may not be able to graciously accept compliments.

In a relationship damaged by criminal conduct and substance abuse, the good things in a friendship or union may get lost. Learning to express appreciation for the good times, giving kind responses, recalling positive moments, is one way to heal a damaged relationship. People whose AOD use or criminal behavior have upset others will often have negative thoughts and feelings about themselves. They find it difficult to receive positive reinforcement and support.

OBJECTIVES OF SESSION AND KEY TERMS

➠ Learn the skills involved in giving and receiving positive support and sincere compliments and praise.

➠ **Key words:** compliments, praise, positive reinforcement, be sincere, open receiver, own the compliment.

WE START THIS SESSION by doing the *CB Map Exercise* and sharing our *TAP Charting*.

SESSION CONTENT AND FOCUS

Feeling good about yourself and about how others feel about you are important as you develop the thoughts and actions that lead to self-control and more responsible living. Two skills that help us feel good about ourselves are:

▶ Giving sincere compliments and praise to others;

▶ Learning to accept praise and compliments from others.

DIFFERENCE BETWEEN PRAISE (COMPLIMENTS) AND THANKS OR APPRECIATION

The skills of giving praise or positive reinforcement are similar to those of giving thanks or gratitude. But here is how they are different.

- **Thanking someone** or giving gratitude is a response to something that someone has done for you. Using the skill of saying "thank you" is important in keeping positive relationships. "Thank you" will focus on the object or favor or the "thing" that was done for you.

- **Positive reinforcements** (praise, compliments) focus on a person's successes and accomplishments, not necessarily on what was done for you. It is easy to recognize what people do for you. It is more difficult to attend to positive behaviors that take place apart from you. This is why it is difficult to give praise.

THE SKILL OF GIVING COMPLIMENTS AND PRAISE

Giving compliments is based on **active listening.** Compliments are effective when you know about the other person. We get to know the other person when we use **open statements** and **open questions.** The actual giving of a compliment involves using the **reflection skill.** A compliment is reflecting back what you see as positive about the other person or about their actions. "I see you doing a really great job." "You really came through this time." Here are some guidelines for giving praise and compliments.

- **Be sincere** in your compliments or positive reinforcement.

- **Be brief.** What is the point you want to recognize?

- **Be specific.** Focus on a specific action or behavior. Rather than saying, "You're a good guy," it is better to be specific about the behavior that makes you think the person is a "good guy." "It was good of you to help your friend get to work."

- **Put thoughts and feelings into the praise.** Don't just state facts as you see them. "It was good of you to help your friend," but also "I felt good to see you being kind to your friend." This helps the person feel the compliment is sincere and comes from you and not only on what they did.

- **Be sensitive to the other person's personality when you give compliments and praise.** A shy person might feel better if you gave them praise when no one is around.

- **Listen to the person's response** to your praise.

THE SKILL OF RECEIVING COMPLIMENTS

This skill is based on the second skill of active sharing - receiving feedback from others about you. Here are the guidelines for receiving positive reinforcement.

- **Be an open receiver and listen to the praise.** We shut down feedback when we get defensive or push away. We sometimes do this when we receive positive reinforcement or praises. Maybe the compliment is embarrassing. Do not deny the praise. Most people find it more difficult to receive a compliment than to give one.

- **Own the compliment** and your positive behaviors. Maybe we don't want to be that responsible since this will mean we have to take responsibility for our negative behaviors. To own a compliment means we may have to take ownership of a criticism or of a correction of our behavior. We may push away a compliment because we don't think a lot of ourselves. If we have poor self-esteem, we will push away compliments. Be gracious. Say: "That makes me feel good."

▶ **Respond** to the compliment or praise. Use clear words. Even though you may not agree, thank the person. Let the person know you like what they said and that you appreciate it.

Exercise: Exchange giving and receiving praise and compliments in the group. Give a compliment to someone and then have that person give you a compliment. Your counselor will help the group in this exercise. Which is easier, giving or receiving the compliment?

Exercise: Group members role play giving compliments to family members or people close to them. Then group members role play giving a compliment to someone they have never praised or complimented but deserved it. The group will then give feedback as to how well group members did.

Exercise: Share an event where you had a chance to compliment or praise someone and you didn't. Use the STEP Method to get a positive outcome.

S SITUATION: Had chance to give a compliment but didn't.

T THINKING CHANGE: Thoughts that lead to a compliment.

E EMOTIONS: Positive feelings or outcomes.

P POSITIVE ACTION: Actions that give praise or compliment.

Giving compliments is taking positive action.

SESSION ACTIVITIES AND PROCESS GROUP

---

1. Update your *Master Skills List*, page 291, and your *MAP*, page 295. Do this week's *TAP charting*.

2. **Homework exercises:** Do *Worksheet 66,* practicing giving compliments; and *Worksheet 67,* practicing receiving compliments.

3. Rate yourself on your skill of receiving and giving compliments or praises.

Your skill level of receiving praise	0	1	2	3	4	5	6	7	8	9	10
	LOW					MEDIUM					HIGH

Your skill level of giving praise or compliments	0	1	2	3	4	5	6	7	8	9	10
	LOW					MEDIUM					HIGH

4. Use the process group to talk about difficulty you might have in receiving positive reinforcement or praise. Why is this?

Practicing giving compliments: Practice giving a compliment or praising someone this coming week and then write down what happened

BEFORE NEXT SESSION, GIVE A COMPLIMENT OR PRAISE TO A FAMILY MEMBER OR FRIEND THAT YOU APPRECIATE.

Who was the person?

What was the compliment you gave?

What specific action or behavior did you compliment?

What feelings or emotions were part of your compliment?

What was the person's response to the compliment?

Practicing receiving compliments this coming week. Write down a specific event where you received a compliment

PAY ATTENTION THIS WEEK TO WORDS OF PRAISE OR A COMPLIMENT THAT SOMEONE GAVE YOU. ANSWER THE QUESTIONS AS TO HOW YOU HANDLED THE PRAISE.

Who complimented you?

What kind of compliment did you receive?

What was the specific action the person complimented?

What feelings did you have when you were complimented?

Did you listen carefully to the praise or compliment?

Did you express your thanks for the compliment?

Did you deserve the compliment?

SESSION INTRODUCTION AND OBJECTIVES

Our most difficult problems involve other people. Problems that touch us emotionally and our core beliefs and attitudes are particularly difficult to solve. Some problems may not involve others. You misplace your car keys. You go through solving the problem to find them. But, most often, solutions do involve other people. Here is an **example.**

One of the authors of this workbook, on his return flight from Hong Kong, discovered he had left his appointment book in the hotel. **Panic:** the book had all of his appointments for the coming week. First thought: "My wife should have checked the hotel room more closely." **Thinking Error** - Blame: not her appointment book! **Problems to solve:** locate the appointment book; specific appointments and times for next week had to be identified. **Apply problem solving skills:** the hotel staff found the appointment book, faxed the appointment pages for the coming two weeks, and the book was mailed to the author. Problem solved!

We often solve problems on the spur of the moment and not see different solutions or not get the facts. We focus on the persons involved rather than the problem. We think getting high or drunk will solve the problem - or help forget it for a while. Good problem solving skills keep us from getting frustrated, angry, depressed. **Good problem solving helps us have positive outcomes in our relationship with others and our community. It is one of the keys to preventing R&R.**

OBJECTIVES OF SESSION AND KEY TERMS

⇒ Learn "what is a problem."

⇒ Learn and practice the basic steps of problem solving.

⇒ Learn how to be solution-focused.

⇒ **Key words:** steps in problem solving, think outside the box, solution-focused.

WE START THIS SESSION by doing the *CB Map Exercise* and sharing our *TAP Charting.* We then look over our homework, *Worksheets 66 and 67,* page 204, *Giving and Receiving Compliments.*

SESSION CONTENT AND FOCUS

TWO BAD WAYS OF PROBLEM SOLVING

▶ Impulsive, careless and not-thought-out rushed style.

▶ Avoiding or putting off solving the problem, or depend on others to do it for you.

Exercise: Think back to the last problem you had. Did you solve it using these two styles?

WHAT IS A PROBLEM?

A problem is an action, situation, or event that causes you difficulty: 1) Not getting your way; 2) Not sure what is expected of you; 3) Conflict over how things should be done or what actions to take; 4) A difference between your goal and the goal of others; 5) Losing something important.

How do we know we have a problem? We may feel it in our **bodies:** our heart beats faster, we sweat, have indigestion. **Emotionally:** we cry, get angry, feel anxious, depressed. **Relationships:** avoid people; people avoid you; don't feel comfortable with others or have conflict with others. **Actions:** arguing, not doing well at work. **Uneasy:** know we have a problem, but not sure what it is.

Our problems begin in our thinking. Here is an example.

Larry is on his way to an appointment with his P.O. He has missed the last three sessions. Suddenly, his car stalls. He'll never make in time. He gets sweaty. Angry. "Why does this happen to me." His first thought is his friend Tim - an old crime buddy. He spots a phone booth and calls him. Tim is there in 20 minutes, but too late to make the appointment. His friend says: "Screw 'em. He'll put you in the slammer. Time you stopped screwing around. I'm heading to L.A. tomorrow. Couple jobs we can do there. Take a ride." Larry thinks: "My P.O. will revoke. I'll go back to prison. Just as well split. But what about Susan. She's pregnant with my baby. I had good reasons for missing my last appointment. But my P.O. didn't like it. He told me I'm on the line. Yet, I've done nothing wrong."

STEPS TO PROBLEM SOLVING

Problem solving begins in our thinking. Often, we solve it in our head before it even takes place in our actions. The steps and methods to problem solving are shown in *Figure 27*.

Step 1: Define the problem. Get all the facts. Study the problem. Have you been here before? Is it similar to one you had before? Ask: "who, what, when, where, how." "A problem defined is a problem half solved."

Step 2: Set your goal or target. What do you want? What is it you don't like? What do you want the outcome to be? Close your eyes and imagine a good outcome.

Step 3: Look at different solutions or options. Brainstorm and come up with every option you can think of. They don't have to be good solutions when brainstorming, just good ideas. What action should I take? Get other people's ideas as to solutions. What gets in the way of solving the problem - the obstacles? Pick four solutions and rate them: Good, fair, poor. Pick the best of those you rated good. Always match the solution with the outcome you want. If others are involved, pick a solution that is win-win for everyone.

Step 4: Choose the solution and start action. As you work the solution, different approaches or new ideas may come up. Stop at times to see how the solution is working. Put the new ideas to work but try to stay with one you have chosen. If it is not working, start over, be flexible.

Step 5: Study the outcome. What was the result? Was it in your best interest? Did everyone gain? Could you have done something different? What will you do next time? Problem solving is a spiral. You never end up where you started. New problems come from solving the old one.

Figure 27 below shows that problem solving outcomes never bring you back to where you started. You arrive at new knowledge and possibly new problems to be solved. As you study the outcome, always ask: "Am I better off?" Was it a win-win outcome?

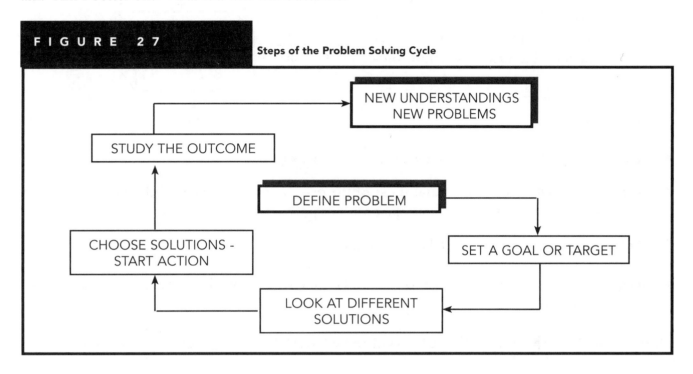

FIGURE 27 Steps of the Problem Solving Cycle

Exercise: Apply the above steps to Larry's problem. What is his best solution? What skills does he need to use to solve the problem? Could refusal skills (page 134) help?

Exercise: Use *Worksheet 68,* page 209, and work at solving a problem that you are having at this time in your life. Share results with your group.

RULES TO KEEP IN MIND

Think outside the box - look at all the choices

Think in different directions. You may always do things in a certain way. Larry usually solved his problems by "going along with his friends." But it led to prison. Change choices. It's your power. Here is how you do this.

▶ **Be mindful or aware you are making a choice: stop and think.** Don't rush into a solution, even in the simple choice of getting gas before going to

Get all the facts.

the grocery store. You choose to look at options.

▶ **Get information and brainstorm.** Details are important. It may take a few seconds but save you, days or years. "What don't I know?" "What else is causing the problem?"

▶ **Look at the outcome.** Replay the tape. Prepare for next time. We often give up making changes because the problem seems too big or you see only one solution. Think outside the box. How can Larry think outside the box?

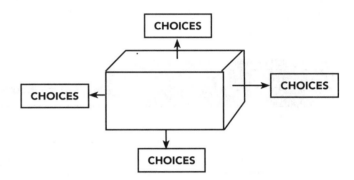

Be solution focused

▶ **Keep your thinking on the problem** and not the person.

▶ **Know your needs and interests and those of the people involved.** Don't feel pressure to take on their position. But, don't argue about the positions people take.

▶ **Pick win-win solutions** where all gain and not just you.

Exercise: Pick a problem you had that led to a bad outcome. Use the STEP Method to make it turn into a positive outcome.

S SITUATIONS → **T** THINKING CHANGE → **E** EMOTIONS → **P** POSITIVE ACTION

The STEP Method to get positive outcomes is different from the steps of problem solving described above.

SESSION ACTIVITIES AND PROCESS GROUP

---

1. Update your *Master Skills List* and your *MAP.* Do this week's *TAP charting.*

2. Complete *Worksheet 68,* Problem solving.

3. Use the SSC Scale to rate yourself on your problem solving skills.

Your problem solving skills

0	1	2	3	4	5	6	7	8	9	10
LOW					MEDIUM					HIGH

4. Use the process group to talk about problems you have in your life and how you can solve some of those problems.

Problem solving: Pick a problem that you are now having. Go through the steps below. Use these simple steps for studying and coming up with solutions to this problem.

1.   Define the problem:

2.   What is your goal?

3.   Look at different solutions - brainstorm:

4.   Pick a solution and take action - put it to work:

5.   Study the outcomes - how did it work?

SESSION INTRODUCTION AND OBJECTIVES

In other sessions we learn that we can have successful and positive relationships with others and our community through the use of effective communication and problem solving skills. These prosocial skills help build healthy and successful relationships. They help us to be responsible to others and to the community. Getting our needs met and helping others get their needs met is also an important prosocial goal. Persons with an AOD abuse and criminal conduct history often need to improve their skills on how to get their needs met in healthy and meaningful ways. They often use aggressive behavior getting needs meet. They have difficulty setting limits on what they expect from others.

We look at three different styles of relating to others that most often do not lead to positive outcomes for yourself and others. We then learn a way to relate to others that increases our chances of positive relationship outcomes. This approach is another key to preventing relapse and recidivism.

OBJECTIVES OF SESSION AND KEY TERMS

➡ Learn three ways of relating that often lead to negative or conflictive outcomes.

➡ Learn and practice the approach of being assertive.

➡ **Key words:** assertiveness, flight, fight, fake, fair.

WE START with the *CB Map Exercise* and sharing our *TAP Charting.* We review how using problem solving skills worked this week.

SESSION CONTENT AND FOCUS

REVIEWING REFUSAL SKILLS

Your counselor will review the refusal skills in *Session 17,* page 134. Refusal skills involve being assertive. Refusal skills are used to specifically prevent R&R (relapse and recidivism). Assertiveness skills go beyond this goal and work to get positive outcomes in all of our relationships.

RELATIONSHIP STYLE CHOICES THAT LEAD TO POOR OUTCOMES

We look at three ways of relating to others that usually do not lead to problem solving, do not resolve conflicts and do not fulfill your needs and the needs of others.

Flight - passive

Flight avoids problems and conflicts in relationships. **Passive persons:** 1) give up their rights when there is a conflict; 2) do not get what they want at their own expense; 3) put out more and "pay" more;

4) do not express thoughts, feelings, needs; 5) let people choose for them.

PASSIVE

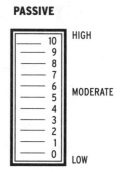

Exercise: Discuss how flight leads to criminal conduct. Rate yourself on this relationship style using the PASSIVE Scale on the right.

Fight - aggressive

Fight dominates, bullies, embarrasses and attacks others. **Aggressive persons:** 1) protect their own rights at the expense of others; 2) make other people "pay;" 3) end up losing closeness, and do not get relationship needs met; 4) violate the rights of others. **Exercise:** Rate yourself on the fight style using the AGGRESSIVE Scale on the right. Discuss how fight leads to criminal conduct.

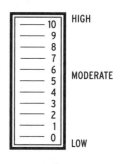

Fake - passive-aggressive

This style falls between avoiding and being aggressive. **Passive-aggressive persons:** 1) are not direct in approaching problems; 2) fail to express needs in a way that other people can respond to; 3) do not get what they want at the expense of themselves and others; 4) make people distrust; 5) prevent problem solving; 6) make everyone "pay." **Exercise:** Rate yourself on the this style of relating using the PASSIVE AGGRESSIVE Scale on the right. Discuss how fake can lead to criminal conduct.

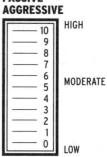

These approaches fail to give positive outcomes or results. They do not help people get their needs met in healthy ways. They drive people away. **AOD use makes people show these styles in more extreme or severe ways. Under AOD influence the aggressive person becomes more aggressive and even violent.**

What do you think about this? Criminal conduct is both passive-aggressive and aggressive behavior. Discuss this in your group.

A HEALTHY CHOICE

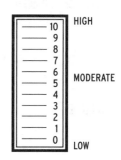

Fair - assertive

A healthy choice is being assertive. This helps you and others get their needs met. It leads to win-win outcomes. It is a way of caring. **Assertive persons:** 1) do not compromise their rights to get their needs met; 2) but, they do not get their needs met at the expense of others; 3) they do not violate the rights of others; 4) are more honest and open and direct; 5) do not make others "pay." **Exercise:** Rate yourself on the ASSERTIVE scale. Discuss how being assertive can prevent R&R.

The 10 keys to being assertive.

Check those that are easy for you. Less than five checks may mean you have a hard time being assertive. The more checks, the more assertive you are.

1) You recognize your rights without trespassing on those of others.

2) You can clearly state your opinions and what you want from others.

3) You keep in mind the needs of others as you get your own needs met.

4) You are flexible, willing to compromise, and give, yet are able to make your position clear.

5) You avoid blaming, avoid using "you" messages.

6) You state how you feel and think by using "I" and "Me" messages.

Clearly state your opinion and what you want from others.

7) You have your goals clearly in mind. You know what you want.

8) You can be part of the solution and not part of the problem.

9) You stick with your decision unless it takes away the rights of others. You don't rehash "what might have been."

10) You can confront the issue head on. You attack the problem, not the person.

SPECIFIC SKILLS IN BEING ASSERTIVE

Skill 1: **Active sharing:** Clearly state your position. Focus on your agenda. State your needs. Use "I" and "me" messages. "**I** need to not be criticized so much." "It's important to **me** to be listened to."

Skill 2: **Active listening:** Listen to the other person's response. Give the person a chance. Most important, hear the other person's needs. Use invitation and reflection skills.

Skill 3: **Make the outcome win-win.** Offer solutions that meet each side's needs. Assertiveness is about getting needs met.

Skill 4: **Keep the door open for further discussion.** Keep the options open. Our needs change. People change.

PRACTICE WHAT YOU HAVE LEARNED

<u>Exercise:</u> Role play the following examples using all four methods to solve the problem: **Avoiding - FLIGHT; aggressive - FIGHT; passive-aggressive - FAKE; and assertive - FAIR.** When using the assertive approach, keep in mind the 10 ways of being assertive. After each method, decide if the goals of the person were met.

▶ **Example:** It is important to you to take Friday afternoon off to attend your son's football game. You have no vacation time. The football game is two weeks away. Work is busy and the boss is not giving time away easy. Group members are asked to role play each of the four ways to handle the problem.

▶ **Example:** Your boss promised you a bonus for working the weekend. The extra money did not appear on your paycheck. The goal is to get the bonus without offending the boss.

▶ **Example:** An old friend calls and wants to borrow money so he can purchase some drugs that he can sell at a very high profit.

Exercise: Read the case of Larry on page 206 of *Session 32.* Members of the group will be asked to role play Larry and Tim, with Larry using all of the four styles of relating to Tim.

Exercise: Use the STEP METHOD to help Larry take part in positive actions and get a good outcome.

S SITUATION → **T** THINKING CHANGE → **E** EMOTIONS → **P** POSITIVE ACTION

SESSION ACTIVITIES AND PROCESS GROUP

1. Update your *Master Skills List.* Look at your *MP, Program Guide 2,* page 292. If you rated yourself high on AOD use to cope with social discomfort and relationships, you need assertiveness training. Update your *MAP,* page 295, based on this need. Do this week's *TAP charting.*

2. Homework: Do a *Thinking Report* on a situation this week in which you could have been assertive but you were not. Then do a *Re-thinking Report* to make it a good outcome.

3. Use the *SSC Scale* to rate yourself on assertiveness skills.

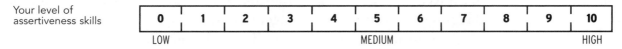

Your level of assertiveness skills: 0 1 2 3 4 5 6 7 8 9 10 — LOW ... MEDIUM ... HIGH

4. Use the process group to talk about what are the situations in which you have a hard time being assertive.

SESSION INTRODUCTION AND OBJECTIVES

Session 27 looks at what triggers anger, and skills to manage anger. In this session we work at understanding and developing skills to prevent destructive relationships anger. *SSC Sessions 27, 34 and 38* present only the basic knowledge and skills in managing anger and preventing nonphysical and physical abuse and violence. Some participants will need or be required to complete more extended treatment in this area.

> ### OBJECTIVES OF SESSION AND KEY TERMS
>
> ➡ Understand the different kinds of anger and the basis of anger in relationships.
>
> ➡ Learn skills to manage and regulate anger and criticism in relationships.
>
> ➡ Understand and manage the guilt-anger cycle.
>
> ➡ **Key terms:** hostility, anger, aggression, violence, the guilt-anger cycle.

GETTING STARTED. This is an important session for you if your *Master Profile* ratings were high on: AOD use to cope with emotional discomfort and relationships; violent and aggressive criminal conduct; behavioral disruption from use; and angry thinking.

SESSION CONTENT AND FOCUS

Managing and regulating anger is a big part of keeping your freedom and preventing relapse and backsliding into criminal behavior. Most criminal conduct clients have problems with anger control. For many, their offense was directly related to anger problems, such as domestic violence. Our focus in this session is on learning prosocial ways to handle anger in relationships. All of the skills we learn in *Session 27* to manage relationship anger we now review. The skills and ideas in this session apply to all relationships.

Exercise: Check all relationships you have that this session on anger will apply to.

❐ My child ❐ Parent or parents ❐ Boss/employer
❐ Friend ❐ Spouse or intimate partner ❐ Other_____

HOSTILITY, ANGER, AGGRESSION, ABUSE AND VIOLENCE

Hostility: an attitude that gets expressed when we experience a harmful action towards us or towards important values and ideas we hold. Hostility is a way of orienting yourself to the outside world. It comes from within: anger and violence are reactions to outside events. But, hostility can feed anger and violence.

Anger: A thought and a feeling. Anger is described in *Session 27*. When anger is directed towards harming or injuring another living being, then it is aggression. Failure to control your anger will lead to aggressive behavior. **Exercise:** Use the work space below and describe yourself when you are angry. How do you act? What is your behavior? Draw your face when you are angry at someone.

DESCRIBE YOURSELF WHEN YOU ARE ANGRY	DRAW YOUR FACE WHEN ANGRY

Nonphysical abuse and aggression: verbal and nonverbal behavior that abuses, attacks, controls, provokes, injures or hurts someone emotionally or psychologically. Non-physical abuse and aggression end up in violence unless controlled and dealt with in a positive manner. We look at this abuse in *Session 38*.

Physical abuse - violence: aggression that becomes physical. Violence does everything that non-physical abuse and aggression do, but it causes physical harm and damage to things and people. We look at abuse and violence in *Session 38*.

Anger that expresses itself in non-physical or physical abuse is not acceptable and must not occur in any relationship.

WHAT CAUSES ANGER IN RELATIONSHIPS?

Relationship conflicts are high-charged events. They lead to anger or are caused by anger. This anger is based on:

▶ not having your expectations met; perception of your needs being blocked or not getting what you want from others;

▶ not being understood, approved of or accepted;

▶ feeling powerless;

▶ extreme rigid thinking, not being able to change your mind - "I'm right, he's/she's wrong";

▶ blaming and attacking the person's personality; name-calling.

SKILLS IN MANAGING RELATIONSHIP ANGER

First, look at the skills of managing and regulating anger outlined in *Session 27,* page 184. Here are the key ones: **1) Mental control skills; 2) Stress management and relaxation skills; and 3) Assertiveness skills.** We now outline the specific strategies and skills to manage relationship anger.

Skill 1: **Know what relationship issues trigger anger.** Know the thoughts that come from those triggers. **Exercise:** Use *Worksheet 69,* page 219, to list relationship triggers and angry thoughts that come from those triggers (columns 1 and 2).

Skill 2: **Use relationship communication skills** to manage and control anger. **1) Active sharing and active listening. 2) Attack the problem, not the person. 3) Express your anger, not act it out; 4) Own your anger. 5) Use it to move towards a solution. 6) Communicate your needs. 7) Listen and hear the other person's position. 8) Imagine positive outcomes.** **Exercise:** Use *Worksheet 69,* column 3 to list relationship skills to handle the triggers and angry thinking.

Skill 3: **"Hear" what the relationship is saying.** It needs to be nurtured and to be heard. It has one goal: to survive, even at the expense of the individuals in the relationship. We look at this in *Session 35.*

Skill 4: **Know when you have reached a dead end.** The clues? 1) There is verbal attack and blame. 2) Can't let go. 3) One follows the other around the house. 4) Both dwell on not being understood, not getting needs met. 5) When the focus is on win-lose, right-wrong. Unless stopped, the outcome is more anger and even violence.

Skill 5: **Use a time-out plan when reaching a dead end.** Make it a part of your relationship agreements. This is not walking away. The purpose is to get to a solution. Don't paint yourself into a corner. Give the other person space. If you reached a "dead end," take responsibility to "step out" of the fight. Here are parts of this plan: 1) **one person** has the right to call off the conflict; 2) **always** keep a physical distance; 3) **know** what you will do in a time-out, such as, going for a walk, visiting a friend; 4) **agree** to go back and try to resolve the conflict when both are cooled off. If time-out doesn't work, use an escape plan. We look at this in *Session 38.*

Skill 6: **Problem solve together.** Ask each other, What is the problem? Look for win-win; state the other's position.

Skill 7: **Begin repairing and fixing during and right after an angry episode.** The basis is **forgiveness.** In the middle of the conflict, imagine a positive outcome: see the two of you going for a walk and holding hands. Reward each other when you have come to a win-win.

A key cause of relationship anger is not getting what you want or expect. **Exercise:** Role play what you want from someone close to you. Be specific. "I want to go bowling." "I want to feel close."

MANAGING CRITICISM

Being critical and criticizing is a part of close relationships. But, they are triggers for anger. We want to avoid criticism, get defensive, deny it is true, make excuses or fight back. Here are some skills for handling criticism.

▶ **Understand what the other person is saying.** Use active listening skills. Reflect back what you heard. Then, sort out what is accurate to you.

▶ **Confirm or support the part you agree with.**

▶ **If you see you need to change, say so.** "I'll work on that." Apologize if necessary. Admit to mistakes.

▶ **If you don't agree,** politely say so, but be firm about it.

▶ **See criticism as a way to improve** your relationship.

<u>Exercise:</u> Role play a situation where someone close to you criticized you and you didn't handle it well. Then use the STEP Method to replay the event to get to a positive action and outcome.

S SITUATIONS → **T** THINKING CHANGE → **E** EMOTIONS → **P** POSITIVE ACTION

THE GUILT-ANGER CYCLE

The guilt-anger cycle, *Figure 28,* page 218, starts when anger builds up. Together, they form a cycle that can be destructive unless stopped. The cycle applies to any relationship and can be triggered by drug use or depression. We use alcohol and an intimate-partner relationship to show the cycle.

You have a conflict with your partner and store up feelings and emotions and push them down inside. You have several drinks and unload your anger, become aggressive and abusive. You go the bar and stay out all night. The next day, she/he is angry and gives you the silent treatment or blows up. You feel depressed and guilty and accept the punishment - even abuse. When your guilt wears off, your anger builds. Your partner senses you are getting angry. Her/his anger turns to guilt. Now you are angry and think: "I've been punished enough." But you don't express it. Those around you are afraid of causing you to drink again. Everything is shoved "under the rug." Tensions build, there's another conflict, you drink and the cycle starts again. Getting involved in criminal conduct adds more intensity to the emotions. Repeating this cycle over and over may lead to a state of depression and violence.

<u>Exercise:</u> Share with the group how you fit the anger-guilt cycle.

What keeps the cycle going? Continue AOD use to express stored emotions. Being passive or passive-aggressive. Losing control over your anger and guilt by being aggressive and hostile. Feeling guilt and shame or denying appropriate guilt, preventing you from seeing right from wrong.

What breaks the cycle? By using the self-control skills, page 160, the relaxation skills in page 180 and the anger management skills, page 184. Your counselor will review those skills. Here are some additional strategies or ways to break the cycle.

1. **Stop or control the thinking and behavior that triggers the cycle.** Don't use alcohol or other drugs. Never get into a conflict when drinking or using other drugs.

2. **Be aware when emotions build and your moods change.** Tune into your self-talk. **Anger:** "they deserve that;" "she's a b...;" "he's an s.o.b.;" **Depression:** "what's the use;" "I don't care." **Guilt:** "I'm a failure." These are thinking errors (page 35) that can cause emotions to build up.

FIGURE 28   **The Guilt-Anger Cycle**

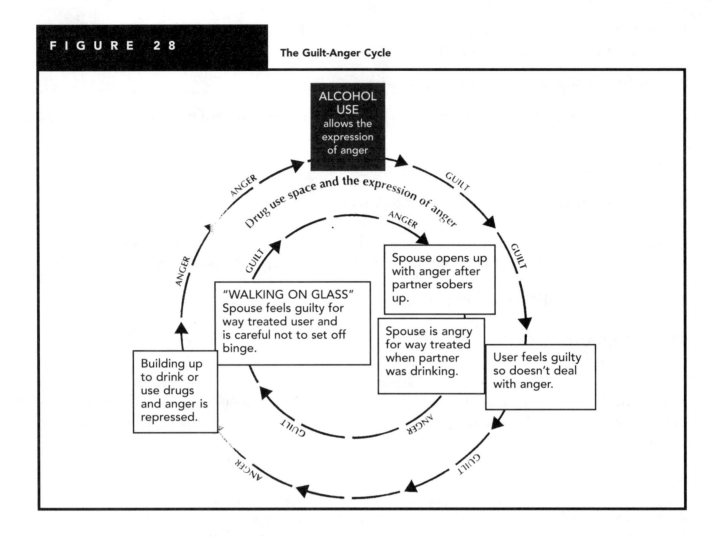

3. **If you sense the feelings first, back into the thoughts.** In angry events, automatic thoughts happen quickly. Many people fail to recognize their angry thoughts and just "blow up." As soon as you feel angry, ask, "what are my thoughts?" Then, "how can I express those thoughts and feelings?"

4. **Express your angry and guilty thoughts and feelings in a safe way.** BUT, NOT WHEN YOU ARE ON DRUGS. Don't act them out.

5. **Use all the mental control and communication skills you learn** to manage your anger and guilt, including relaxation skills.

6. **Work at repairing the relationship.** Being AOD and crime-free is 90 percent of the repair. Be gentle, kind, caring.

Work at repairing the relationship.

SESSION ACTIVITIES AND PROCESS GROUP

1. Do *Worksheet 69.*

2. Update your *Master Skills List,* page 291. Look at your MP, *Program Guide 2,* page 292. Update your *MAP* based on what you have learned about your anger. Do this week's *TAP charting,* page 300.

3. Use the *SSC Scale* to rate yourself on your level of skill in managing your anger in relationships.

Your skills in managing your anger in relationships

0	1	2	3	4	5	6	7	8	9	10
LOW					MEDIUM					HIGH

4. Use the process group to talk about the areas of anger you are struggling with.

WORKSHEET 69

List relationship triggers that set off angry thoughts and feelings: Write down angry thoughts or beliefs that come from those triggers. Then, put some relationship skills you can use to manage relationship anger.

RELATIONSHIP TRIGGERS	ANGRY THOUGHTS/BELIEFS	RELATIONSHIP SKILLS

SESSION INTRODUCTION AND OBJECTIVES

Conflict in our close and intimate relationships and loneliness are big triggers for relapse and recidivism. People who are lonely and who have relationship problems often seek "a second family" in drug using or criminal associates. The purpose of this session is to learn skills in developing and keeping close relationships. Part of good communication between people in intimate relationships is to deal openly with sexual problems or issues. You may want to deal with this in a separate session with your counselor and your intimate partner. If possible, bring your "significant other," spouse, roommate or intimate partner to this session.

OBJECTIVES OF SESSION AND KEY TERMS

➠ Look at ways to improve closeness in our intimate partner relationship.

➠ Understand the conflict between our need for closeness and separateness.

➠ Learn skills that keep a healthy balance between closeness and separateness in our intimate partner relationships.

➠ **Key words:** enmeshment, separateness, relationship balance.

WE START by introducing our significant other guests, doing the *CB Map Exercise* and updating your *MAP*.

SESSION CONTENT AND FOCUS

CONFLICT BETWEEN NEED FOR CLOSENESS AND NEED FOR SEPARATENESS

We have a powerful need to be part of people, **to belong,** to share with others, to be close to someone. We also have a powerful need to be ourselves, **to be separate,** different and unique. Society places more value on closeness. We are led to believe that closeness is what makes us OK. Think about the words to most popular songs. "I can't live without you," "You're my whole life," "Without you I'm nothing." But, what about separateness? How often do you hear: "Leave me alone and I'll love you forever," "I'd rather sleep alone tonight." Frank Sinatra's song: "I Did It My Way," says this. Being ourselves and separate is very important. How can we be ourselves, separate and individual, and still be close to another person?

DEFINING OUR BASIC NEEDS

A famous psychologist, Abraham Maslow, concluded that people have five basic needs.

1. **Physical needs:** food, air, sleep, elimination and water.

2. **Safety Needs:** protection from danger and threat.

3. **Social Needs:** friendship, acceptance, love.

4. **Esteem Needs:** self-confidence, self-respect, to be important.

5. **Self-Actualization Needs:** to fulfill our talents and to bring out the best from within ourselves.

This list again tells us about the two important needs: 1) to be loved and close to people, and 2) to be an individual with self-esteem, self-importance and to develop the best within ourselves.

UNDERSTANDING RELATIONSHIP

A relationship is like a person. It thinks, feels, acts. It has needs and wants. It fights to survive. It can give wonderful things to people. It can also control, dominate, crush the individual. When couples get angry or aggressive in relationships, they are not only trying to hurt the other person; they are striking out at the control of the relationship. **Exercise:** Group members will be asked to share a recent conversation with their intimate partner or someone close. From that sharing, have the group figure out what the relationship was thinking, feeling, doing. This is very hard to do. Your counselor will help you.

THE STAGES OF CHANGE OF A RELATIONSHIP

Healthy intimacy and closeness means keeping a balance between the needs of the relationship and the separateness needs of the persons in that relationship. Here are the stages that most relationships go through to get to a balance.

▶ **First stage, enmeshment:** being "swallowed up." Our need for closeness is so great that we allow relationships to swallow us up and we become enmeshed. First, we hold our relationship responsible for our OKness - the beginning of enmeshment. Then we hold the other person and the relationship responsible for our not-OKness. That deepens the enmeshment. One day we find we have lost our separateness, our individuality. We can't go fishing, read the paper, or have lunch with a friend without the other person (the relationship) saying, "where are you going?" The relationship is in control. This stage is represented by the **first set of circles** in *Figure 29,* page 223. We seek relief from the **control of enmeshment** through work, sports, community events. Or, we drink with friends, at the bar or alone to get relief. The eventual result is the second stage.

▶ **Second Stage, detachment:** "throwing up" the relationship. Your separateness is threatened. You feel stressed and controlled. You seek a temporary "divorce" by drinking or being with friends to get separateness. **The bar becomes your second home.** You can be "yourself" there. No pressures. You get drunk and say "screw the relationship." It works until you sober up and find you are just as enmeshed. You may seek a permanent separation; or counseling to try to develop a better balance between total enmeshment and separateness. You might go through several relationships. Each time you get enmeshed. Each time you seek separateness. The **second set of circles** in *Figure 29* shows this separateness - where energy is directed only at oneself. However, this kind of relationship will not allow closeness or meet intimacy needs.

▶ **Third stage: balanced or synthesis.** The **third set of circles** in *Figure 29* shows a balance; there is separateness and there is closeness. Closeness means we give up a part of ourselves. We "can't always have it my way." There is a "we" as well as an "I" and "you" in all healthy relationships.

We have a need to be loved and to be ourselves.

TEN TIPS FOR KEEPING A HEALTHY CLOSENESS

1. **Be proactive and active.** Put energy into the relationship. Make things happen. Do your share of planning activities.

2. **Let your partner be proactive and active.** Respect and support your partner's effort to energize the relationship.

3. **Interact rather than react to what your partner does.** Use active listing and active sharing to interact. When you react, you make your partner responsible rather than taking responsibility.

4. **Keep a balance between closeness and separateness.** Be OK even when your partner is not OK. When you are not OK, let your partner be OK. Each safeguards the self and the relationship.

5. **Always work for a win-win when working on settling conflicts.** Keep the focus on the problem, not on the other person. State the other person's side. Talk about yourself, not the other person. Use "I" messages, not "you" messages. After a conflict is resolved, be sure that each of you is better off.

6. **Help the other person be successful and celebrate that success.**

7. **Combine strengths for the good of each other and the relationship.** Be proud of and profit from the other person's achievements. What attracted you to each other was the strength of your differences.

8. **Don't let things build up between you.** Tell your partner what bothers you. Don't expect your partner to read your mind, to know what you want or feel or think.

9. **Keep your relationship fresh and romantic.** Take trips, go to different places, have fun. Keep up the romance. Remember, romance brought you together. See physical and sexual intimacy as more than having sex. Take part in healthy play - to move freely in space together.

10. **Give and receive compliments and praise.** Show that you appreciate the other person. Make the positive outweigh the negative. Otherwise, it will be a negative relationship. All parts of the relationship are better when there are positive expressions. It is true for sexual intimacy. Sexual intimacy occurs when there are positive feelings between the couple.

KEEPING THE BALANCE

Communication skills are keys to building and keeping a healthy relationship balance: active sharing; active listening; starting conversations, giving and receiving compliments and problem solving.

Exercise: Using *Worksheet 70,* page 224, draw your relationship with your intimate partner or spouse like those in *Figure 29.* How would your "significant other" draw the relationship? If you feel comfortable doing so, discuss your findings with that person (if your significant other is present) and with the group.

Exercise: Do *Worksheet 71,* looking at your closeness and separateness needs. If present, have your intimate partner do the *Worksheet.*

Exercise: If your significant other is present in the session, practice the skills of active sharing and active listening. Have one do the active sharing and the other do the active listening. Change roles. If you do not have a significant other present, have someone play the role of that significant other.

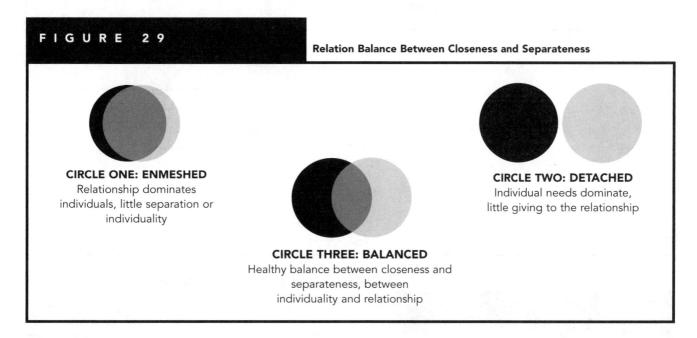

FIGURE 29

Relation Balance Between Closeness and Separateness

CIRCLE ONE: ENMESHED
Relationship dominates individuals, little separation or individuality

CIRCLE THREE: BALANCED
Healthy balance between closeness and separateness, between individuality and relationship

CIRCLE TWO: DETACHED
Individual needs dominate, little giving to the relationship

SESSION ACTIVITIES AND PROCESS GROUP

1. Do *Worksheets 70 and 71.* Update your *Master Skills List.* Update your *MAP* based on what you have learned about your intimate relationships. Do this week's *TAP charting.*

2. Use the *SSC Scale* to rate yourself on skills to build and keep a healthy intimate relationship.

Your skills in keeping a healthy close relationship	0	1	2	3	4	5	6	7	8	9	10
	LOW					MEDIUM					HIGH

3. Use the process group to talk about your needs for closeness and your needs for separateness.

The relationship with your significant other or intimate partner. Draw the relationship you and your intimate partner have. If you are not in an intimate relationship, pick someone you are close to in your life.

A. DRAW CIRCLES HERE:

B. REFLECT ON:

1. What do you think about what you see?

_____

_____

2. Why are things like they are?

_____

_____

3. How would you like the relationship? Draw another set of circles below if you want a different balance between closeness and separateness.

Looking at your closeness and separateness needs. In column one, write those things that represent intimacy and closeness (for example, going to movies together). Then list those things that you do separate from the relationship that keep your own sense of self and identity.

MAKE A LIST OF YOUR MOST IMPORTANT CLOSENESS NEEDS	MAKE A LIST OF YOUR MOST IMPORTANT SEPARATENESS NEEDS

MODULE 10

Skills for Social and Community Responsibility

Criminal conduct is antisocial behavior - actions that go against society and the community. The most important goal of *SSC* is to prevent backsliding into criminal conduct and live in harmony with your community. We reach this goal through prosocial attitudes and behaviors and moral reasoning that lead to responsible living. Part of this prevention process is to strengthen your character and prosocial behaviors. Understanding and preventing both nonphysical and physical abuse and aggression are important steps to responsible living. A prosocial lifestyle hinges on having empathy and understanding of others, on knowing how to resolve conflicts in a positive way, and on giving to the good of the community. Being a responsible and careful driver are important parts of being prosocial. Finally, preventing relapse is one key that locks out recidivism.

We use the *STEP* method that focuses on the positive change process of the CB Map:
S SITUATIONS → **T** THINKING CHANGE → **E** EMOTIONS → **P** POSITIVE ACTION AND OUTCOMES. Here are the goals of this module.

▶ Understand your past procriminal and antisocial attitudes and behaviors.

▶ Know the meaning of empathy and put it to work in your life.

▶ Understand the different kinds of aggression and learn skills to prevent non-physical and physical aggression and abuse.

▶ Know how to resolve conflicts for positive outcomes for others and your community.

▶ Improve attitudes and skills that increase driving with CARE.

▶ Know how to add to the good of your community and society.

Module 10 has six sessions.

Session 36: Strengthen Character and Prosocial Attitudes and Behavior
Session 37: Understanding and Practicing Empathy
Session 38: Understanding Aggression, Abuse and Violence
Session 39: Preventing Aggression, Abuse and Violence
Session 40: Settling Conflict and Getting to a Win-Win
Session 41: Values and Morals for Responsible Living: The Moral Dilemma
Session 42: Giving to the Community and Driving with CARE

SESSION 36: Strengthening Character and Prosocial Attitudes and Behaviors

SESSION INTRODUCTION AND OBJECTIVES

Throughout SSC, we have worked on building moral character and prosocial values through changing our thinking for both positive emotional and action outcomes. Positive emotional outcomes strengthen our prosocial thinking and actions. These are keys to preventing recidivism. In this session we focus on strengthening our moral character and prosocial values with the goal of developing responsible attitudes and behaviors in our community.

OBJECTIVES OF SESSION AND KEY TERMS

➡ Review the work we did on antisocial and prosocial thinking and behavior in Sessions 9 and 10.

➡ Look at ways to strengthen our moral character and prosocial attitudes and behaviors.

➡ **Key terms:** antisocial, prosocial, strengthening character.

WE START THIS SESSION with the *CB Map Exercise,* using a situation involving a positive experience with our intimate partner or someone close to us. We share our *TAP Charting* for the week.

SESSION CONTENT AND FOCUS

REVIEW OF CRIMINAL THINKING AND CONDUCT

Your counselor will review the most important parts of *Sessions 9 and 10.* **Exercise:** Redo *Worksheet 24,* page 87, your past and present risk for criminal conduct. Score your new answers. Your past risk score should be the same. Did your score change on your present risk? If *SSC* is working, your score should be lower.

Your counselor will review the *Criminal Conduct Cycle* in *Session 10, Figure 14,* page 90. **Exercise:** Go back over *Worksheet 26,* page 93, your own criminal conduct cycle. Add or make changes to the work you did in that worksheet.

UNDERSTANDING ANTISOCIAL, MORAL CHARACTER AND PROSOCIAL

One important goal of *SSC* is to change antisocial thinking to prosocial thinking and attitudes.

1. **Antisocial.** Involves disregarding and violating the rights of others, doing harm to others and going against the rules of laws and society. **Exercise:** Redo *Worksheet 23,* page 86. Put a different mark for your new answers. Rescore your test. Are your scores lower? Remember, scores above 20 to 25 mean high risk for antisocial behaviors unless you change your thinking and actions. For each of the antisocial behaviors and attitudes, identify an emotion that goes with it.

3. **Moral character.** This is the moral and ethical features of a person. It is our thinking and feeling sense of what is right and wrong and the strength to stick by what we see as right. Our conscience is the basis of our moral character and the basis of being prosocial and morally responsible.

2. **Prosocial.** Is respecting the rights of others, complying with the norms, rules and laws of society and living in harmony with the community. Prosocial also includes: having positive regard for and caring about the welfare and safety of others; and contributing to the good of society. **Exercise:** Redo *Worksheet 27,* page 94, your *Prosocial Strengths.* Put a different mark for your new answers. Score the answers you gave the first time. "Not a Strength" = 0; "Somewhat a Strength" = 1; and "Definitely a Strength" = 2. Score the answers you gave the second time. Is your second score higher? **For each prosocial strength, identify a feeling that goes with that strength.**

Exercise: Group members give a situation that leads to the antisocial behavior or attitudes in *Worksheet 23,* page 86. Use the *STEP Method* to change thinking and get a positive emotion and action outcome. **Example:** No. 1: Impulsive, fail to plan ahead.

S **SITUATION:** Never have enough money for rent at end of month.

T **THINKING CHANGE:** I'll put first paycheck away for rent, and go without some things for the first week of the month.

E **EMOTION:** Feels good the first week, and will feel better when I stick by my plan - nice not to have to worry at end of month.

P **POSITIVE ACTION AND OUTCOME:** Pay rent on time; no hassle from landlord.

TEN WAYS TO STRENGTHENING MORAL CHARACTER AND PROSOCIAL BEHAVIOR

1. **Change thinking errors** that lead to antisocial actions. **Exercise:** Use the *STEP Method* to change the thinking errors on *Worksheet 25,* page 92, to thoughts that lead to positive feelings and actions. First, think of a situation that can lead to each of the thinking errors.

2. **Developing empathy** or understanding the position of others - how they think and how they feel. Active listening is a key to developing empathy. We work on empathy in *Session 37.*

3. **Understand you are part of society. When you hurt society, you hurt yourself.** When you commit a crime, it costs you, your children, spouse, parents. You "slip on your own spills."

4. **Think how your AOD abuse and criminal conduct affect other people.** This is part of empathy. Or even simple things, like throwing a pop can out the window or a cigarette butt on the street. You become more prosocial and build character when you change these actions.

5. **You are a role model,** whether you model good or bad behavior. People watch and copy you - your children, your friends.

6. **Think of yourself as important.** Increase your self-esteem.

7. **Be part of the solution** and not part of society's problem.

8. **Think of yourself as a CARETAKER** of your community, your society, the earth.

9. **Do something each day that shows respect, consideration and kindness.** Hold the door open for someone; let people change lanes in front of you; thank people for their service; pick up trash on the street; give someone a smile.

10. **Give to your community.** Give time to a charity, a church, an agency that serves people. That is the topic in *Session 42.*

Understand that you are part of society.

Exercise: Read again the story of John, page 32. Apply the above approaches to help John make different choices, prevent backsliding into criminal conduct, and strengthen his character.

Exercise: Read again the story of Larry on page 206. How could Larry use the above ways and strategies to change his antisocial thinking to prosocial thinking and actions?

SESSION ACTIVITIES AND PROCESS GROUP

1. Update your *Master Skills List,* page 291, and *MAP,* page 295, based on what you have learned about the antisocial and prosocial parts of your character. Do this week's *TAP charting.*

2. Use the *SSC Scale* to rate your ability to use the above ways and skills to strengthen your moral and prosocial character.

Ability to use skills to strengthen your prosocial character.

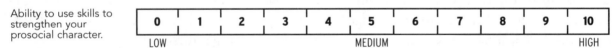

0	1	2	3	4	5	6	7	8	9	10
LOW					MEDIUM					HIGH

3. In your process group, talk about the strengths and weaknesses of your moral character. Take some risks and be as honest as you can in this area. Share the changes you have made in becoming more prosocial.

SESSION INTRODUCTION AND OBJECTIVES

Empathy is basic to the concern for the safety and welfare of others. It is an important part of moral character, prosocial behavior and responsibile living. This topic is important because AOD abuse and criminal conduct blocks us from putting ourselves in the place of others and hurts others. Preventing relapse and recidivism is having empathy for others and society.

> ### OBJECTIVES OF SESSION AND KEY TERMS
>
> ➡ Understand the difference between sympathy and empathy.
>
> ➡ Learn to consider the position of others - practice empathy.
>
> ➡ Understand how empathy is the basis of prosocial behavior.
>
> ➡ **Key words:** sympathy, empathy, "walking in another's shoes."

WE START THIS SESSION with the *CB Map Exercise,* using a situation involving a prosocial act. We also share our *TAP Charting.*

SESSION CONTENT AND FOCUS

SYMPATHY

Both sympathy and empathy help us care about others. But they are different. Sympathy is an emotional response to something outside of ourselves. It is feeling sorry for another living being. It is having awareness, compassion, and feeling the pain or hurt of another person. It does not have to involve the knowledge of the other person's pain. **Sympathy is "your pain, my heart." Sympathy takes place after the fact - after you see someone's hurt and pain.**

EMPATHY

Empathy **feels and knows** the other person's pain. It is **"your pain, my heart and head."** It is putting yourself in the place of another person, particularly people we may have hurt or who have been victims of our actions. Empathy understands another person's thoughts, feelings and beliefs. **It is "walking in the shoes" of the other person.**

Empathy takes place before the fact, before someone is in pain. It understands the pain another person **can** have. It prevents harmful actions. It is seeing a child and imagine the child being struck by a car and in a hospital suffering. Here are the empathy skills.

Skill 1: Center on the person: Look, listen, understand.

Skill 2: Think and imagine being in that person's place.

Skill 3: Accept - don't judge or blame.

Skill 4: Reflect or state the other person's position, to yourself or to that person.

Skill 5: Listen back to your own and the other person's response. How correct was your empathy?

PRACTICING EMPATHY

Exercise: *Worksheet 72* gives four stories telling about something that happened to another person. Put yourself in that person's place. Note what the other person is thinking and feeling.

Exercise: In small groups, use newspaper stories to practice making empathy statements about the persons in the stories.

Empathy is one of the most important values we can learn.

Exercise: Using *Worksheet 73,* list four people who were affected by your AOD abuse and four people affected by your antisocial behavior and criminal conduct. Put how they were affected and their response. **Don't put names,** only who they represent, such as child, father, a victim of your crime.

Exercise: You are asked to take the role of one of the persons you put on *Worksheet 73.* Another group member will be you. As that person on your list, tell the person playing you how that person was affected by your AOD abuse or criminal conduct. Get in touch with that person's feelings and thoughts. You will then change roles and you be you and the other group member be the person on *Worksheet 73.* Respond to that person's feelings and thoughts. This is a difficult exercise. If you do not feel comfortable doing this, that's ok.

SESSION ACTIVITIES AND PROCESS GROUP

---

1. Do *Worksheets 72 and 73.* Update your *Master Skills List.* On your MP, put an EM by those rating scales that require empathy to change. Do you need to add to your MAP based on what you learned in this session? Do this week's *TAP charting.*

2. Use the *SSC Scale* to rate yourself on your skills of having empathy.

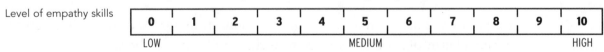

Level of empathy skills

0	1	2	3	4	5	6	7	8	9	10
LOW					MEDIUM					HIGH

3. In your process group, talk about the strengths and weaknesses of your moral character. Take some risks and be as honest as you can.

Practicing empathy. Read each brief story. Close your eyes and put yourself in the place of the person in the story. What is the person thinking? Feeling? Then write the thoughts and feelings you had when you put yourself in the place of the other person.

BELOW ARE FOUR STORIES. EACH STORY IS ABOUT A PARTICULAR INDIVIDUAL WHO HAS EXPERIENCED SOMETHING OF GREAT IMPORTANCE IN HIS OR HER LIFE. READ EACH STORY CAREFULLY.	PUT YOURSELF IN THE PLACE OF THE PERSON IN THE STORY. THEN WRITE DOWN WHAT YOU THINK THE OTHER PERSON WAS THINKING AND FEELING.
John is nine years old. He was hit by a car and was in the hospital for two months. He lost his right leg in the accident. He loved baseball, was a very good player and was feeling a great deal of sadness because he knew he would never play baseball again.	
Marie, who is 45 years old, struggled all of her life to make a living and support her family of four children. Her husband died just after the youngest was born. She works as a cook in a high school. Her oldest son is very smart and will be finishing high school this year. He wants to be a doctor, but Marie knows she does not and never will have the money to send him to college. The other day her son came home and told her that he received a full four year scholarship to attend college.	
Hank, age 30, a house framer and carpenter, was leaving work when a robber hit him on the head and stole his car. The robber then drove over Hank when getting away. Hank has been in the hospital for two months. He has severe spinal injuries and will have to be in rehab for many months, and he may never walk again.	
Karen is 48, has six children and does not work out of the house. Her husband drives a city bus. Yesterday she bought a lottery ticket. She and her husband checked the numbers today and found that they won a million dollars.	

Persons affected by your AOD abuse and your criminal conduct.
Don't put their names but only who they represent, such as child, spouse, father, victim.

PERSONS AFFECTED BY YOUR ALCOHOL AND OTHER DRUG ABUSE BEHAVIOR

Persons affected	How were they affected?	What was their response?

PERSONS AFFECTED BY YOUR PAST ANTISOCIAL AND CRIMINAL CONDUCT

Persons affected	How were they affected?	What was their response?

SESSION 38: Understanding Aggression, Abuse and Violence

SESSION INTRODUCTION AND OBJECTIVES

Abuse and violence are antisocial behaviors that begin with angry thinking. The goal of this session is to promote prosocial and peaceful involvement with others and your community through a better understanding of abuse and violence. In *Session 39,* we learn skills to prevent aggressive and violent behavior. **The rule: Nonphysical or physical abuse is not acceptable and must not occur in any relationship or situation.** They are an attack on people and on society.

OBJECTIVES OF SESSION AND KEY TERMS

➠ Understand the different kinds of nonphysical and physical abuse.

➠ Understand the cycle of violence.

➠ **Key terms:** nonphysical abuse and aggression, physical abuse or violence, power and control, cycle of violence, arousal.

WE START WITH the *CB Map Exercise.* We then review the important ideas and skills of *Sessions 27,* page 184, *and 34,* page 215, to manage and regulate anger.

SESSION CONTENT AND FOCUS

Most persons with a history of criminal conduct (CC) do not engage in a physically violent lifestyle. Yet many persons with a CC history have been involved in some form of abuse or violence.

NONPHYSICAL AGGRESSION AND ABUSE

This is verbal and nonverbal behavior that attacks, controls or hurts others emotionally, psychologically or sexually. It damages the self-esteem of others, causing lasting injury. It can be calculated or impulsive, controlled or uncontrolled. There are several kinds of nonphysical abuse.

Emotional abuse harms the feelings and sense of self of others. It includes: isolating; controlling; insults; being critical; having affairs; blaming; drinking and doing drugs; going through belongings; putting down; forcing others into certain actions; entitling self because of being a man or a woman.

Verbal abuse is the use of words, voice or tone to control or harm others. It includes: name calling, sarcasm, blaming, threatening, accusing, insulting.

Nonphysical sexual abuse is the nonphysical abuse and control of sexual relationships. It includes: refusing to use birth control; verbally forcing sexual fantasies; having affairs; becoming angry and demanding when denied sex.

PHYSICAL AGGRESSION AND ABUSE - VIOLENCE

Non-person physical abuse and violence: Aggression involving smashing and breaking objects of others or society. This violence is usually about someone or in relationship to others and society.

Person physical abuse and violence involves contact between two or more persons resulting in physical hurt. That hurt may not show physical signs, but involves physical contact. Legally, it includes the threat to harm others and includes forms of nonphysical contact abuse such as blocking someone's path; taking objects from another person; clenching or shaking fist; getting nose to nose. Physical contact abuse includes: hitting, slapping, grabbing, shoving, pushing, kicking, choking, scratching, punching, pulling hair, hitting with objects, physical force.

Physical sexual abuse is the physical control of sexual relationships to meet the abuser's personal needs. It includes: rape and any forced physical sexual contact.

ABUSE AND VIOLENCE FOCUS ON:

▶ the **position of strength or power of others** - the victims have the strength and power to get in the way of the violent person's needs or goals and the violent person is initially weak;

▶ the **position of weakness of others** - this is when the victims are weak and the violent person has to maintain a position of strength;

▶ the **position of sex** - victims are a target of the violent person's distorted sexual drives.

THE PARTS OF ABUSE AND VIOLENCE

▶ **Power and control over another person or persons.** Conflict starts when others resist control. When control slips, anger becomes the way to get control. "I'm in charge." The abuser puts other people down, blames.

▶ **Power and control over the relationship or relationships.** Violence tries to destroy the controlling relationship. The relationship is the victim. That is why abusers and victims get into another abusive relationship after getting out of one. They never solve the problem of being controlled by relationship. Developing skills to promote a healthy relationship (*Sessions 34 and 35*) is one key to preventing violence.

▶ **There is the victim and perpetrator or abuser. But remember, society is also the victim.**

REALTIONSHIP CYCLE OF VIOLENCE - LIKE THE GUILT-ANGER CYCLE, PAGE 218

Stage 1: **Build-up stage: tension, stress, anger, guilt builds.** Abuser is moody, blames, gets sullen, yells, uses drugs. Victim tries to calm, protect people, reasons, supports.

Stage 2: **Release or explosion stage:** Includes nonphysical and physical abuse. Abuser hits, yells, gets verbally abusive, gets violent; Victim tries to protect self, family, calls police, leaves, fights back.

Stage 3: **Calm, quiet, guilt stage:** The abuser is apologetic, makes up, wants to make love, promises won't happen again, tries to undo what has happen. Victim is angry, has mixed feelings of hope and despair. The cycles get closer together and more abusive, particularly when the abuser justifies the violence, feels less guilty.

JEALOUSY

Based on not having what others have, or losing what someone can give you, such as affection; when someone else gets your partner's attention more than you do. Jealousy leads to power and control. I'll control her/him. Being dependent will feed jealousy.

Sexual jealousy is most powerful. Sexual intimacy is a special connection, a blending together, and boundaries dissolve. Since loss is an important part of jealousy, losing sexual intimacy is a powerful stimulant for jealousy and resentment.

Jealousy is also a positive emotion. It helps keep commitments; contributes to the bond, the closeness. But when it becomes controlling, it becomes destructive.

<u>Exercise:</u> Group does a *Thinking Report* on an event of jealousy.

AROUSAL

Arousal is anger starting to wind-up. We may need to deal with the arousal first, and then back into the thoughts. In *Session 27* we learn signs that indicate anger such as flushed face, heart beats fast, sweating, agitated, fly off the handle. Managing anger when it builds is the key to preventing aggression. We look at the skills for arousal control in *Session 39*.

SELF-ASSESSMENT OF ABUSE AND VIOLENCE

This part of the session may be difficult. **Share only what you feel comfortable sharing.**

The profile for abuse and violence

Check each of the 10 items that applies to you. The more checks you have, the higher your risk for being involved in uncontrolled anger and abuse. Six or more checks is high risk.

- ❏ Overly dependent on partner
- ❏ Low self-esteem, do not think a lot of self
- ❏ Unable to express self in words
- ❏ In relationship where you feel dominated or controlled
- ❏ Angry at society for how you think you have been mistreated
- ❏ Have a history of exploding or losing temper
- ❏ Open up with anger when you drink or use substances
- ❏ Do not feel in control of self
- ❏ Have a history of hitting or striking out physically
- ❏ Prior arrest for domestic violence, assault, harming others

Describing anger, abuse and aggression you have witnessed

Exercise: On *Worksheet 74*, you are asked to give one episode of nonphysical abuse and aggression and one episode of physical abuse and aggression **you have witnessed or seen.** Describe the episode in a few words. Give what the victim was feeling and thinking.

SESSION ACTIVITIES AND PROCESS GROUP

---

1. Do *Worksheets 74.* Update your *Master Skills List* and MAP based on what you have learned about your intimate relationships. Do this week's *TAP charting.*

2. Use the *SSC Scale* to rate yourself on your understanding of nonphysical and physical abuse and violence.

Your understanding of abuse and violence.

0	1	2	3	4	5	6	7	8	9	10
LOW					MEDIUM					HIGH

3. In your process group, take some risks and share some of your past involvement in abusive and violent behaviors. It may be reporting being in a fight.

WORKSHEET 74	Describe episodes of abuse and violence you have seen
EPISODE OF NONPHYSICAL ABUSE/AGGRESSION	WHAT VICTIM THOUGHT AND FELT
EPISODE OF NONPHYSICAL ABUSE/AGGRESSION	WHAT VICTIM THOUGHT AND FELT

SESSION INTRODUCTION AND OBJECTIVES

Session 38 gives an understanding of aggression, abuse and violence. In this session, we look at how to prevent abuse and violence. The basis of violence is uncontrolled anger. Our goal is not only to prevent violence but to develop beliefs and skills that lead to a prosocial and peaceful relationship with others and the community.

OBJECTIVES OF SESSION AND KEY TERMS

➡ Learn skills to prevent abuse and violence and to have peaceful relationships.

➡ **Key terms:** time out, escape plan, jealousy control, arousal control, anger and aggression journal.

WE START WITH the *CB Map Exercise.* We then review the important ideas of *Session 38.*

SESSION CONTENT AND FOCUS

SKILLS IN PREVENTING VIOLENCE

Approaches that don't work: Stuffing the anger and rage; or stepping up the anger by blaming or seeing the cause outside of you. **Self-talk** is probably the most powerful method of preventing abuse and violence. In addition to the skills in *Session 27,* page 184, and *Session 34,* page 215, in managing anger, here are some skills that can be used to prevent abuse and violence. These skills can be used to prevent violence with people in the community or in a close relationship.

❯ **Time out.** The guidelines are in *Skill 5,* page 216.

❯ **Escape plan:** Sometimes, walking away is the solution. It is always better than staying in a dead end situation that will result in a violent outcome. It is effective if you and the other person agree ahead of time that this is best when you reach a deadlock. Don't spend time mulling over the interaction, but quickly remove yourself from an explosive situation.

❯ **Think trust rather than distrust.** Focus on the parts of the relationship that give you proof of trust. Rather than focus on your partner getting home 20 minutes late, focus on the times she/he was home when expected. Trust builds gradually.

❯ **Focus on the relationship.** You can change the relationship easier than you can change each other. **Rather than think:** "It's her/his fault." Think: "There's a problem in the relationship. We can change that."

❯ **Take responsibility for your own actions, not those of the other person.** This is owning your behavior, a big step to change. The only area you have the power to change is yourself.

▶ **See the strengths in the other person and relationship.**

▶ **Always think:** "When we have sex, is it always 100 percent shared." This works towards a positive sexual relationship. Always think, "I don't own her/him. She/he is her/his own person.

▶ **See relationship as a partnership.** This means working at **becoming cooperative and not controlling.** This means being a partner in all areas that are important to both of you: money and finances, sex, children, leisure time, taking trips, staying clean and sober, being prosocial.

▶ **Always think:** "There is always an alternative to nonphysical and physical aggression." **And, "Do I want to keep my freedom?"**

RULES AND GUIDELINES TO PREVENTING AGGRESSION AND VIOLENCE

Rule 1: Abuse and violence are never justified.

Rule 2: Abuse and violence start with angry thinking.

Rule 3: Preventing violence means changing thoughts and beliefs.

Rule 4: We can only be in control of ourselves, no one else.

Rule 5: Both partners are equal in the relationship.

When we get high, we blow up or hurt others emotionally or physically.

Rule 6: There are always signs of anger that causes violence.

Rule 7: You can always use the time-out rule.

Rule 8: Abuse and violence can **always** be prevented.

JEALOUSY CONTROL AND GETTING TO HARMONY

Review what we learned about jealousy in *Session 38,* page 235. Jealousy is anger based on not having what other people have such as your partner's affection and love. Jealousy is often based on loss. Managing jealousy is done through the *SSC* self-control and relationship skills. Here are some specific skills to handle Jealousy and getting to harmony.

▶ **Confront the jealousy,** not the other person, and share it with your partner.

▶ **Under stress, you are more apt to be jealous.** Use self-talk: "I'm tired tonight. My thoughts are not rational. I'll look at my feelings tomorrow."

▶ **Know the other person is separate and unique.** You don't own her/him. Your partner is her/his own person. You have ownership in the relationship, but you don't own your partner.

▶ **Use the self-control and relationship skills** that help you control anger and jealousy.

▶ **Confront your insecurity,** change the insecure thoughts. If your dependency on your partner is threatened, you get more insecure. Make your security more independent of your partner.

ANGER AROUSAL CONTROL AND GETTING TO HARMONY

When anger is aroused or starts to build, apply the self-control skills. We review the basic skills.

▶ **Relaxation skills** of deep breathing, calming breaths, calm scenes, tensing and relaxing muscles.

▶ **Calming self-talk:** acknowledge the feelings of anger. In your head, rate your anger on the *Anger Scale.* Where are you? A 10, a 6, a 1? Use the *thought-stopping skill* to stop arousing anger.

▶ **Change your angry thoughts.** You may feel arousal first. **Back into your thoughts.** "What's making me so angry? How rational are my thoughts? Is she really out with another guy?" Use thoughts that end up in positive action. Calmly walk away. Announce you need time out.

▶ **Look at the bad results:** jail, hurting someone, having an accident, losing your freedom.

Exercise: Role play starting to get angry with someone in the community such as a neighbor or store clerk. Use the above skills to prevent a violent situation.

ANGER JOURNAL

The first step to prevention is being aware. **Exercise:** Do *Worksheet 75, Anger and Aggression Journal.* Each day, track your angry thoughts, anger level, control skills and outcome **over the next two weeks.** List some angry thoughts you had during the day. If no angry thoughts, put NONE. Rate the level of anger from zero to 10. What skills did you use to manage the anger and prevent it from leading to aggression? Note if the outcome was positive or negative. If the skills worked, then you will put a plus (+). If the outcome was bad, put a minus (-). Our goal is to have harmony with others.

SESSION ACTIVITIES AND PROCESS GROUP

1. Do *Worksheet 75.* Update your *Master Skills List,* page 291. Update your *MAP,* page 295, based on what you have learned about your anger, aggression, violence. Do this week's *TAP charting.*

2. Use the *SSC Scale* to rate your skill level in preventing aggression, abuse and violence.

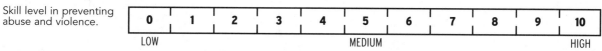

Skill level in preventing abuse and violence.

0	1	2	3	4	5	6	7	8	9	10
LOW					MEDIUM					HIGH

3. Talk about how successful you are in managing your anger and preventing abuse and violence.

Anger and Aggression Journal

DATE	ANGRY THOUGHTS	ANGER LEVEL	SKILL USED	OUTCOME

SESSION INTRODUCTION AND OBJECTIVES

The social and interpersonal skills we learn help us have better outcomes in our relationships and to be responsible members of the community. In this session we look at some important ideas and skills for settling conflicts. This helps us in our relationship with others and with the community. Persons with a history of AOD problems and criminal conduct are less apt to relapse or backslide if they master skills to settle conflicts and manage stress.

OBJECTIVES OF SESSION AND KEY TERMS

➡ Learn that resolving conflicts contributes to positive relationships with others and with the community.

➡ Learn guidelines to settle conflicts.

➡ Learn how to achieve a win-win solution.

➡ **Key words:** conflict resolution, win-win solutions, negotiation, knowing what you can and cannot change.

WE START THIS SESSION going over your *Anger Journal*. If this is your first session in *Phase II*, your counselor will help you start your *Anger Journal*. We also share our *TAP Charting*.

SESSION CONTENT AND FOCUS

It is almost impossible to live without conflict. You may find yourself in conflict because of the changes you have made in SSC. Standing up for what you believe makes you a better person but it can put you in conflict. Conflict leads to stress. It can test your goal of living in harmony with others and the community.

WIN-WIN OUTCOMES

Most conflicts are solved by someone being right and someone being wrong. The most common way people settle disputes is through the adversarial approach - or **going to court.** *SSC* takes the **win-win approach** of settling conflicts so that you and others feel good about the outcome. This gives you self-control.

WHAT IS INVOLVED IN SETTLING CONFLICTS OR PROBLEM SOLVING?

▶ The **makeup** or the situation and persons involved.

▶ The **idea** or what it is about.

▶ The **give and take** or what happens among those involved. Positive give and take leads to positive outcomes.

GUIDELINES FOR WORKING OUT A CONFLICT

▶ **Work to a win-win** outcome: Solving conflicts does not require someone being wrong and someone being right.

▶ **There is usually no one truth.** We hold our own truths. We see the world from our own point of view.

▶ **Two people can both be partly right and partly wrong.**

▶ **Be part of the solution,** not part of the problem.

▶ **Focus on the problem,** not the person.

▶ **Use the assertive or FAIR approach.** Avoid: FIGHT - being aggressive only increases the conflict; FLIGHT - run away and nothing is solved; FAKE - you go along with the other person but then do what you want and things are left up in the air.

SKILLS FOR GETTING A WIN-WIN OUTCOME

Here are skills that lead to win-win and positive outcomes. Everyone gains. No one loses.

Skill 1. STATE-ASK: Tell the other persons your position, thoughts, feelings, sharing your story; hear the other persons' thoughts, feelings, goals and ideas.

Skill 2. LISTEN-REFLECT: Understand their position and then reflect or state their position or what you hear them saying. Be open-minded. Listen to feedback.

Skill 3. COMPARE-CONTRAST: State why you think your solution is best and give evidence. Find out why the other persons think their solution is best and ask for evidence. Compare the solutions. Decide what you agree on and put that aside.

Skill 4. OFFER-COMPROMISE: Decide what you disagree on. Decide what you can give up and still feel you have won. The other side decides the same. Be flexible. Offer a solution or answer. Listen to the other persons' offer. Discuss the offers or options.

Skill 5. CHOOSE-AGREE: Decide what is best for both sides. Do both sides feel they have won enough? In most cases, the conflict is settled.

<u>Exercise:</u> Do *Worksheet 76.* Describe a conflict you had in which you practice skills outlined above.

AN APPROACH FOR SETTLING CONFLICTS

Dr. Reinhold Niebuhr wrote a prayer that has become known as the serenity prayer of Alcoholics Anonymous.

God, grant me the serenity to accept the things I cannot change,
Courage to change the things I can,
And the wisdom to know the difference.

Clearly understand each conflict that you may be a part of. Ask yourself the question: can I change the situation or negotiate a settlement? Or, is it simply impossible to change what exists? If you decide that change and settlement are possible, then negotiate with strength and courage. If you truly see that change is not possible and there is no hope for negotiation, then accept what is with serenity and patience. But most important - use your wisdom and intelligence to know the difference.

SESSION ACTIVITIES AND PROCESS GROUP

1. Do *Worksheet 76.* Update your *Master Skills List.* Do this week's *TAP charting.*

2. Use the *SSC Scale* to rate yourself on skills to settle conflicts.

Level of skills to settle conflicts	0	1	2	3	4	5	6	7	8	9	10
	LOW					MEDIUM					HIGH

3. In your process group, share some of the biggest conflicts you have had in your life.

WORKSHEET 76	**Settling conflict skills: Working for a win-win outcome.** Describe a conflict you had recently. Apply the skills and the following steps.

1. STATE-ASK: What was your position? The other person's position?
2. LISTEN-REFLECT: What did you hear and reflect back to the other person?
3. COMPARE-CONTRAST: What did you agree on? What did you disagree on?
4. OFFER-COMPROMISE: What did you offer? What did the other person offer?
5. CHOOSE-AGREE: What was the solution or outcome? Was it win-win?

SESSION INTRODUCTION AND OBJECTIVES

Our values and morals determine how we relate to ourselves, others and our community. Values and morals are two of the most important pieces of our beliefs and attitudes. In this session we look deeper into values and morals.

OBJECTIVES OF SESSION AND KEY TERMS

➡ Understand the values that SSC is based on.

➡ Work on identifying your values, morals and community norms that lead to prosocial behavior.

➡ Understand and resolve the value and moral dilemma.

➡ **Key words:** *SSC* values, personal values, personal morals, community norms, the moral and value dilemma.

WE START THIS SESSION with sharing your *Anger Journal.* This is the last week for doing your journal. We also share our *TAP Charting.*

SESSION CONTENT AND FOCUS

VALUES WE HAVE STRESSED IN SSC

▶ **The value of change:** Where are you now as to making changes that will prevent relapse and recidivism and that support responsible living? Are you still being challenged to change? Are you committed to preventing relapse and recidivism? Do you have ownership of the changes you have made? **Exercise:** Rerate yourself on the stages of change in the area of AOD use, *Worksheet 46,* page 143, and criminal thinking and conduct, *Worksheet 47,* page 144. Share with the group how you have changed.

▶ **The value of freedom:** Many of the skills that we have learned will help keep your freedom.

▶ **The value of self-control over your thoughts, feelings and actions.**

▶ **The value of being prosocial** - building positive relationships with others and your community.

WHAT GUIDES RESPONSIBLE AND PROSOCIAL BEHAVIOR?

When you respect the rights of others and follow the rules and laws of society and live in harmony with your community, you are being **prosocial.** When you violate the rights of others and go against the rules and laws of society, you are being **antisocial.** There are three kinds of values that guide prosocial thinking and behavior.

▶ **Personal values:** Something that is worthwhile, means a lot, and is important to us; guiding principles of life. For example: family, freedom, work. **Exercise:** Use *Work Sheet 77* to list your most important personal values. Check "yes" or "no" as to whether your AOD abuse and criminal conduct go against these personal values.

▶ **Personal Morals:** Has to do with what is right or wrong **for you;** what you expect to live by; it is what you think is good or correct. **Exercise:** Use *Work Sheet 78* to list your most important personal morals. Check "yes" or "no" as to whether your AOD abuse and your criminal conduct go against these morals.

▶ **Community moral norms or standards of conduct:** These are the rules that our community or society expects us to live by. **Exercise:** Do *Work Sheet 79*. Make a list of what you see as the important moral norms or standards of conduct of your community. Check "yes" or "no" as to whether your AOD abuse and your criminal conduct go against these value and morals.

THE VALUE OR MORAL DILEMMA

The value and moral dilemma put you in conflict with a value or moral that you hold and a value, rule or expectation placed on you by another person, a group or society. It could be two moral beliefs that are in conflict with each other. When you resolve the value and moral dilemma so that you stay in harmony with yourself and society, you are being prosocial. Some examples of value and moral dilemmas.

▶ **You value being loyal to friends.** A close friend wants you to hold on to his drugs while he spends 60 days in county jail. But you have made a commitment to go straight and not break the law.

▶ **Your boss wants you to work the weekend.** You value family and it's when your son has the most important game of the season.

▶ **You have a moral value that you don't lend money to anyone.** But a close friend desperately needs some money to pay his rent.

Exercise: Share with the group a moral dilemma you have faced this past month. How did you resolve it?

Exercise: A security guard patrolling the grounds of a hospital came across a man lying on the ground with a gunshot wound in his chest, was bleeding heavily, and unconscious. He had to have immediate medical attention. The guard ran into the hospital emergency room, where the only people he saw were a mother and a child who appeared to have a broken arm. He was able to find a nurse. The nurse said she could not leave the emergency room. "This man will die if you don't help him," the guard insisted. The nurse pointed to a sign on the wall that said "HOSPITAL EMPLOYEES MAY NOT LEAVE THE BUILDING WHEN ON DUTY."

Dilemma: Should she stay on duty or go help the wounded man? If you were the nurse, what would you do? Discuss the dilemma.

SESSION ACTIVITIES AND PROCESS GROUP

1. Do *Worksheets 77 through 79.* Update your *Master Skills List.* Do this week's *TAP charting.*

2. Use the *SSC Scale* to rate yourself on skills to handle moral dilemmas in your life.

Level of skills to handle moral dilemmas	0	1	2	3	4	5	6	7	8	9	10
	LOW					MEDIUM					HIGH

3. **Homework:** Do a *Thinking Report* on a moral or value dilemma you face this coming week. Remember the parts: Situation, Thoughts, Beliefs, Emotions and Outcome.

4. In your process group, share some of moral dilemmas that you think you will face in the coming months.

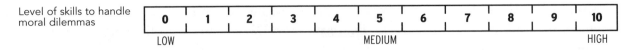

WORKSHEET 77	**List your most important personal values.** Then check whether your AOD abuse and criminal conduct have gone against these values.			
LIST YOUR MOST IMPORTANT PERSONAL VALUES	DOES YOUR AOD USE GO AGAINST THESE VALUES?		DOES YOUR CRIMINAL CONDUCT GO AGAINST THESE VALUES?	
	YES	**NO**	**YES**	**NO**

List your most important personal morals. Then check whether your AOD use or abuse and your criminal conduct have gone against these.

LIST YOUR MOST IMPORTANT PERSONAL MORALS	DOES YOUR AOD ABUSE GO AGAINST THESE MORALS?		DOES YOUR CRIMINAL CONDUCT GO AGAINST THESE MORALS?	
	YES	**NO**	**YES**	**NO**

List the most important moral norms and standards of your community. Then check whether your AOD use or abuse and your criminal conduct have gone against these.

LIST IMPORTANT NORMS AND STANDARDS OF CONDUCT THAT PEOPLE SHOULD FOLLOW IN YOUR COMMUNITY.	DOES YOUR AOD USE GO AGAINST THESE NORMS AND STANDARDS?		DOES YOUR CRIMINAL CONDUCT GO AGAINST THESE NORMS AND STANDARDS?	
	YES	**NO**	**YES**	**NO**

SESSION INTRODUCTION AND OBJECTIVES

Prosocial behavior and moral responsibility involve more than respecting the rights of others and following the rules and laws of society. They are also about contributing to the good and welfare of the community and society, and caring about the safety and welfare of others.

OBJECTIVES OF SESSION AND KEY TERMS

➡ Gain knowledge and skills in giving to the good of society.

➡ See that driving with care is an important way to show concern for the safety and welfare of others.

➡ **Key words:** reaching out, giving to community, road risk, road hazard, driving with care.

WE START THIS SESSION by doing the *STEP Method* around an experience that a group member had this past week that had a bad outcome. Review the moral dilemma *Thinking Report* homework. Share your *TAP Charting* for this week.

SESSION CONTENT AND FOCUS

REACHING OUT AND GIVING TO THE COMMUNITY

There is an old saying: "leave a place better than you found it." Ask yourself: "Will the world be better or worse off because of me?" Prosocial behavior is about making the world a better place to live.

Substance abuse, antisocial behavior and criminal conduct take energy, resources and time from society. *SSC* challenges you to give back to society and to commit to improving not only yourself, but the community in which you live, to reach out and help others.

Here are some ways to give to the good of your community.

▶ **Engage people in a positive and constructive way each day.** Contribute to their positive well-being rather than increase their stress. Share a smile each day.

▶ **Make your surroundings a better place.** It is more than not littering. It is picking up litter left by others. Have pride in your community. Take care of your own belongings and property. This is the "face" you present to the community.

▶ **Set aside time for spiritual growth,** searching for deeper meaning in your life, and connecting with values that go beyond your own needs.

- **Join a group whose purpose is to help people grow and change,** such as Alcoholics Anonymous, Cocaine Anonymous, a church or a spiritual growth group.

- **Think about giving time to a service group:** a homeless shelter, animal shelter, "adopt a highway" group, nursing home, hospital or school. You may not be ready for this or want to. That's OK. **Exercise:** Discuss with your group the problems you might run into by offering to volunteer with a community agency group because you have a judicial record.

Exercise: Using *Worksheet 80,* page 250, make a list of activities you would like to do and groups you would like to attend and join that reach out and help others or give to the good of society.

CARING ABOUT THE WELFARE AND SAFETY OF OTHERS - DRIVING WITH CARE

There are many ways to care for the safety and welfare of others. One important way is to **drive with CARE.** You put yourself and others at more risk driving than in any other activity in your life. Over 40,000 people die each year in auto crashes at a cost of over 125 billion dollars a year. More people are killed every six years driving motor vehicles than were killed in all of the four major wars this country has fought. You have a 1 in 3 chance of being in a serious accident during your lifetime.

Impaired driving is antisocial.

We do not intend to give you a course in driving safety. But here are the basics.

- **Driving is a privilege.** Yet, it is neither simple nor easy. The most dangerous activity we take part in is driving a car.

- **Careful driving requires top sensory and motor skills.**

- **Alcohol and other drugs impair or block these skills,** even in small amounts. Impaired driving is antisocial behavior.

- **Careful driving involves a positive attitude.** Angry driving attitudes are the most dangerous and contribute to road rage.

- **Defensive driving** uses all of the skills of SAFE driving and DEFENDS AGAINST CARELESS AND IRRESPONSIBLE DRIVERS.

- **It is your thoughts** that lead to either safe or dangerous driving.

- **Risk taking** or taking chances when driving is a dangerous driving habit.

- **You become a road hazard when you take risks.** You are a danger to yourself and others. Rate your level of driving risk and being a road hazard.

  ❏ Low   ❏ Moderate   ❏ High   ❏ Very high

WHEN YOU DRIVE WITH CARE YOU WILL FEEL PRIDE AND POWER. IT IS THE POWER OF SELF-CONTROL. IT IS THE PRIDE OF CARING.

Exercise: Use *Worksheet 81* to describe the driving skills, habits and attitudes that you think you should improve or change in order to be a more careful and responsible driver. Be honest. It is for your use only.

Exercise: Complete the Driving Assessment Survey (*DAS*) and score it in class. Plot your profile, *Worksheet 82.* You are comparing yourself with 395 impaired driving offenders. Are you high on POWER, HAZARD, IMPULSE, STRESS? You may fit one or even all of the patterns. What kind of risk taker are you? If your GENRISK score is higher than 12 (50th percentile or higher), you are bordering the at-risk level. If your GENRISK is from 16 to 22, you are in the moderate to high risk range. If your GENRISK is higher than 22, you are definitely high at-risk. You might even be a ROAD HAZARD.

SESSION ACTIVITIES AND PROCESS GROUP

1. Do *Worksheets 81 through 83.* Update your *Master Skills List,* page 291. Do this week's *TAP charting.*

2. Use the *SSC Scale* to rate yourself on your desire to give to the good of community.

Level of your desire to give to the good of your community.	**0**	**1**	**2**	**3**	**4**	**5**	**6**	**7**	**8**	**9**	**10**
	LOW					MEDIUM					HIGH

3. In your process group, share concerns you might have in giving to the good of society and volunteering your time with a helping agency.

WORKSHEET 80	Make a list of activities you would like to do and groups you would like to attend or join that reach out and help others or give to the good of society

ACTIVITIES YOU WANT TO DO OR GROUPS TO JOIN OR ATTEND THAT HELP OTHERS
1.
2.
3.
4.
5.
6.
7.
8.

List driving skills, habits and attitudes you need to improve or change.

LIST DRIVING **SKILLS** YOU THINK YOU SHOULD IMPROVE:

LIST SOME DRIVING **HABITS** YOU THINK YOU SHOULD CHANGE:

LIST SOME DRIVING **ATTITUDES** YOU THINK YOU SHOULD CHANGE:

W O R K S H E E T   8 2

Driving Assessment Profile

SCALE NAME	RAW SCORE	Low			Low-medium			High-medium		High		NUMBER IN NORM SAMPLE
		1	2	3	4	5	6	7	8	9	10	
1. POWER			0		1	2		3	4	5	6 7 8 9 19	392
2. HAZARD		0	1	2	3	4	5	6	7	8 9 10 11	13 21	393
3. IMPULSE		0	1	2	3	4		5	6	7 8	9 10 18	393
4. STRESS		0	1	2	3	4		5	6	7 8	9 11 15	395
5. RELAX		0 1	2	3	4		5	6	7 8	9	10 15	395
5. REBEL		0	1		2		3		4	5 6	7 8 17	393
6. CONVIVIAL		0 1 2	3	4	5		6	7	8	9	10 11 12 22	395
7. GENRISK		0 1 2 3	4 5	6 7	8 9	10 11	12 13	14 15	16 17 18	19 21 22	23 27 42	385

DECILE RANK

```
0        10        20        30        40        50        60        70        80        90        100
                                      PERCENTILE
```

NORMATIVE GROUP
The normative group is made up of 395 individuals who were being assessed by the district court probation department after being convicted of an alcohol-related driving offense.

SUMMARY OF DRIVING ASSESSMENT SURVEY SCALES

Scale 1: POWER measures the extent to which the driver experiences power when driving, e.g., feel powerful behind the wheel, feeling powerful when driving at high speeds.

Scale 2: HAZARD measures the degree to which an individual takes part in hazardous or high-risk driving behavior such as beating a red light, driving fast, outrunning others.

Scale 3: IMPULSE measures the driver who is impatient and impulsive, e.g., honks horn, swears at other drivers, loses temper, etc.

Scale 4: STRESS measures the driver who, when under stress or is upset, tends to have accidents, pays less attention to driving, is less cautious, gets annoyed.

Scale 5: RELAX indicates that a driver uses driving as means of relaxing, e.g., forgets pressure, blows off steam, calms down when driving.

Scale 6: REBEL measures the driver who feels rebellious towards authority, who breaks the rules, gets into fights, etc.

Scale 7: CONVIVIAL measures a pattern of attending drinking parties, drinks at bars, attends "keggers" and drinks with people away from home.

Scale 8: GENRISK is a general or broad measure of high risk driving behavior. It is composed only of driving-related measures.

PHASE II CLOSURE: LOOKING FORWARD TO PHASE III - OWNERSHIP OF CHANGE

You have completed the *Phase II* leg of your journey through *Strategies for Self-Improvement and Change: Pathways to Responsible Living.* You worked hard in *Phase II.* You learned and changed a lot. Again, you have come to a fork in the road. The question: do you want to continue into *Phase III of SSC?*

Again, you may be saying, "I've done all I can. I'm OK, I'll stop here." Some of you may have to continue because that is the condition of your probation, parole or sentencing. We still want you to take an honest look at how open you are to continuing in *SSC.*

You do your closing moments in your last *Phase II SSC* group. You will also have a review session with your counselor. We ask you to share these thoughts.

▶ The progress and important changes you made so far.

▶ The problems and issues that you still need to work on.

▶ The most important ideas and skills you learned?

▶ Share your thoughts about continuing into *Phase III.*

The group will give you feedback as to how they have seen you change, and the strengths they see in you.

Using the questionnaires and surveys you and your counselor filled out during Phase II, you will meet with your counselor to get feedback on your progress and change.

If this is your last session, and you choose not to go on into *Phase III,* or you are unable to do so, you are asked to read the *Program Closure Session* on page 290.

Now, we want you to rate yourself on what stage you see yourself in as to your stage of change in your AOD use patterns and in your criminal conduct and thinking.

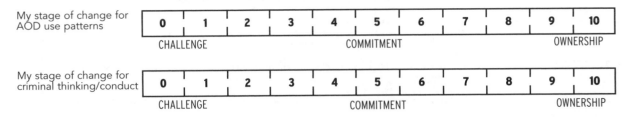

My stage of change for AOD use patterns

0	1	2	3	4	5	6	7	8	9	10
CHALLENGE					COMMITMENT					OWNERSHIP

My stage of change for criminal thinking/conduct

0	1	2	3	4	5	6	7	8	9	10
CHALLENGE					COMMITMENT					OWNERSHIP

YOUR DECISION? WILL YOU COMMIT YOURSELF TO PHASE III - OWNERSHIP OF CHANGE?

We are all related. -LAKOTA BELIEF

PHASE III
ownership of change

Taking Ownership of Change: Lifestyle Balance and Healthy Living

Happiness and moral duty are inseparably connected.
-GEORGE WASHINGTON

Phase I challenged you to change. The **challenge** was self-disclosure - telling your thoughts, beliefs, emotions and behaviors. The challenge was building self-control skills for responsible living. You met this challenge by finishing *Phase I*. You worked hard and gave time and energy to preventing relapse and recidivism.

Phase II is your **commitment** to change your thinking, attitudes and beliefs which lead to drug abuse and to criminal conduct. It involved building and strengthening skills to continue on the path of self-correction and responsible living. *Phase II* includes 22 sessions that focus on specific knowledge and skills to increase self-control and positive outcomes in your relationship with others and with the community.

Phase III is about taking **ownership** of change. It is strengthening your relapse and recidivism prevention skills and establishing a pattern of healthy and happy living that supports your living free of criminal conduct and AOD problems. It is made up eight sessions that build on your life management skills for a balanced and healthy lifestyle.

The *Phase III Orientation Session* is done in a small group or in an individual session. Some programs merge *Phase II and III* into one program. Most programs, however, will have separate groups for both *Phase II* and *Phase III*.

There are two modules in *Phase III*.

Module 11: Relapse and Recidivism Prevention: Strategies for a Balanced Lifestyle

Module 12: Strengthening Ownership of Change: Skills for a Healthy Lifestyle

Looking Back at Phase I and II

Your counselor reviews the work we did in *Phase I and II*. This includes a review of the goals of *SSC*, the *CB Map Exercise*, the *STEP Method* for positive outcomes, and the four *Program Guides*. You go over the skills you worked on by reviewing your *Master Skills List*. You again rate yourself on the *SSC Scales* at the end of each *Phase II* session. Your counselor will walk you through these, giving you the page numbers.

Overlook of Phase III

Congratulations on starting *Phase III: Ownership of Change*. You have shown a commitment to change, to responsible living and to continue a lifestyle free of AOD problems and criminal conduct. You learned the skills and attitudes for self-control, building close and caring relationships, and living in peace and harmony with your community. *Ownership of Change* means using the knowledge and skills to maintain a positive and healthy lifestyle and a sense of purpose throughout the life span. Ownership means you maintain these changes because you want to, not because you have to. *Phase III* is about strengthening positive actions that lead to positive outcomes. It gives you time to think back on the changes you own, and how these changes help you live a positive, meaningful and fulfilling life.

Goals and Objectives of Phase III

Taking ownership of change means having a firm grip on preventing relapse and recidivism (R&R). You take another look at your own pathways to R&R and the prevention skills your are using. Part of preventing R&R is doing critical reasoning and doing your own thinking so that your own values and morals guide your behavior. *Module 11* works on strengthening R&R prevention in your life.

An important part of keeping your ownership of change is to develop knowledge and skills for a healthy lifestyle. This means being productive in your work and job, taking part in healthy play, eating healthy, having good personal care, being physically active, and learning to relax. A healthy lifestyle involves sharing the joy and power of change. You do this by receiving and giving support. This means being an example and mentor for others. We do this by being part of a group where members support each other in the changes they have made. *Module 12* is about learning strategies for healthy living.

Here are the goals of Phase III.

▶ Review relapse and recidivism and R&R prevention.

▶ Review your high-risk exposures that could lead to R&R and strengthen prevention skills.

▶ Develop a good understanding and approaches for healthy living.

▶ Learn to give and receive support from others.

HAVE A GREAT JOURNEY IN YOUR FINAL SESSIONS OF SSC.

MODULE 11

Each day you remain AOD free and free of criminal acts, you will feel power and strength. Your self-confidence grows and gives you ownership of your changes. This ownership means you take responsibility for managing the high-risk exposures - thoughts, situations, feelings attitudes, beliefs - that lead to relapse and recidivism (R&R). We revisit and review the important ideas about relapse and recidivism you learned in *Module 6.* You look again at your R&R prevention goals, your own high-risk pathways and the skills that work best for you. We then develop a plan for self-control and balance in our effort to prevent R&R.

Taking ownership of your changes means doing critical thinking so your own values and morals guide your actions. We look again at being assertive and using refusal skills.

The specific goals for this module:

Relapse and Recidivism Prevention: Strategies for a Balanced Lifestyle

Remember good things come from being AOD and crime free.

- Take another look at your R&R prevention goals.
- Review your present high-risk exposures that put you at risk.
- Zero-in on the R&R prevention skills that are working for you.
- Develop a plan of lifestyle self-control and balance.
- Learn critical reasoning.

Module 11 has three sessions.

Session 43: Strengthening Your Relapse and Recidivism Prevention Skills

Session 44: Strengthening Your Relapse and Recidivism Plan

Session 45: Strengthening R&R Prevention Through Critical Reasoning

SESSION INTRODUCTION AND OBJECTIVES

Most of this session reviews the important ideas and work you did in *Sessions 15 and 16*. Using the skills to prevent relapse and recidivism (R&R) is a daily process. It follows the practice of Alcoholics Anonymous - "one day at a time."

OBJECTIVES OF SESSION AND KEY TERMS

➡ Update your *Master Profile* and *Master Assessment Plan*.

➡ Review the work you did on R&R and R&R prevention in *Sessions 15 and 16*.

➡ Restate your R&R goals.

➡ Look at the R&R prevention skills that have worked for you.

➡ **Key words:** impact of AOD abuse and CC, R&R high-risk exposures, R&R prevention skills.

WE START BY having each group member share a recent situation that was high risk for recidivism. Apply the *STEP Method* to one member's situation. Share your *TAP* Charting for this week.

SESSION CONTENT AND FOCUS

UPDATING YOUR MP AND MAP

Look at the *Alcohol and Other Drug Use Assessment* part of your *Master Profile, Program Guide 2*, page 292. The higher your scores on the level of involvement and the negative consequences from AOD use, the greater your risk for recidivism and relapse. Now, look at parts II and III of your *MAP, Program Guide 3*, page 295. What problems have you resolved in this part of your *MAP*? Are there any new problems that you need to add?

REVIEW OF THE PATHWAYS TO RECIDIVISM AND RELAPSE

R&R begin when you are confronted with high-risk exposures: high-risk thinking; high-risk situations; high-risk feelings; and high-risk attitudes. These high-risk exposures are the marker points of the pathways to R&R. Relapse and recidivism have their own pathways but they are linked together.

Exercise: Review *Figure 18*, page 121, which shows the pathways to R&R. Each of the high-risk exposures are discussed. Group members share their own specific exposures. For example, each member will be asked to share a high-risk situation, high-risk thought, etc.

Exercise: Review your work on *Worksheet 37,* page 122, examples of high-risk exposures that could lead to relapse and recidivism for you. Go over the ones you listed. Update and add new ones.

Exercise: Review *Worksheet 39,* page 124, mapping your own unique R&R path. Go over each of the exposures you put the first time. Add new high-risk exposures you face at this time.

REVIEW OF YOUR R&R GOALS

In the *Orientation Session* to *SSC* and in *Session 16,* you stated your R&R prevention goals.

Exercise: Once again, review your statement of these goals on page 126 for recidivism and page 127 for relapse. Do you want to change those goals? If you do, write in a goal that best fits you at this time. Share your findings with the group.

R&R PREVENTION SKILLS THAT ARE WORKING FOR YOU

Persons with **strong coping skills and self-mastery in dealing with high-risk exposures** are not likely to relapse or backslide into criminal thinking and conduct. The fact that you have stayed in *SSC* means you have been successful in using R&R prevention skills. These are: mental change skills; relationship skills; and skills in having a positive relationship with your community. We will do several exercises to strengthen our R&R skills.

Exercise: First, the group reviews the *Process of R&R Prevention, Figure 19,* page 129. You will go over each part of that map.

Exercise: Second, using *Worksheet 83,* page 258, write in the skills you have used to handle the high-risk exposures for R&R. Use the skills you learned in *Modules 8 through 10.*

SESSION ACTIVITIES AND PROCESS GROUP

---

1. Do *Worksheet 83.* Update your *Master Skills List,* page 291. Do this week's *TAP charting.*

2. Use the *SSC Scale* to rate yourself on your skills in preventing recidivism and relapse.

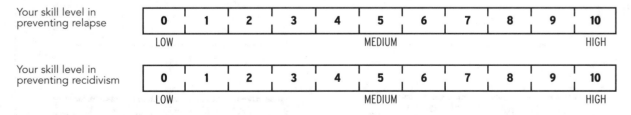

3. Use the process group to share the concerns you are having at this time in your life.

Your skills in handling high-risk exposures that could lead to relapse or recidivism

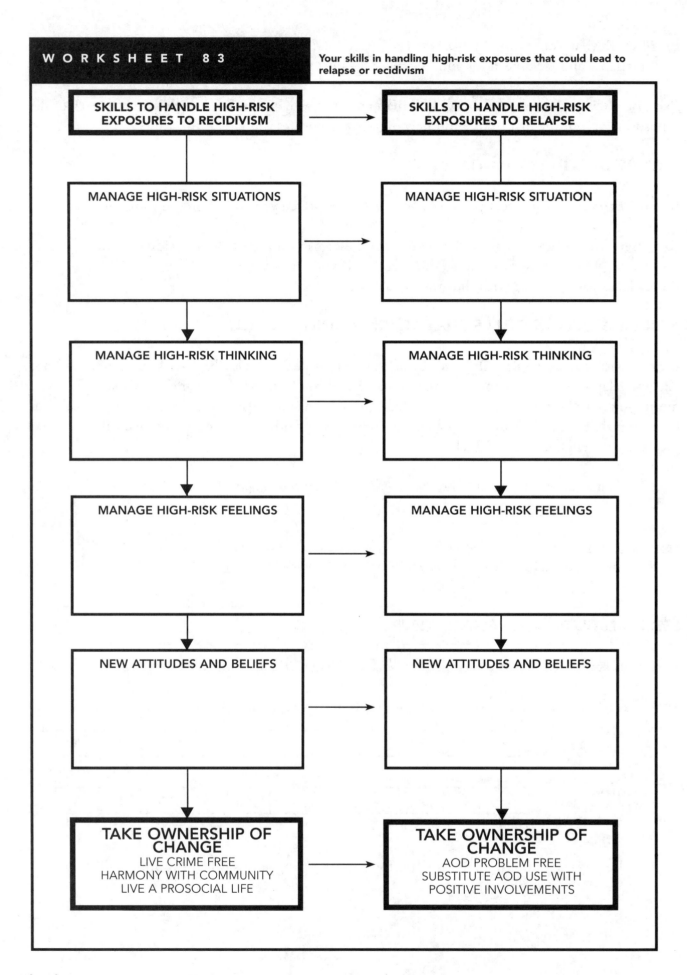

SKILLS TO HANDLE HIGH-RISK EXPOSURES TO RECIDIVISM

SKILLS TO HANDLE HIGH-RISK EXPOSURES TO RELAPSE

MANAGE HIGH-RISK SITUATIONS

MANAGE HIGH-RISK SITUATION

MANAGE HIGH-RISK THINKING

MANAGE HIGH-RISK THINKING

MANAGE HIGH-RISK FEELINGS

MANAGE HIGH-RISK FEELINGS

NEW ATTITUDES AND BELIEFS

NEW ATTITUDES AND BELIEFS

TAKE OWNERSHIP OF CHANGE
LIVE CRIME FREE
HARMONY WITH COMMUNITY
LIVE A PROSOCIAL LIFE

TAKE OWNERSHIP OF CHANGE
AOD PROBLEM FREE
SUBSTITUTE AOD USE WITH
POSITIVE INVOLVEMENTS

SESSION INTRODUCTION AND OBJECTIVES

You have worked hard preventing relapse and recidivism (R&R). You developed your (R&R) prevention goals. You have a good understanding of the R&R process. In this session we work on reviewing and strengthening your R&R plan. We look at the outcomes for decisions we can make about AOD use and criminal conduct - the *Decision Window*. We look at developing and maintaining a *balanced* lifestyle.

> ### OBJECTIVES OF SESSION AND KEY TERMS
>
> ➠ Review and update your stages of change.
>
> ➠ Look at the outcomes of your R&R prevention decisions.
>
> ➠ Develop a plan to maintain a lifestyle balance.
>
> ➠ Commit yourself to stay on the road to responsible living.
>
> ➠ **Key words:** stages of change, R&R plan, decision window, lifestyle balance.

WE START THIS SESSION by role playing a situation where you used SSC skills to prevent AOD relapse. Share your *TAP Charting.*

SESSION CONTENT AND FOCUS

REVIEWING YOUR STAGES OF CHANGE

As you work on your R&R prevention, remember how people change and the stages of change: **Challenge to Change, Commitment to Change** and **Ownership of Change.**

Exercise: Go to *Worksheets 46 and 47,* pages 143 and 144. Rate yourself again on the stages of change for AOD use, and criminal conduct and thinking. Share with the group what you found.

REVIEW YOUR R&R PLAN

In *Session 16,* you developed a R&R plan to manage high-risk exposures, meet your needs and cravings in a **positive way and work for a better balanced lifestyle.**

Exercise: Review *Worksheets 41 and 42,* pages 131 and 132. Update and add to those plans based on what you learned in *Phase II.* Share your changes with the group.

THE DECISION WINDOW

Your prevention goals have short and long-term outcomes. Many of these will be positive. Some negative. Take a realistic look at these outcomes.

Exercise: *Worksheet 84,* page 263, provides a **decision window** for AOD use and *Worksheet 85* for criminal conduct involvement. For the AOD decision window, put your relapse prevention goal. **Examples:** Your relapse prevention goal is being AOD free. What do you get right now and later by abstaining from AOD use? What do you miss out on by not drinking or using drugs, both in the short and long run? For the criminal conduct recidivism window, do the same. Share your findings.

You may decide to choose the relapse prevention goal of preventing further alcohol use problems rather than the goal of living alcohol free - abstinence. This may mean that you choose to continue alcohol use, but avoid alcohol problems.

The SSC relapse prevention goal for its clients is total abstinence from the use of illegal drugs or the abuse of legal prescription drugs. It is not OK to use illegal drugs. This represents a form of criminal conduct. *SSC* **also strongly recommends that clients with a history of alcohol problems, disruption, abuse or dependence should choose to live alcohol-free. Its simple: if you never use alcohol or other drugs again, you will never again have another problem from AOD use.**

HOW LIFESTYLE IMBALANCES LEAD TO RELAPSE

The demands of living AOD and crime-free, and living a prosocial life may cause imbalances in your life. You may feel pressured, hassled and controlled by family, boss, your P.O. You feel pressured by shoulds or oughts to stay on the R&R prevention path. You are living free of AOD problems, but you begin to feel cheated. You have no time for yourself. The demands of everything and everyone are too much. **You say, "I felt more balanced when drinking or not worrying about going straight."**

This imbalance might bring on desires to meet your needs right away, to indulge or satisfy yourself **now.** As these desires increase, so does the need to get back to the "balance" you had when drinking or using other drugs. You may have cravings and urges for alcohol or other drugs. You think, "I deserve more than this," "I deserve a good time - a few drinks," "I have a right to drink with my friends."

This thinking leads to relapse. It is gradual, like erosion. It sneaks up on you. You make small choices that don't seem important. You say, "I'll just go by the bar (where your old crime buddies are) and pick up something to go. They have good fried chicken." We call this *Seemingly Irrelevant Decisions* (SIDS). You may engage in high-risk thinking. You think, "I'll just have a coke while I wait for my order to go." Then you decide to have a beer. "One won't hurt me." Get immediate rewards. High-risk thinking, high-risk situation, high-risk actions.

Given this, how can you get your own needs met and still meet your R&R goals? You can do this by building a healthy balance between activities that cause you pressure and stress and activities that bring you pleasure and self-fulfillment.

ADDING TO YOUR R&R PLAN: DEVELOPING A BALANCE

Your R&R prevention plan that you just reviewed and updated is based on the skills you would use to deal with high risk thinking and high risk situations. We add to that plan a balanced lifestyle. *Figure 30*, page 262, gives you the outline for this. The circled parts help handle the boxed parts. The circles on the right represent the strategies and on the left, the skills.

Balanced daily lifestyle - Positive involvements: We build a balanced lifestyle by living a healthy lifestyle. We work on this in *Module 12*. Write in a couple positive involvements.

Substituting desires - mental control skills: Put other activities in the place of AOD use or CC. Be ready with those when you need them. These are activities that provide immediate self-gratification (such as eating a nice meal, getting a massage). CAUTION: DON'T SUBSTITUTE ADDICTIONS. Discuss this in group.

Detach and label - mental-social-community skills: Cravings and urges surprise us. We smell alcohol or see people use. You can detach from the situation. Use the cravings and urges coping skills on page 134. Put a label on the urge and "ride it out," "urge surf." The urge does go away.

Label SIDS as warning - Change decision window (SIDS): A powerful part of R&R is making excuses, not to own up, to defend. You should now see that the choices you make that move towards R&R are *Seemingly Irrelevant Decisions* (SIDS). Label these as "warnings." You think, "I deserve it." Label it "poor excuse" (PE). You think, "I can get by with it." Label it "big fool" (BF). These warn that you are moving towards relapse. Look at your *Decision Window*. What's the long run outcome of committing a crime? Of using?

<u>Exercise:</u> Use *Figure 30*, and fill in the circles. Your counselor will help you.

Handle or avoid high-risk exposures: Use all of your *SSC* skills.

REVIEW YOUR HIGHWAY MAP TO RESPONSIBLE LIVING

Your R&R prevention plans are maps for responsible living. Look at *Figure 21*, page 136. Where are you on this highway now? On **Relapse Road 000.** Or on **R&R Prevention Road 101?** Remember: **YOU ARE IN THE DRIVER'S SEAT.**

SESSION ACTIVITIES AND PROCESS GROUP

---

1. Do Worksheet *84 and 85*. Update your *Master Skills List*. Do this week's TAP charting.

2. Use the *SSC Scale* to rate yourself on your skills of making your R&R prevention plan work for you.

Level of skills making your R&R plan work	0	1	2	3	4	5	6	7	8	9	10
	LOW					MEDIUM					HIGH

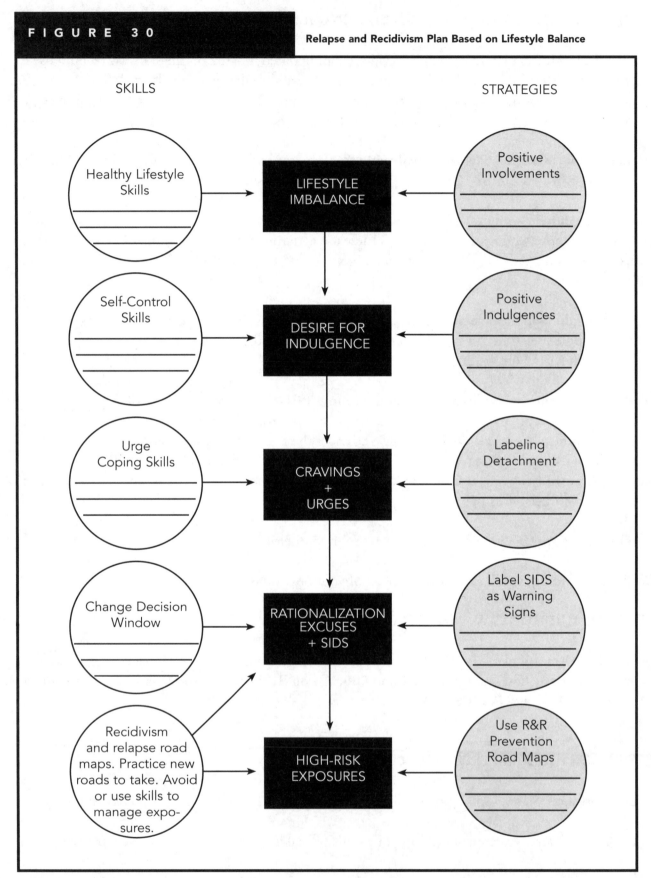

Adapted with permission from G.H. Marlatt, 1985, Relapse Prevention: Theoretical Rationale and Overview. In G.A. Marlatt, & J.R. Gordon (Eds.), *Relapse Prevention: Maintenance Strategies in the Treatment of Addictive Behaviors* (p. 61), Guilford Press.

WORKSHEET 84

Relapse Decision Window for AOD use and abuse outcomes

YOUR RELAPSE PREVENTION GOAL:	IMMEDIATE OUTCOME (SHORT RUN)		DELAYED OUTCOME (LONG RUN)	
	POSITIVE	NEGATIVE	POSITIVE	NEGATIVE
❑ Living free of alcohol or other drugs (AOD) ❑ Living free of alcohol problem outcomes and free of all illegal drugs				
CONTINUE TO USE AND ABUSE ALCOHOL AND OTHER DRUGS				

WORKSHEET 85

Recidivism Decision Window for criminal conduct outcomes

YOUR RECIDIVISM PREVENTION GOAL:	IMMEDIATE OUTCOME (SHORT RUN)		DELAYED OUTCOME (LONG RUN)	
	POSITIVE	NEGATIVE	POSITIVE	NEGATIVE
❑ Crime free ❑ Crime free and prosocial				
CONTINUE ANTISOCIAL AND CRIMINAL BEHAVIOR				

Adapted with permission from G.H. Marlatt, 1985, Relapse Prevention: Theoretical Rationale and Overview. In G.A. Marlatt, & J.R. Gordon (Eds.), *Relapse Prevention: Maintenance Strategies in the Treatment of Addictive Behaviors* (p. 58), Guilford Press.

SESSION INTRODUCTION AND OBJECTIVES

Critical reasoning helps you make good decisions. It keeps you from being talked into actions that lead to bad outcomes. You take ownership when your **own** values and morals guide your behavior.

> ### OBJECTIVES OF SESSION AND KEY TERMS
>
> ➠ Learn the skills and guidelines for critical reasoning.
>
> ➠ Spot propaganda or being talked into actions that lead to bad outcomes and see how this relates to relapse and recidivism.
>
> ➠ **Key words:** critical thinking, creative thinking, propaganda.

WE START THIS SESSION by role playing a situation where using *SSC* skills prevented AOD relapse. Share your *TAP Charting.*

SESSION CONTENT AND FOCUS

SKILLS IN CRITICAL AND CREATIVE THINKING

Critical or logical thinking is making sense and getting the facts before making decisions. It builds on problem solving skills. Here are seven guides for critical and creative thinking.

Guide 1: Look at all sides. Be mentally flexible. Rigid thinking blocks problem solving.

Guide 2: Get the facts first. The goal is to come to conclusions that are based on correct information.

Guide 3: Stick with thoughts, not emotions. Don't make a decision because you are angry. "The clerk was a jerk. I'm not going back." Change thinking: "That store may have what I might need sometime. A clerk's not getting to me."

Guide 4: Make sense of the facts. So how do the facts fit together. What do the facts tell you?

Guide 5: Ask, "Am I being conned?" Making decisions because of being swayed by others is being conned (tricked). People trying to convince you to agree with them regardless of the facts are using propaganda.

Guide 6: People often don't say what they really mean: Don't assume. Ask questions if you don't understand. Pay attention. Few people say what they mean in a CLEAR way. Use active listening to figure out what is being said. Pay attention to body language and facial expressions.

Guide 7: Sort out fact from opinion. These are opinions. **Soft statements:** "In my opinion," "I think," "It seems to me." **Emotional statements:** "I hate that person." **Extreme statements:** "He always does that."

RECOGNIZING PROPAGANDA: BEING TALKED INTO THOUGHTS AND ACTIONS

Critical thinking spots approaches that get you to meet other people's needs - being talked into acting. The following are ways to con.

ONE-SIDED ARGUMENTS: Person tells a friend taking a job out of town: "This is an awful job. You'll live in a one horse town. Nothing to do."

THE BANDWAGON APPROACH: You're not "in" if you don't buy the product. Everybody does it. Boyfriend: "Let's get some speed and shoot up." Girlfriend "I won't do that. Using drugs isn't smart." Boyfriend: "Everybody does it."

REPETITION: Mentioning the product over and over. Tobacco advertisements do this: LSMFT: "Lucky Strike Means Fine Tobacco." "Let's get high." "Let's get high."

TRANSFER: Associating an appealing person with a product. Tobacco ads show the attractive, young and healthy smoking cigarettes.

TESTIMONIAL: A famous person advertises a product to get you to transfer loyalty to the product. A famous athlete wears the product being advertised.

EMERGENCY OR CRISIS: You are told there is limited time to buy the product at the reduced price; or, there are only a few left for sale. "This offer is good until Friday."

BARGAIN: "Buy one, get one free. Lowest prices in town. Everything is on sale at half price."

Exercise: Using a newspaper, and in small groups, find advertisements that are examples of these propaganda methods.

RELATING RELAPSE AND RECIDIVISM TO THESE PROPAGANDA METHODS

Exercise: In group, take each propaganda method and discuss how they can lead to AOD use and criminal conduct. Discuss and complete *Worksheet 86,* page 266, to see how these methods are related to your AOD use and criminal conduct. How can they lead to R&R?

Exercise: Use the *STEP Method* on a situation where you were pressured to use drugs.

S SITUATIONS → **T** THINKING CHANGE → **E** EMOTIONS → **P** POSITIVE ACTION

SESSION ACTIVITIES AND PROCESS GROUP

1. Do *Worksheet 86.* Update your *Master Skills List.* Do this week's TAP charting.

2. Use the *SSC Scale* to rate yourself on the skills of critical thinking or reasoning.

Level of skills to do critical thinking

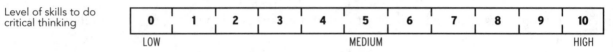

| 0 | 1 | 2 | 3 | 4 | 5 | 6 | 7 | 8 | 9 | 10 |

LOW   MEDIUM   HIGH

3. Share in the group where you are on the highway to responsible living.

WORKSHEET 86	**Relating propaganda to your drug use and criminal conduct:** For each of the methods of propaganda listed below, write a statement as to how that method has led you to AOD use or criminal conduct.
PROPAGANDA METHOD	HOW HAS THIS METHOD BEEN USED ON YOU TO GET YOU TO USE ALCOHOL OR OTHER DRUGS OR TO GET YOU INVOLVED IN CRIMINAL CONDUCT?
One-Sided Arguments	
The Bandwagon Approach	
Repetition	
Transfer	
Testimonial	
Emergency or Crisis	
Bargain	

MODULE 12

In *Phase III,* you are working on taking ownership of the changes you have made. But how do we make those changes stick? We do this by tying the changes we have made into our whole lifestyle of healthy living. This means we are doing more than preventing relapse and recidivism. We are changing the way we approach life.

For many who have abused drugs and committed crimes, AOD use is at the center of their lives. And, for many, antisocial and criminal behavior is a big part of their lives. Now, you are challenged to develop alternatives to AOD use and criminal conduct and take ownership of a heathy lifestyle. We want you to learn or strengthen four alternatives, the objectives of this module.

- ▶ Productive and satisfying work.
- ▶ Healthy play, leisure time and relaxation.
- ▶ Healthy eating and exercise.
- ▶ Mentor and role model healthy living.

There are five sessions in *Module 12.*

Session 46: Managing Work, Job and Time

Session 47: Healthy Play and Leisure Time

Session 48: Relaxation Skills for a Healthy Lifestyle

Session 49: Healthy Eating, Personal Care and Physical Activity

Session 50: Receiving and Giving Support for Change and Responsible Living

Strengthening Ownership of Change: Skills for a Healthy Lifestyle

Take ownership of a healthy lifestyle.

SESSION INTRODUCTION AND OBJECTIVES

You use your work and job to express yourself in healthy ways and as a way of replacing AOD use and involvement in criminal conduct. There is a difference between your work and your job. **Your work** is the means through which you practice your skills, fulfill your talents and earn your livelihood. **Your job** is what you go to in order to fulfill your work. You take your work to your job. You own your work. You don't own your job; it is given to you in order to do your work. Work is one way you fulfill a healthy lifestyle.

OBJECTIVES OF SESSION AND KEY TERMS

➡ Learn what's in your work "tool kit." Learn the difference between your work and your job.

➡ Learn skills to look for a job.

➡ Look at education and work goals for the next three years.

➡ Learn skills to manage time and completing tasks.

➡ **Key words:** work, job, time management, task-frame, time-frame.

WE START THIS SESSION doing the *STEP Method* around a situation where group members had a problem at their job. Share your *TAP Charting*.

SESSION CONTENT AND FOCUS

KNOW WHAT'S IN YOUR "TOOL KIT" - THE BASICS

▶ **Specific skills** to do your job. Do the skills match your job?

▶ **Schedule and plan** to approach your job each day - start with what is important first. You lead yourself.

▶ **Positive attitude** towards your job.

▶ **Cooperative spirit** with your coworkers.

▶ **Sharpener** to keep your skills sharp, up to date, fresh, renewed.

▶ **Evaluation sheet:** Each day, evaluate how you are doing

WHAT IS YOUR WORK? DOES YOUR JOB MATCH YOUR WORK?

<u>Exercise:</u> Identify your work using *Worksheet 87*, page 271. Give a name to the work and write down

as many things as you can that define your work. Check each that you like doing. If you check most of the items, you like your work. You may not like your job; but you can love your work. Feel power in that. If you check that you like only a few things about your work, you may want to look for or train for another kind of work.

Exercise: Does your job match your work? In the right column of *Worksheet 87* check each item that matches the job you now have. If you check most of the statements, then your job matches your work. If not, you may not be happy in the job you have. You may want to look for a different job that better matches your work.

LOOKING FOR OR CHANGING JOBS

Here are the tasks and skills in looking for or changing a job. You may not be looking for a job, but you can practice these skills and tasks for a time when you may be looking. Or, you can help a group member do the worksheets.

▶ **Developing a resumé** that describes your work history and desire for work. Explain periods of time when you were not working. Have the document typed and include a cover letter.

▶ **The job application** emphasizes personal strengths and skills.

▶ **Job leads:** Use *Worksheet 88,* page 272, to make a list of 10 possible jobs and employers. Job seeking is a full time job. Practice using the Internet to look for jobs.

▶ **Practice telephone skills** to ask for the person in charge of hiring and to set up an appointment.

▶ **Practice job interviewing** to introduce and sell yourself. You can't buy the job, but you can sell your work which you own.

▶ **Set goals** that are short-term and long-term. Look at your plan for school and/or work for the next three years. Use *Worksheet 89,* page 273.

▶ **Use the Internet** to search and apply for jobs.

Exercise: Group members roleplay the tasks of looking for a job.

TIME AND TASK MANAGEMENT

Emotional stress comes when we feel pressure to get our work and tasks done. It is usually a matter of time and task management.

▶ **Plan ahead:** Take a few deep breaths and relax. Take a few minutes each evening or at the beginning of each day to plan the day, even if it is your day off from work. Plan it.

▶ **Set goals and plan outcomes.** Know what do you want to finish.

▶ **Put what is important first.** Start with what needs to get done. You will have less stress. Don't put the most important last and then go crazy trying to get it done. If buying a birthday present is most important, do it first.

▶ **Timing is the key** and is nine-tenths of success. Start early. Know the time it takes to do certain jobs. If you are cooking, figure the time you will need. Add time. We always give ourselves less time than we need to finish a task.

▶ **Time-framing** gives time each day to work on a task that has a deadline. Waiting to the last minute will make you task-frame - work until it is done. That causes stress.

▶ **Task-framing:** This may be necessary for the last big push to finish a task. To make task-framing work, you will have to use time-framing for much of the task or project. If you task-frame, give yourself enough time.

▶ **Have fun, enjoy and look back:** Give yourself time to enjoy the task or job. Look back. Did you meet your goals for the day? How was your timing? Did you feel stress? Did you use the above skills? Did you enjoy yourself?

<u>Exercise:</u> Plan your next day off from work. What activity will you do? What is your goal? Will you time-frame or task-frame what you do? What would you like your outcome to be?

SESSION ACTIVITIES AND PROCESS GROUP

1. Do *Worksheets 87 through 89.* Update your *Master Skills List.* Do this week's *TAP Charting.*

2. Use the *SSC Scale* to rate your ability and skills to do your work. Then, rate yourself on whether you like your job. If you rate yourself low on skills to do your work, and low on liking your job, you may want to seek job training or counseling.

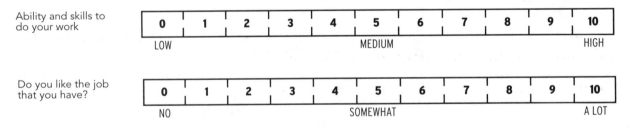

3. Talk in group about your work and job. Do you like them? Do you think you need to make some changes?

What is your work? First, give a name to your work. The following are some examples: Truck Driver, Tile Setter, Bookkeeper, Sales Person, etc. Then, write down everything you think of that defines your work or the important parts of your work. Use extra paper if you run out of room in this worksheet.

NAME OF MY WORK

List what defines your work or the important parts of your work.	Check if you like doing this	Check if work matches your job

Job Search Plan. Make a list of 10 possible jobs including the employer, date contacted, phone number, and the result of your call.

NAME OF JOB	NAME OF EMPLOYER	DATE CONTACTED	CONTACT NAMES AND NUMBERS	RESULT

School and Work Plan for the Next Three Years. List your specific objectives for education, schooling and work for the next three years. Share this with your group.

LIST SPECIFIC OBJECTIVES IN SCHOOL AND WORK PLAN FOR THE NEXT THREE YEARS

SESSION INTRODUCTION AND OBJECTIVES

Involvement in AOD use and criminal activities filled a lot of space in your life. Giving up those activities may leave you feeling empty. Unless you replace that void with healthy play and leisure time, there is a greater chance you will experience loneliness, boredom and depression. In maintaining a drug-free and crime-free lifestyle, healthy play is vital.

OBJECTIVES OF SESSION AND KEY TERMS

➠ Understanding the meaning of play.

➠ Identify healthy play activities you have been doing.

➠ Learn the activities that bring you the most pleasure.

➠ List healthy play activities you plan to do in the future.

➠ **Key words:** healthy play; *Personal Pleasure Inventory.*

WE START THIS SESSION by doing the *STEP Method* around a situation where group members failed to use critical reasoning and were talked into actions that lead to bad outcomes. Share your *TAP Charting.*

SESSION CONTENT AND FOCUS

WHAT IS HEALTHY PLAY?

To play is to take part in fun, to have pleasure, to be amused, to enjoy an activity or recreation. An important part of the meaning of play is to **move freely within a space.** But the lifestyle alternative we refer to is **healthy** play. This play:

▶ Moves freely within boundaries. It sets limits on time, cost, how much energy you put out;

▶ Replaces unhealthy activities such as AOD use patterns that cause harm to you, others and your community; and

▶ Is prosocial and moral. It respects the rights, welfare and safety of others. It is play that is responsible to others and your community. It benefits you and others around you. And, you feel fulfilled when you finish healthy play.

Exercise: Using the above ideas, share with the group what kinds of healthy and unhealthy play you have been involved in. Then, complete the top part of *Worksheet 90,* page 276, and list what healthy play and leisure time activities you have been doing in the past few months. Put the number of times a month you do the activity and if it has replaced AOD use and criminal activities. Make sure the activity fits what *SSC* sees as healthy play.

FULFILLING OUR PLEASURES - PERSONAL PLEASURE INVENTORY

The better you feel about yourself, the more pleasant activities you will take part in. People who spend most of their time doing the "shoulds" and "oughts," will experience less reward in life. They are likely to feel they deserve to reward themselves with "a drink, a hit, or a night out with old criminal buddies."

One way to learn healthy play is to know what activities give you pleasure. This will help your healthy play to be more fulfilling. The *Personal Pleasure Inventory* (PPI) can help discover this. The PPI is in *Worksheet 91*, page 277. Complete the PPI and then add up the score for each area of activity. Put your scores on the *PPI Profile, Worksheet 92*, page 279. Your counselor will help you do this and explain how to read the profile. There are four broad areas of pleasure.

▶ Physical expression.

▶ Focus on the self.

▶ Artistic or aesthetic activities.

▶ Cooperative harmony or working together.

Where are your high scores? You can have high scores across all of these areas. Discuss your profile with the group.

Healthy play is prosocial.

COMPLETE YOUR LIST OF HEALTHY PLAY ACTIVITIES

<u>Exercise:</u> Using your *PPI Profile*, complete *Worksheet 90*, page 276. **List healthy play activities you plan or would like to do in addition to the ones you are doing.** Put down the number of times a month you plan to do these activities. If you plan to increase your past activities, change the times a month you plan to do them.

This helps develop a balance between work and play. What kind of problems will you have finding ways other than AOD activities to fill your time? Have you been successful in finding new friends and acquaintances with whom to share leisure time and fun?

SESSION ACTIVITIES AND PROCESS GROUP

1. Do *Worksheets 90 through 92*. Update your *Master Skills List*. Do this week's *TAP charting*.

2. Use the *SSC Scale* to rate your ability and skills in taking part in healthy play and leisure activities.

Ability to take part in healthy play.

0	1	2	3	4	5	6	7	8	9	10

LOW   MEDIUM   HIGH

3. Share in the group problems you have taking part in healthy play and leisure time activities.

WORKSHEET 90

Healthy play and leisure time activities: In the first part of this worksheet, list the healthy play activities you have been doing, the number of times a month you did them, and check if they replaced AOD use activities. In the second part, add to those you would like to do, how many times a month, and if they will replace AOD use activities.

HEALTHY PLAY AND LEISURE TIME ACTIVITIES YOU HAVE BEEN DOING AND WILL CONTINUE DOING	TIMES PER MONTH	REPLACES AOD ACTIVITIES

HEALTHY PLAY AND LEISURE TIME ACTIVITIES YOU WANT TO ADD TO YOUR LIST	TIMES PER MONTH	REPLACES AOD ACTIVITIES

Personal Pleasure Inventory: Using one of the five choices below, rate the degree of pleasure you get from each activity. Place the number (0 through 4) of your choice on the blank line by activity.

0 = Never engaged in activity or no pleasure derived from activity
1 = Low degree of pleasure derived
2 = Moderate degree of pleasure derived
3 = High degree of pleasure derived
4 = Very high degree of pleasure derived

1.   **SPORTS**
____ Playing basketball
____ Tennis
____ Watching sports
____ Softball
____ Going to football games
____ Playing golf
____ Playing football and soccer
____ Playing volleyball

Total Score_____

2.   **CHALLENGING NATURE**
____ Floating on a raft
____ Canoeing
____ White water rafting
____ Camping out
____ Hiking
____ Skiing

Total Score_____

3.   **PHYSICAL FITNESS**
____ Eating healthy foods
____ Exercising
____ Biking
____ Stretching
____ Walking

Total Score_____

4.   **ROMANCE**
____ Making love
____ Kissing and cuddling
____ Giving flowers to your lover
____ Feeling and touching
____ Go to the beach

Total Score_____

5.   **CALMING SENSATIONS**
____ Listening to soft music
____ Warming self by fire
____ Soaking in hot tub
____ Having back rubbed
____ Massage
____ Eating in nice restaurant

Total Score_____

6.   **MATERIAL COMFORTS**
____ Make money
____ Shopping
____ Spend money
____ Go out for an evening
____ Improve outward appearance

Total Score_____

7.   **SEEKING ADVENTURE**
____ Driving to new places
____ Visiting different cities
____ Experiencing new places
____ Experiencing new things
____ Traveling to foreign cities
____ Visiting different cultures.

Total Score_____

8.   **ENJOYING NATURE**
____ Being in nature
____ Being in the woods
____ Watching wildlife
____ Watching the stars
____ Watching the sunrise

Total Score_____

9.   **HOME INVOLVEMENT**

   ____   Redecorate your home
   ____   Remodel your home
   ____   Work on home projects
   ____   Painting your house
   ____   Working in the yard and gardening

Total Score_____

10.   **MENTAL RELAXATION**

   ____   Meditation
   ____   Relaxation exercises
   ____   Daily meditations
   ____   Self-reflection
   ____   Journal writing

Total Score_____

11.   **ARTISTIC STIMULATION**

   ____   Going to movies/theater
   ____   Attending symphony
   ____   Creating art work
   ____   Reading books/poetry/fiction
   ____   Writing poetry/fiction
   ____   Playing musical instrument

Total Score_____

12.   **MENTAL EXERCISE**

   ____   Word games
   ____   Playing cards
   ____   Crossword puzzles
   ____   Solving mystery games
   ____   Sewing

Total Score_____

13.   **PEOPLE CLOSENESS**

   ____   Helping family members
   ____   Playing with children
   ____   Being with family
   ____   Time with friends
   ____   Hugging
   ____   Being with your partner

Total Score_____

14.   **RELIGIOUS INVOLVEMENT**

   ____   Spiritual thinking
   ____   Worship
   ____   Bible study
   ____   Church work
   ____   Going to church
   ____   Praying

Total Score_____

15.   **HELPING OTHERS**

   ____   Counseling others
   ____   Helping others
   ____   Teaching others
   ____   Volunteering services
   ____   Writing letters to friends or family

END OF INVENTORY

When you have finished, put the total score for each group of activities on the Total Score line. Then, put that score on the PPI Profile, Worksheet 92. Find your score on the row for each activity and mark it with an X. Find your percentile rank for that activity. The percentile score shows how you compare with a sample of adult men and women. For example, if your raw score for ATHLETIC PROWESS is 15, you enjoy this pleasure activity more than 65 percent of the people in that sample.

Personal Pleasure Inventory Profile

NAME: _____ DATE: _____ GENDER: ☐ MALE ☐ FEMALE AGE: _____

DECILE RANK

		RAW SCORE	LOW			LOW-MEDIUM		HIGH-MEDIUM			HIGH		
	SCALE NAME		1	2	3	4	5	6	7	8	9	10
1.	SPORTS		0 2 3 4	5 6 7	8 9 10	11 12	13	14 15	16 17	18 19 20	21 22 23	24 26 32
2.	CHALLENGING NATURE		0 2 3 5	6 7	8	9 10	11 12	13	14 15	16 17	18 19	20 21 24
3.	PHYSICAL FITNESS		2 5 6 7	8	10	11		12	13	14	15	16 18 20
4.	ROMANCE		1 6 8 9	10 11 12	13	14	15	16	17	18		19 20
5.	CALMING SENSATIONS		4 10 11	12 13 14	15	16	17	18	19	20	21 22	23 24
6.	MATERIAL COMFORTS		4 7 8 9	10 11	12	13	14	15	16	17	18	19 20
7.	SEEKING ADVENTURE		4 7 8 9	10 11 12	13	14 15	16	17 18	19	20 21	22	23 24
8.	ENJOYING NATURE		1 6 7 8	9 10	11	12	13	14	15	16 17	18	19 20
9.	HOME INVOLVEMENT		0 1 2	3	4	5 6	7	8	9	10	11 12 13	14 15 20
10.	MENTAL RELAXATION		0 1 2	3	4	5	6	7	8	9 10	11 12	13 15 20
11.	ARTISTIC STIMUALTION		0 2 3	4 5 6	7	8	9	10 11	12	13 14	15 16 17	18 20 24
12.	MENTAL EXERCISE		0 1 2	3 4	5	6	7		8	9	10 11	12 14 20
13.	PEOPLE CLOSENESS		4 11 12	13 14	15 16	17	18	19	20	21	22	23 24
14.	RELIGIOUS INVOLVEMENT		0	1 2	3	4 5	6	7 8	9 10	11 12	13 14 15	16 19 24
15.	HELPING OTHERS		1 6 7	8	9	10	11	12	13	14	15	16 17 20
			0	10	20	30	40	50	60	70	80	90 99

PERCENTILE

Categories (left margin): PHYSICAL (1–3), SELF FOCUS (4–6), AESTHETIC DISCOVERY (7–11), HARMONY (12–15)

Source: *The Personal Pleasure Inventory,* Wanberg, Milkman and Harrison.
Copyright 1992 © K.W. Wanberg and H.B. Milkman

SESSION INTRODUCTION AND OBJECTIVES

Many people use drugs to relax. But, drug use also increases stress. This session is about using natural and simple activities in our daily lives to relax. In *Sessions 25 and 26,* we learned skills to manage stress. It is best to see stress management as part of an overall program of relaxation. And, relaxation is seen as a part of an overall healthy lifestyle.

OBJECTIVES OF SESSION AND KEY TERMS

➠ See relaxation as part of a healthy lifestyle.

➠ Practice the relaxation strategies already learned.

➠ Develop a weekly relaxation plan.

➠ **Key words:** lifestyle relaxation, daily relaxation plan.

WE START THIS SESSION by doing the *STEP Method* around a situation where a group member had lots of stress that lead to bad outcomes. Share your *TAP Charting.*

SESSION CONTENT AND FOCUS

THE ROLE OF RELAXATION IN DAILY LIVING

Relaxation reverses the negative results of stress and gives you balance in living. Daily relaxation gives you these outcomes.

▶ It prepares you for stressful events. Athletes train each day. At game time - stress time - they are ready. Relaxing each day prepares us for stress.

▶ It reduces stress as it comes up.

▶ Lets tension flow from our minds and body.

▶ Brings body and mind together as one.

▶ Gives you energy.

WAYS THAT WE RELAX

There are three kinds of relaxation activities.

1. **Informal or unplanned activities.** Watching T.V., going to a movie, talking with a friend. Going for a walk.

2. **Formal or planned healthy play.** Going to a sport event, a vacation, playing a sport, going out to dinner, a movie.

3. **Planned relaxation exercises and skills.** This is building in a specific time to do the relaxation exercises in *Table 7,* page 180. These not only prepare you for stress, but bring joy and pleasure to your overall life.

Exercise: Review and practice the relaxation exercises in *Table 7,* page 180. Group members may want to take turns leading in some of these.

SPECIAL ACTIVITIES THAT INCREASE RELAXATION AND PREPARE FOR STRESS

▶ Treat yourself with a massage. Do self-massages such as rubbing your shoulders, your leg muscles, your feet.

▶ Sit upright with legs crossed, close your eyes, relax and let your mind go blank.

▶ Sit in a hot bath or hot tub.

▶ Develop good sleep patterns.

▶ Keep your house relaxed with music and pleasant aromas.

Have some quiet time each day.

▶ Have a quiet time each day and make time for yourself.

▶ Enjoy nature. Take walks in the woods, down a pleasant path, in the mountains, in a park. Look at the flowers. Smell the roses.

Exercise: Using the above relaxation strategies and *Worksheet 93,* page 282, make a weekly relaxation plan. Each day, plan to do some stretches, mental relaxation and take a walk. You might do active relaxation three times a week. Follow this plan. Change it every so often. Make notes as to your success.

SESSION ACTIVITIES AND PROCESS GROUP

1. Do *Worksheet 93.* Update your *Master Skills List.* Do this week's *TAP charting.*

2. Use the SSC Scale to rate the degree to which you use relaxation activities in your daily life.

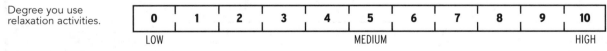

Degree you use relaxation activities.

0	1	2	3	4	5	6	7	8	9	10
LOW					MEDIUM					HIGH

3. Share with the group the most relaxing moments you spend in your daily life.

Your Weekly Relaxation Plan: Planned healthy play would be watching T.V., going to movie, out to dinner. Formal relaxation exercises are based on *Table 7*, page 180.

DAY OF WEEK	PLANNED HEALTHY PLAY ACTIVITIES	FORMAL RELAXATION EXERCISES
Monday		
Tuesday		
Wednesday		
Thursday		
Friday		
Saturday		
Sunday		

SESSION INTRODUCTION AND OBJECTIVES

A healthy lifestyle involves healthy eating, personal care and physical activity. This session only introduces you to this area. You may want to take a special class on these topics.

OBJECTIVES OF SESSION AND KEY TERMS

➡ Learn basic ideas of healthy eating.

➡ Identify basic approaches to personal care.

➡ Understand the value of regular exercise.

➡ **Key words:** diet, food groups, personal care, activity levels.

WE START THIS SESSION by doing the *STEP Method* around an experience that a group member had this past week that had a bad outcome. Share your *TAP Charting* for this week.

SESSION CONTENT AND FOCUS

The benefits of making healthy choices when eating and exercising are looking and feeling good, a higher energy level, being a positive role model, and preventing heart problems, high blood pressure, diabetes, some cancers and other illnesses.

Eating a balance of healthy foods and calories is basic. Almost two-thirds of Americans are overweight or obese because of unhealthy lifestyles, which include improper nutrition and lack of regular physical activity. Replace the bad effects of choosing smoking and/or junk foods with healthy choices that contribute to a lifestyle of well-being. Your food and physical activity choices each day affect your health – how you feel today, tomorrow, and in the future. **Always consult with your health care provider before starting an exercise program.**

MANAGING WEIGHT AND HEALTHY EATING

To maintain your ideal healthy body weight and fitness, balance portions from each of The Five Basic Food Groups.

▶ **Grains:** Examples: whole-grain cereals, breads, crackers, rice or pasta.

▶ **Vegetables:** Select from all five vegetable subgroups (dark green, orange, legumes, starchy vegetables, other vegetables).

▶ **Fruits:** Eat different kinds; best if fresh or fresh-frozen, canned or dried; limit fruit juices.

- **Dairy:** Fat-free or low-fat milk or equivalent milk products.

- **Meat and Beans:** Examples: low fat, lean meats, fish, beans, peas, nuts.

Ask your health care provider for a daily vitamin plan. Follow the *My Pyramid Plan* at http://www.mypyramid.gov to help you choose the foods and amounts that are appropriate for your age, gender, and activity level. Know the limits on fats, sugars, and salt. When planning meals, use moderation, your personal tastes, right amounts, and different kinds. *My Pyramid Plan* gives you a variety of eating and activity suggestions and resources that can help move towards a healthier you.

Exercise: On the left side of *Worksheet 94,* page 286, put what you would typically eat for breakfast, lunch and evening meal. Using the five basic food groups listed above and material provided by your counselor, or http://www.mypyramid.gov, fill in healthy foods for the three meals. Figure your calories for your typical and healthy meal. How do the two compare?

BASIC PERSONAL CARE

These may be obvious and simple, but many people do not follow these personal care habits.

Foods: Here are just a few ideas. Wash hands before preparing food and after handling raw meats. Wash fruits and vegetables. Wash chicken and fish before cooking. Keep location of rinsing and preparing meat completely separate from where you prepare uncooked vegetables, fruits, etc., so you don't contaminate those uncooked foods. Even when shopping, keep these foods separate. Cook foods at a safe temperate to kill germs. Keep foods that perish properly cooled, and defrost properly. Avoid using raw (unpasteurized) milk, raw or partially cooked eggs, raw or undercooked meat, unpasteurized juices and raw sprouts. **Exercise:** Have group list other ideas not noted here.

Personal care and protection: Here are just a few ideas. Clean teeth after meals and floss and rinse with mouth wash before bed. Wash hands after going to bathroom. Avoid touching objects in public rest rooms. Almost 70 percent of men don't wash their hands after going to the bathroom. Don't drink from someone's unwashed container. Don't put your hands to mouth or face when in public. Avoid having contact of bare feet and other parts of skin with floors and streets in public places. Protect against air, surface and food-born germs. Go to bed and get up at same time each day. **Exercise:** Have group share their ideas on good personal care and protection. Put ideas on a flipchart.

PHYSICAL ACTIVITY

Take part in regular physical activity and reduce lazy activities in order to have better health, psychological well-being and a healthy body weight. **ALWAYS CONSULT YOUR HEALTH CARE PROVIDER BEFORE CHANGING YOUR NORMAL LEVEL OF PHYSICAL ACTIVITY.**

- Engage in at least 30 minutes of physical activity, above usual activity, at work or home on most days of the week, such as walking, working in the yard or gardening.

- For most people, greater health benefits can be obtained by engaging in physical activity of more vigorous intensity or longer duration.

▶ Get physically fit by including cardiovascular conditioning, stretching exercises, weight-bearing (walking), and resistance exercises or calisthenics for muscle strength and endurance.

▶ Choose activities that you enjoy and can do regularly: brisk 10 minute walks, join an exercise class. What's important is to be active most days of the week and make it part of your daily routine.

<u>Exercise:</u> Using charts provided to you by your counselor, complete *Worksheet 95,* page 286, a weekly physical activity plan. **Are there any activities you should not do because of a medical condition you have?**

Greater health benefits come for most people in more vigorous activities.

SESSION ACTIVITIES AND PROCESS GROUP

1. Do *Worksheets 94 and 95.* Update your *Master Skills List.* Do this week's *TAP charting.*

2. Use the *SSC Scale* to rate yourself on your level of healthy eating and your level of physical activity.

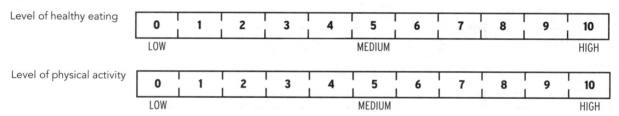

Level of healthy eating

| 0 | 1 | 2 | 3 | 4 | 5 | 6 | 7 | 8 | 9 | 10 |
| LOW | | | | | MEDIUM | | | | | HIGH |

Level of physical activity

| 0 | 1 | 2 | 3 | 4 | 5 | 6 | 7 | 8 | 9 | 10 |
| LOW | | | | | MEDIUM | | | | | HIGH |

3. Discuss in your process group how important it is for you to keep healthy, to eat healthy and to be physically active.

WORKSHEET 94

Your typical meals and healthy meals

MEAL	TYPICAL FOODS YOU EAT	HEALTHY EATING MEAL
BREAKFAST		
LUNCH		
EVENING MEAL		

WORKSHEET 95

Weekly Activity Plan: Put type of physical activity and amount of time you will spend in minutes

DAY OF WEEK	TYPE OF PHYSICAL ACTIVITY	MINUTES
MONDAY		
TUESDAY		
WEDNESDAY		
THURSDAY		
FRIDAY		
SATURDAY		
SUNDAY		

SESSION INTRODUCTION AND OBJECTIVES

Receiving and giving support is a two-way road in the process of self-improvement and change. This two-way process strengthens our prosocial attitudes and actions.

OBJECTIVES OF SESSION AND KEY TERMS

➠ Learn about different support groups.

➠ Know the guidelines for being a role model or mentor.

➠ **Key words:** self-help groups, mentoring, sponsoring.

WE START THIS SESSION doing the *STEP Method* around a disappointing event or situation. Share your *TAP Charting* for this week.

SESSION CONTENT AND FOCUS

RECEIVING HELP AND SUPPORT: BEING MENTORED AND SUPPORTED

We were often taught to solve our own problems, to "not hang our dirty linen in public." But, ownership of change means we are secure enough to seek help and support from others. We have done this within our *SSC* group and with our program counselor. There are outside resources to help you keep up the changes you have made. It is easier to receive support from those who have problems similar to ours. There are two kinds of support groups.

❱ Those that give direct support such as Alcoholics Anonymous (AA).

❱ Those that support you indirectly in your efforts to change and help you live healthy and prosocial - such as a hiking club, health club or spa, church.

Exercise: Use *Worksheet 96,* page 289, to make a list of different support and self-help groups in your community. Have the list include the above two kinds of support groups. Call some of these groups and talk with their members. Or, look them up on the Internet.

GIVING SUPPORT AND HELP: MENTORING AND ROLE MODELING

The changes people make become more stable and permanent when they become teachers and mentors of that change. But it is only when we own something that we can share it. Full ownership of responsible living and prosocial actions makes us secure enough to share with other people the joy and power of the changes we have made.

We do this by being an example or a model for others who are starting to live free of AOD problems and legal problems. This is the wisdom of the 12th step of AA. There are two kinds of mentoring.

Informal mentoring or role modeling: You present yourself as having control of your life with respect to living drug and crime-free. People identify with you and want to be "like you."

Formal mentoring is sponsoring someone who wants to change. You become available for supportive contacts and involvement. Here are six simple guides for becoming a mentor, teacher or tutor.

1. **Feel secure in the ownership of the changes you have made.** Be a mentor or sponsor only if you are secure in doing this.

2. **Know your strengths** as to the changes you have made. You might get over-stressed trying to help someone with a lot of problems.

3. **Know your weaknesses.** If vulnerable in a bar, keep in mind you are there only to help another person.

4. **Find someone who needs support** and be available to them. Use the *SSC* skills to build a supportive relationship.

5. **Find your own mentor,** counselor or sponsor that you can get support from as you mentor or sponsor another person.

6. **Go slow and set limits.** Support only one person to begin with.

Giving and receiving help makes us more prosocial.

Exercise: Use *Worksheet 97* to list the strengths and weaknesses you bring into mentorship or sponsorship. These are areas to watch closely when you are mentoring or sponsoring someone else.

SESSION ACTIVITIES AND PROCESS GROUP

1. Do *Worksheets 96 and 97.*

2. Use the SSC Scales to rate your willingness to be helped by a sponsor or mentor and your readiness to help, mentor or sponsor another person with a history of AOD and legal problems.

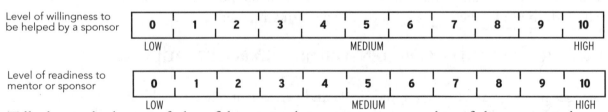

Level of willingness to be helped by a sponsor	0	1	2	3	4	5	6	7	8	9	10
	LOW					MEDIUM					HIGH

Level of readiness to mentor or sponsor	0	1	2	3	4	5	6	7	8	9	10
	LOW					MEDIUM					HIGH

3. Talk about whether you feel confident enough in your own ownership of change to reach out and mentor another person.

Make a list of community support and self-help groups: Use all possible resources. Include groups that support you directly in your R&R prevention goals such as AA and groups that support you indirectly such as a hiking club, church, etc.

NAME OF SELF-HELP GROUP	PHONE NO.	DATE CONTACTED	YOUR REACTIONS AND COMMENTS

Your strong and weak areas: Make a list of those areas in which you feel the strongest that you can bring to mentoring and role modeling and areas you feel weak and vulnerable in. Discuss these in group.

AREAS OF STRENGTH IN MENTORING	AREAS OF WEAKNESS IN MENTORING

PROGRAM CLOSURE: CONTINUING YOUR JOURNEY OF RESPONSIBLE LIVING

"And when you have reached the mountain top, then you shall begin to climb." - KAHLIL GIBRAN, THE PROPHET

Your journey through *Strategies for Self-Improvement and Change* has come to an end. You have worked hard, learned and experienced a lot. You have received and given a lot. But your journey of change and responsible living is now only beginning.

Your life has great promise and opportunity. But you are in charge. You are in the driver's seat. You make the decision of staying on the road to responsible city or to collapse city. You have the tools, the attitude and the strengths to make your life journey successful, meaningful and happy.

You are asked to complete the SSC Program Closure Inventory (PCI) and then meet with your counselor to go over and receive feedback on your progress and change. In your last *SSC* group, you are asked to share these thoughts.

▶ The progress and important changes you made.

▶ The most important ideas and skills you learned.

▶ Farewell statements to your group.

Group members will then give you feedback on the strengths and promise they see in you.

At the end of every session, you were asked to rate yourself on the skills your learned in that session. We called this the *SSC Scale.* We want you to keep a picture of that scale inside of your head. Using that scale, we want you to rate yourself at the end of each day as to the kind of day that you had. But the picture of that scale will have only two ratings:

▶ A good day.

▶ A great day.

Your journey of change continues.

We want your inside SSC Scale to always result in good or great outcomes for yourself. You can make this happen. Because, remember the most important part of SSC: **It's not the outside situations or events that give you a bad or good day. It's your thoughts, attitudes and beliefs about those events and experiences of the day. Through the power of your thinking, attitudes and beliefs, you can make your feelings, actions and life outcomes positive and good.**

GOOD DAY AND GOOD THINKING.

Master Skills List for Self-management, Responsible Living and Change: Put the dates and rate your mastery level. Update your level of mastery after each session. Make Good to Very Good your goal for each skill.

	DESCRIPTION OF SKILLS	DATES	LEVEL OF SKILL MASTERY			
			POOR	FAIR	GOOD	VERY GOOD
MENTAL SKILLS	1. Using the cognitive behavioral map					
	2. Mental self-control/change skills					
	3. Relaxation skills					
	4. Changing AOD use patterns					
	5. Preventing AOD problems/relapse					
	6. Managing urges/cravings					
	7. Changing negative thinking					
	8. Changing thinking errors					
	9. Managing stress/anxiety					
	10. Managing depression					
	11. Use CB STEP method					
RELATIONSHIP SKILLS	12. Anger management skills					
	13. Reading nonverbal cues					
	14. Active sharing skills					
	15. Active listening skills					
	16. Starting a conversation					
	17. Giving compliments/praise					
	18. Receiving compliments					
	19. Problem-solving skills					
	20. Assertiveness skills					
	21. Close relationship skills					
	22. Managing high-risk exposures					
SOCIETY SKILLS	23. Refusal skills					
	24. Change criminal thinking					
	25. Prevent agression/violence					
	26. Lifestyle balance skills					
	27. Preventing recidivism					
	28. Prosocial skills					
	29. Strengthening moral character					
	30. Empathy skills					
	31. Conflict resolution skills					
	32. Negotiation skills					

I. ALCOHOL AND DRUG USE ASSESSMENT

LEVEL OF INVOLVEMENT IN DRUG USE	NONE OR LOW			MODERATE				HIGH		
Alcohol involvement	1	2	3	4	5	6	7	8	9	10
Marijuana involvement	1	2	3	4	5	6	7	8	9	10
Cocaine involvement	1	2	3	4	5	6	7	8	9	10
Amphetamine/meth involvement	1	2	3	4	5	6	7	8	9	10
Other drug involvement	1	2	3	4	5	6	7	8	9	10

STYLE OF ALCOHOL/OTHER DRUG USE	NONE OR LOW			MODERATE				HIGH		
Gregarious or social use	1	2	3	4	5	6	7	8	9	10
Solo or use by yourself	1	2	3	4	5	6	7	8	9	10
Sustained or continuous use	1	2	3	4	5	6	7	8	9	10

BENEFITS FROM AOD USE	NONE OR LOW			MODERATE				HIGH		
Cope with social discomfort	1	2	3	4	5	6	7	8	9	10
Cope with emotional discomfort	1	2	3	4	5	6	7	8	9	10
Cope with relationship problems	1	2	3	4	5	6	7	8	9	10
Cope with physical distress	1	2	3	4	5	6	7	8	9	10

NEGATIVE CONSEQUENCES FROM USE	NONE OR LOW			MODERATE				HIGH		
Loss of behavioral control	1	2	3	4	5	6	7	8	9	10
Loss of emotional control	1	2	3	4	5	6	7	8	9	10
Problems with family/partner	1	2	3	4	5	6	7	8	9	10
Social irresponsibility	1	2	3	4	5	6	7	8	9	10
Physical problems from use	1	2	3	4	5	6	7	8	9	10

CATEGORIES OF AOD USE PROBLEMS	NONE OR LOW			MODERATE				HIGH		
Alcohol/drug use problem	1	2	3	4	5	6	7	8	9	10
Problem drinking or drug user	1	2	3	4	5	6	7	8	9	10
Alcohol/drug abuse disorder	1	2	3	4	5	6	7	8	9	10
Alcohol/drug dependent disorder	1	2	3	4	5	6	7	8	9	10

II. CRIMINAL CONDUCT (CC) AND BEHAVIOR

LEVEL OF INVOLVMENT IN CC	LOW			MODERATE				HIGH		
Motor vehicle - non-DUI offenses	1	2	3	4	5	6	7	8	9	10
Motor vehicle - DUI offenses	1	2	3	4	5	6	7	8	9	10
Offenses against persons	1	2	3	4	5	6	7	8	9	10
Offenses against property	1	2	3	4	5	6	7	8	9	10
Assaultive/violence to others	1	2	3	4	5	6	7	8	9	10
Possession/transporting drugs	1	2	3	4	5	6	7	8	9	10
Selling/making drugs	1	2	3	4	5	6	7	8	9	10
Prostitution/solicitation	1	2	3	4	5	6	7	8	9	10
Overall problems from CC	1	2	3	4	5	6	7	8	9	10

III. THOUGHTS, ATTITUDES, FEELINGS AND ACTIONS THAT LEAD TO CRIMINAL CONDUCT AND AOD ABUSE

THOUGHTS, ATTITUDES, FEELINGS, ACTIONS	LOW			MODERATE				HIGH		
Blame others for problems	1	2	3	4	5	6	7	8	9	10
Victim stance	1	2	3	4	5	6	7	8	9	10
Careless: don't care	1	2	3	4	5	6	7	8	9	10
Think: better than others	1	2	3	4	5	6	7	8	9	10
Irresponsible thinking	1	2	3	4	5	6	7	8	9	10
Act without thinking	1	2	3	4	5	6	7	8	9	10
Angry and aggressive thoughts	1	2	3	4	5	6	7	8	9	10
Think: they have it coming	1	2	3	4	5	6	7	8	9	10
Rebellious/against authority	1	2	3	4	5	6	7	8	9	10
Time with drinking friends	1	2	3	4	5	6	7	8	9	10
Friends angry at laws/society	1	2	3	4	5	6	7	8	9	10
Time with criminal friends	1	2	3	4	5	6	7	8	9	10
Distrust of other people	1	2	3	4	5	6	7	8	9	10
Thoughts of being cheated	1	2	3	4	5	6	7	8	9	10
Don't tell the truth/lie a lot	1	2	3	4	5	6	7	8	9	10
Lack of guilt when hurt others	1	2	3	4	5	6	7	8	9	10
Don't follow the rules/norms	1	2	3	4	5	6	7	8	9	10
Violate the rights of others	1	2	3	4	5	6	7	8	9	10
Con others for personal gain	1	2	3	4	5	6	7	8	9	10

IV. BACKGROUND: PROBLEMS OF CHILDHOOD AND DEVELOPMENT

PROBLEMS IN CHILDHOOD AND TEENS	LOW			MODERATE				HIGH		
Teenage alcohol/drug use	1	2	3	4	5	6	7	8	9	10
Problems with law during teens	1	2	3	4	5	6	7	8	9	10
Problems with parents/family	1	2	3	4	5	6	7	8	9	10
Emotional problems	1	2	3	4	5	6	7	8	9	10
School adjustment problems	1	2	3	4	5	6	7	8	9	10
Physical illness in childhood	1	2	3	4	5	6	7	8	9	10

V. CURRENT LIFE SITUATION PROBLEMS

AREAS OF ADULT PROBLEMS	LOW			MODERATE				HIGH		
Job and employment problems	1	2	3	4	5	6	7	8	9	10
Financial and money problems	1	2	3	4	5	6	7	8	9	10
Unstable living situation	1	2	3	4	5	6	7	8	9	10
Social-relationship problems	1	2	3	4	5	6	7	8	9	10
Marital-family problems	1	2	3	4	5	6	7	8	9	10
Emotional-psychological problems	1	2	3	4	5	6	7	8	9	10
Problems with the law	1	2	3	4	5	6	7	8	9	10
Physical health problems	1	2	3	4	5	6	7	8	9	10

VI. AWARENESS OF PROBLEM AND READINESS FOR TREATMENT

AWARENESS AND READINESS	LOW			MODERATE				HIGH		
Awareness of AOD problem	1	2	3	4	5	6	7	8	9	10
Awareness of criminal conduct problems	1	2	3	4	5	6	7	8	9	10
Degree of help that you need	1	2	3	4	5	6	7	8	9	10
Your willingness to accept help	1	2	3	4	5	6	7	8	9	10
Willingness to change	1	2	3	4	5	6	7	8	9	10
Willingness to change	1	2	3	4	5	6	7	8	9	10
Willingness for CC/AOD treatment	1	2	3	4	5	6	7	8	9	10

I. THOUGHTS AND BELIEFS ABOUT YOUR CHILDHOOD AND YOUTH

SPECIFIC PROBLEM AREAS AND DESCRIPTION	GOALS: CHANGES NEEDED IN THOUGHTS, BELIEFS AND ACTIONS	METHODS: TOOLS, SKILLS AND PROGRAMS TO BE USED FOR CHANGE	RESULTS AND OUTCOME

II. ALCOHOL AND OTHER DRUG USE AND ABUSE THINKING, BELIEFS AND BEHAVIORS

SPECIFIC PROBLEM AREAS AND DESCRIPTION	GOALS: CHANGES NEEDED IN THOUGHTS, BELIEFS AND ACTIONS	METHODS: TOOLS, SKILLS AND PROGRAMS TO BE USED FOR CHANGE	RESULTS AND OUTCOME

III. CRIMINAL AND ANTISOCIAL THINKING AND CONDUCT

SPECIFIC PROBLEM AREAS AND DESCRIPTION	GOALS: CHANGES NEEDED IN THOUGHTS, BELIEFS AND ACTIONS	METHODS: TOOLS, SKILLS AND PROGRAMS TO BE USED FOR CHANGE	RESULTS AND OUTCOME

IV. CURRENT LIFE SITUATION PROBLEMS: INCLUDES EMPLOYMENT AND JOB, LIVING STABILITY, RELATIONSHIPS, MARITAL-FAMILY, HEALTH, EMOTIONAL AND HANDLING INCARCERATION

SPECIFIC PROBLEM AREAS AND DESCRIPTION	GOALS: CHANGES NEEDED IN THOUGHTS, BELIEFS AND ACTIONS	METHODS: TOOLS, SKILLS AND PROGRAMS TO BE USED FOR CHANGE	RESULTS AND OUTCOME

V. CORE BELIEFS THAT LEAD TO AOD ABUSE AND PROBLEMS

SPECIFIC BELIEFS THAT LEAD TO AOD ABUSE	GOALS: NEW BELIEFS TO REDUCE RISK OF AOD PROBLEMS	METHODS: TOOLS, SKILLS AND PROGRAMS TO BE USED FOR CHANGE	RESULTS AND OUTCOME

VI. CORE BELIEFS THAT LEAD TO ANTISOCIAL/CRIMINAL THINKING AND CONDUCT

SPECIFIC BELIEFS THAT LEAD TO ANTISOCIAL AND CRIMINAL CONDUCT	GOALS: NEW BELIEFS TO REDUCE RISK OF ANTISOCIAL AND CRIMINAL CONDUCT	METHODS: TOOLS, SKILLS AND PROGRAMS TO BE USED FOR CHANGE	RESULTS AND OUTCOME

Weekly Thinking and Action Patterns (TAP) Charting: Before each session, you are asked to think back on your thinking and action patterns (TAP) for the past week. In column 1, put the date of this session. Then, thinking back on the week, check yes or no for the questions in each column. In the last column, write down the skills you used to prevent AOD use (or further use) and to prevent criminal conduct.

PROGRAM GUIDE 4

DATE:	Did you think about drinking or using drugs?		Were you where you could drink or use drugs?		Did you drink or use other drugs?		Did you think about commiting a crime?		NAME THE SKILLS THAT YOU USED TO PREVENT AOD USE OR PREVENT CRIMINAL CONDUCT DURING THIS PAST WEEK.
	NO	YES	NO	YES	NO	YES	NO	YES	

P R O G R A M   G U I D E   4

DATE:	Did you think about drinking or using drugs?		Were you where you could drink or use drugs?		Did you drink or use other drugs?		Did you think about commiting a crime?		NAME THE SKILLS THAT YOU USED TO PREVENT AOD USE OR PREVENT CRIMINAL CONDUCT DURING THIS PAST WEEK.
	NO	YES	NO	YES	NO	YES	NO	YES	

Weekly Thinking and Action Patterns (TAP) Charting: Before each session, you are asked to think back on your thinking and action patterns (TAP) for the past week. In column 1, put the date of this session. Then, thinking back on the week, check yes or no for the questions in each column. In the last column, write down the skills you used to prevent AOD use (or further use) and to prevent criminal conduct.

PROGRAM GUIDE 4

DATE:	Did you think about drinking or using drugs?		Were you where you could drink or use drugs?		Did you drink or use other drugs?		Did you think about commiting a crime?		NAME THE SKILLS THAT YOU USED TO PREVENT AOD USE OR PREVENT CRIMINAL CONDUCT DURING THIS PAST WEEK.
	NO	YES	NO	YES	NO	YES	NO	YES	